The History
and
HauNtiNg
of
Lemp Mansion

Lemp Mansion St. Louis, Mo. Circa 1892

Rebecca F. Pittman

Cover design:
©Copyright 2015 by Rebecca F. Pittman

 Published by:
Wonderland Productions, Inc.
Loveland, Colorado

Visit *The History and Haunting of Lemp Mansion* Facebook page for ongoing discussions, photos and more.
Website: www.rebeccafpittmanbooks.com (Sign up for free *Ghost Writings* monthly newsletter at the website home page.)

ISBN: 978-0-578-16009-2

DEDICATION

This book is dedicated to the people who made it possible:

The Lemp Family:

William, Julia, Annie, Billy, Hilda, Louis, Charles, Frederick, Elsa and Edwin Lemp, who left a legacy.

The Pointer Family:

Paul, Patty, Carolyn, Richard L., Sr., Richard "Dick", Jr., Tom, Matt, Mary, Mathew and Rachael, who gave this author the chance of a lifetime to tell the Lemp story.

That two families of nine children each have been the caretakers of Lemp Mansion is truly synchronicity in evidence.

****

And for Ron Bueker: for all the support, and working with me on research, documentation and photography.

****

In Memory
Of
Steve DeBellis
"Historian Extraordinaire"

ACKNOWLEDGMENTS

This book is the direct result of countless people giving of their time, talent and resources. I can't say enough about the hospitality of the people of St. Louis. Every government agency, library, historical society and private enterprise went out of their way to help me create what I hope you will find to be a comprehensive history of the Lemp family, their home and brewery. My immense gratitude to the following people:

The Pointer family, Shashi Palamand, Ron Bueker, Tom Stockman, Karl Lemp, Jr., Christy Hawes Bond, Richard Lay and Amie Bossi—Bellefontaine Cemetery, Missouri Historical Society, St. Louis Library, Missouri Legends, Musee Gailleria, Eon Images, KristenKoster.com, John Eastberg/Director of Development & Senior Historian at Pabst Mansion—Milwaukee, Donald L. Roussin, Jr.—BeerHistory.com, Glamourdaze.com, Molly Brown House— Denver, Co., Tom McLellan—Fort Collins, Colorado Police Service Captain (Ret), James Parrish—St. Petersburg Museum of History, DeMenil Mansion, Beverly Houston—St. Louis Police Department Records, Betsy Burnett-Belanger, Falstaff Museum of Brewing, Teresa Huelsing—Keller Williams Realty St. Louis, Jordan Woerndle—trickykegstands.com, One Hundred Years of Brewing, Terry Gambill—Ghosts and Haunts, St. Louis Archives and Deeds, Assessor's Office of St. Louis, St. Louis Building Division, Dana McDonough—Custodian of Records Medical Examiner's Office City of St. Louis, Ron Elz, Cherokee/Benton Park Association, Missouri History Museum, Captain Dan Rechtein—St. Louis Police

Records Division, Nancy Oliver—St. Louis Genealogy Library, Frank
Oswold—St. Louis Building Division, St. Louis Preservation Board,
Jensen & Halstead Architects—Chicago, Illinois, Andrew Weil—
Landmarks Association of St. Louis, Mackay/Mitchell Architects— St. Louis, St. Louis Assessor's Office, St. Louis Housing Authority, and the St. Louis Mercantile Library.

If I have omitted anyone, please forgive me. I appreciated all the referrals and correspondence that helped me check off everything on the To-Do List.

Please see the back of the book for the listing of newspapers, periodicals, websites and other areas of interest, that helped facilitate the creation of this book.

Contents

PART I: THE HISTORY OF LEMP MANSION

PART II: THE HAUNTING OF LEMP MANSION

Disclaimer:

All newspaper reports, police investigations, dialogue and quoted remarks are presented here without editing by the author. Any misspellings or grammatical errors are maintained to insure the integrity of the report.

Prologue-

When I stepped through the doors of Lemp Mansion in May of 2012, I knew two things: that I had to know its story, and I had to write about it.

With the kind permission of the Pointer family, I began two years of extensive research. It seemed each historic newspaper article, coroner's report, police investigation, and family remembrance, turned up another mystery concerning this amazing legacy. Their influence on St. Louis, and the world, was undeniable. The tragic events that shattered their lives also formed the indelible story that is the Lemps' heritage.

It was my desire, and that of the Pointer family, that the story of William J. Lemp's legacy be told from the viewpoint of compassion. These people lived, they created a brewing empire that, at one time, was the largest and best in St. Louis, and ranked 9th in the country. They set records that still stand in beer brewing history. They laughed, loved, married, divorced, raised children, traveled and dreamed. There is so much more to their stories than a few of their tragic endings.

While it is the sensationalism of four deaths in one family by gunshot, three of which were suicides, and the other still cloaked in mysterious circumstances, that draws the world's attention to this mansion, it is but a small piece of the story. Lemp Mansion's haunted reputation, that landed it in the top ten most-haunted venues in America, only adds to its infamy.

In an effort to bring the Lemps to life, I have taken the liberty of writing a prelude to each in my own words. These snippets are based on things we know about them, St. Louis history at the time, current traditions and fads. These short paragraphs appear in italics. It is a nod to Truman Capote's style of writing dubbed a "non-fiction novel." Here is the story of the Lemp family, complete with never-before-seen photographs, courtesy of Lemp Mansion.

Rebecca F. Pittman

March, 2015

THE HISTORY

Chapter One

William J. Lemp, Sr.
The Keeper of the Keys

William Jacob Lemp
Photo courtesy of Missouri Historical Society

St. Louis, Missouri: 1878

*W*illiam Jacob Lemp awoke to the sounds of the houseman lighting the kindling that had been laid in his bedroom fireplace the night before. Frederick Wachter, age 22, was only one of two men working at the Lemp residence and it was his responsibility to see to the male head of the house, and perform other duties such as that of butler. The other male serving the family, was Henry Hurstmann, age 36. Henry was in charge of the horses and carriages, and typically transported the Lemp's around town. His and Frederick Wachter's rooms were in the upper floor of the two-story carriage house out back.

Frederick set the trade publication of Western Brewer on the table near the fire in the master bedroom, along with the St. Louis Post, and smoothed Mr. Lemp's dressing robe that lay tossed over the high-back chair. He laid out the shirt, waistcoat, trousers, and short black tie Mr. Lemp had requested, and quietly retreated from the room.

Typical Victorian bedroom for a man.
Photo courtesy of CR3AT.com

William lay beneath the covers for a moment, waiting for the fire to take the February chill from the room. The stirrings of the house could be heard coming from various rooms above and below him in the palatial home. His wife, Julia, was speaking softly to the maid in her room on the other side of the closed pocket doors that separated the two master bedrooms. Above him, one flight up, in the servants' attic quarters, came the sounds of an occasional thump and water running. Across the hallway, he could hear his four sons already roughhousing, their laughter echoing throughout the first floor. He smiled, although he was sure his oldest daughter, Annie, would be complaining to her mother once again about the racket. She was constantly awakened each morning from the rambunctious sounds coming from the other side of the pocket doors separating her room from her brothers. It was bad enough she was sharing a room at her age, she would complain. A girl thirteen years old should have her own room, yet here she was sharing it with her much younger sister, Hilda, who was only three years of age. It would be the ubiquitous conversation at breakfast this morning; he was sure of it.

William rose, wrapped himself in his dressing robe and stood before the fire, his hands held out to the warmth. Today was an important day. Only a block down the street from where he stood, something amazing was happening at his brewery—something that would revolutionize the beer brewing industry. Western Brewery, the company his father, Johann Adam Lemp, had created from nothing 38 years ago, was not only the largest brewery in St. Louis, it was ranked 19th in the country, and turning out 100,000 barrels of beer a year, resulting in 1.5 million dollars in sales.

Today, however, would turn the brewing industry on its ear. The first artificial refrigeration machine would be installed in his brewery. It had cost a great deal of money as he allowed several inventors to test their products at his expense, only to come up short. Finally, Theodore Krausch designed an ammonia compression-type that revolutionized the way beer could be stored.

The brewery was growing faster than he could hire men to lay bricks for a new addition. Only last year, he had begun bottling their famous beer instead of carrying it in kegs by wagon to local restaurants, saloons and hotels. Lemp's new slogan, "Bottled in the Brewery," heralded his ability to greatly extend the distribution reach beyond the boundaries of St. Louis. Now, with this new industrial advancement of refrigeration, the caves with their outdated method of keeping the beer cold would no longer be needed. And it had all happened under his helmsmanship.

He walked to the west-facing window of his bedroom and drew aside the heavy velvet drapery. Pushing aside the eyelet sheer, he peered out over the houses to the south of him with twinkling blue-grey eyes. Towering above the home of Edward Hoppe at 3321 2nd Carondolet was the tall brick edifice of the Hop Drying Plant; an American flag flying proudly from the cupola adorning her rooftop. Today, the new Filter House, Stock House and Bottling Plant would begin their construction, adding to the already present Brew House, Malt House, Steep House and Offices.

Smoke from the brewery's twin chimneys was wafting into the winter sky, impregnating the low-lying clouds with the smell of brewing malt. Above the house's rooflines he could just glimpse the brick arch leading into the brewery compound. Across its façade his name was indelibly chiseled: William J. Lemp. He wished his father could have lived to see this. He thought of Adam Lemp every day and the heritage he had left him. Although he passed away in 1862, he still felt his presence when he toured the giant plant, signed a new order for their lager beer, or walked through the cave Adam had originally carved out to house his wooden kegs of beer.

Johann Adam Lemp
Photo courtesy Missouri Historical Society

Western Brewery 1878 --A Tour of St. Louis

To the south of the Hoppe residence was his step-mother's home: Louise Bauer Lemp, at 3335 2nd Carondolet. William*

15

was happy that his half-brother, Otto, had moved in with her. (Otto was listed as her "adopted son" on the 1880 Census.) She was now 65 and living in the large house with only one servant, Tilly, age 19. Louise was his father's second wife and William made sure she was well taken care of. His own mother, Justine Clermont, had died earlier in 1854, of yellow fever. Adam Lemp married Louise the same year.

Louise Bauer Lemp
Courtesy St. Louis Library

* It is possible William, Julia and the children lived with Louise Bauer Lemp at 3335 Carondolet (later to be changed to 3343 S. 13th St.) before they moved into Lemp Mansion, which was just across the street. 3335 was literally steps from the brewery and the 1875 drawing of the street shows it as a stately home. It was owned by the brewery and later became Billy and Lillian Lemp's home after their marriage. (Please see chapter on Billy Lemp for a photo of the house.)

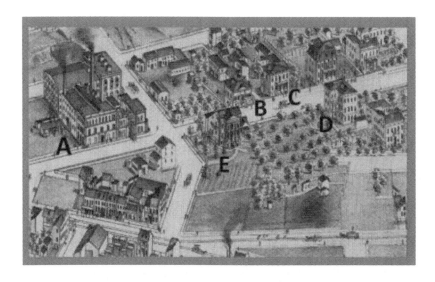

(A)William J. Lemp Brewery, B) Louise Bauer Lemp's home (later home of Billy and Lillian Lemp, at 3335) (C) Edward Hoppe's home at 3321, D) Lemp Mansion at 3322, and E) DeMenil Mansion at 3352. These are the address numbers when the street was 2nd  Carondolet. Most changed later when it became Thirteenth Street in 1880. The street is now called DeMenil Place. While Louise Bauer's home was razed, the Edward Hoppe residence, Lemp Mansion, DeMenil Mansion, and the brewery are still standing. Above is a close-up of the Bauer house (left) and Hoppe residence.

William glanced down from his bedroom window at the street activity below. The clip-clop sound of horse's hooves echoed hollowly on the cobblestones. He watched as an ice wagon passed, the driver hunched against the winter air. A Landau *(no doubt carrying one of his wealthy neighbors) rolled by. He glanced with appreciation at the four-wheeled carriage with a hood at each end. Two seats faced each other with the driver riding up front. It was pulled by two prancing horses. Going in the opposite direction was an even more resplendent Barouche (bearing yet another well-to-do family). It differed from the Landau in that it had one hood instead of two and was slightly larger. It was the fancy carriage of the 19th century, reminding William that the street where he resided was dubbed "Mansion Row." The two passing drivers doffed their top hats at one another and continued on. A Hackney, serving as a form of Taxi, followed in a form of unscripted parade. Several drays rattled by, carrying various goods upon their sideless carts. The horses' breath came in cold bursts, lacing the frigid air with their moisture.*

The pounding sound of hooves was echoed across the street as one of Mr. Hoppe's boarders stood on the front porch and beat his pipe against the railing; a puff of used tobacco cascaded down into the bushes flanking the front walk.

It was one of the moments when a person stopped the never ceasing progression of time and stood, for one full measure of a minute, taking it all in. The sights, sounds, feelings—everything that marked this frozen vignette as momentous. Today, William Jacob Lemp was a happy man, a blessed man, and he knew it. Standing all of 5' 4" tall, the room's 12' ceiling towering above him, he felt like a King among men.

Backing away from the window he picked up the two publications left for him and exited the room. He stepped into the hallway and made his way to the back stairway leading to his private bathroom on the first floor. He could hear his wife running water in the bathroom that adjoined her bedroom as he passed the door.

Double doors leading to the Master Suite on the 2ⁿᵈ Floor.
(Today it is named the Lavender Suite)

Just then, Willie (age 11), Louis (age 8), Charles (age 7),
and Frederick (age 5) came tearing from their room, racing
past him. They took the corner to the main staircase in a
flurry of arms and legs, declaring they were going to the
basement to play nine pins until breakfast was ready. The
smell of sizzling cured bacon wafted up the back stairs from
the basement kitchen below, masking the smell of new paint,
rugs and wall hangings from the recent renovation and
expansion William had ordered for his family's arrival. It had
taken almost two years to complete, but it was worth it. He
had purchased the home from his wife's parents, Jacob and
Elizabeth Feickert, who were, even now, stirring in the large
bedroom to his right at the top of the main staircase.

It was Wednesday, February 13, 1878, and at 42 years of
age, all was well with William Lemp and his household. He
had arranged for a special Valentine card to be created by
the local stationary shop for his 36-year-old bride for
tomorrow's festivities. He had fathered four strapping heirs
to his throne, two beautiful daughters, and employed five
servants. Over 70 laborers residing in the dormitories of his

brewery owed him their livelihood. Drawings for a new railroad line were lying atop his desk in the library below. The headline of the newspaper he carried beneath his arm reminded Americans that Rutherford B. Hayes was President, and the First Lady was hosting the first Easter Egg Rolling Contest to be held on the White House lawn on April 21st. The advent of telephone communication had been announced, a funny-looking contraption called a bicycle was the latest craze, and female suffrage was on the march.

As William J. Lemp happily descended the winding stairs to begin his preparations for the day, no one could foresee the fall of his carefully built empire twenty-six years in the future, marked by the report of a single gunshot coming from his bedroom. Nor, was he aware that his suicide, and that of three other members of his family, would become front page fodder for a newspaper that wouldn't see its first publication for another ten months.

The newly formed publication merger called the **St. Louis Post-Dispatch** would release its first edition of only 4 pages on December 12, 1878, reaching 4,020 customers; its journalistic reach going beyond the confines of St. Louis boundaries. It would doggedly print the ongoing competition of the city's two main breweries: Anheuser-Busch, and the Western Brewery (later to be incorporated as the William J. Lemp Brewery). But as the years passed, the headlines touting the huge triumphs of the Lemp brewing empire would bleed into the more sensational tales of the family's demise.

A Dream and a Prayer: How It All Began

Johann Adam Lemp arrived in America from Eschwege, Germany, in 1836. In his efforts to create a better life for himself and his family, he temporarily left behind his wife, Justine Clermont Lemp, and his young son, William, who had just entered the world that same year. A daughter, Johanette Catharina Lemp, was born September 11, 1816, in Germany. She married Justus Brauneck in 1840 at the age of 24. They had two sons, Charles and Martin Brauneck. Justus died in 1849, and Johanette married Carl Vetter that same year. She was 33. She died one year later in 1850, in St. Louis. She was William's only sibling from Adam and Justine Lemp's union.

Adam Lemp's Original Brew House & Office c. 1840 Courtesy of: *One Hundred Years of Brewing*

Johann, or Adam as he preferred to be called upon setting foot on American soil, had followed many of his kinsmen in hopes of finding a better way of life. America beckoned to foreign places with promises of freedom, plentiful land, and best of all, the chance for a man to own and operate his own business, if he worked hard and persevered. One did not associate this brave new world with famines and poor work conditions. It glittered with hope and fortune.

It must have been daunting to enter a country where your native tongue was not commonly used or understood. Yet, many Germans were coming by the boatloads to begin a new life; many leaving family behind until they had secured a lifestyle and could send for them.

Adam first found his way to Cincinnati, and finally to St. Louis, in 1838, where his wondering star would set its place in the firmament. He set up a small store at the corner of Sixth and Morgan. Here he sold groceries, vinegar and sundries. It made a modest living. At this time, he was also offering a beer he had learned to brew in Germany where he worked as a brewmaster—a crisp, refreshing beverage called "lager" beer. The German population of St. Louis was soon patronizing Adam's little shop. Word was spreading about this new beer with the lighter taste and color. Compared to the heavy, dark ales that permeated the local saloons, this beer was more effervescent, with a wonderful hop flavor.

A bag of hops

Encouraged by the increasing demand for his lager beer, Adam tossed aside the store shelves of flour, sugar, and canned goods and set his sights on the future: brewing beer. He purchased a site at 37 South Second Street (the current site of the south leg of the Gateway Arch) and began his business with a small brewery and an office. Dubbing his newfound enterprise, the Western Brewery Company, he put his German knowledge of brewing into effect. A modest production of 100 barrels of beer marked his first year's ledgers. But his name was becoming well known and the locals were lined up at his door. Always a man who capitalized on a good thing, Adam built a saloon and christened it Lemp Hall. It was soon a burgeoning success, known throughout St. Louis.

One of the obstacles to brewing beer is the lagering process and keeping it cool while it undergoes its fermentation stages.

With St. Louis's humid hot summers, Adam came to a fortunate conclusion. Why not utilize the caves that were literally the foundation of the city? They were cold, maintained a consistent temperature and they were roomy. He found all that he needed in a cave near the Mississippi River called the Cherokee Caves. He expanded the entrance and began storing his popular brew in the cool caverns. Twenty, thirty barrel casks made of oak were delivered to the cave via wagon from Adam's brewery site.

An undeveloped entrance to Cherokee Cave Courtesy of the Saint Louis Public Library

More Germans poured into St. Louis— 450,000 in the mid-1800s alone. And with them, came a taste for their homeland. Soon St. Louisans were hearing the sounds of accordions, unfamiliar songs, and the clinking of beer steins, as German beer gardens, called "beirgartens," began springing up all over town. This was a new way of enjoying an alcoholic beverage. It catered to families and welcomed all to come and sit in the shade of a large tree, or beneath the roof of a small hostel and enjoy this golden nectar called "lagerbier".

A popular newspaper of the day entitled *The St. Louis Republic* laid out in black-and-white the thoughts of the St. Louis populace, as to this influx of European immigrants:

"When they did come in it was tempestuously; a sudden and almost unexpected wave of immigration swept over us, and we found the town inundated with breweries, sausage shops, Apollo gardens, Sunday concerts, Swiss cheese, and Holland herrings. We found it almost necessary to learn the German language before we could ride the omnibus or buy a pair of breeches, and absolutely necessary to drink beer at a Sunday concert... The spacious beer halls and extensive gardens nightly show that Americans are as fond of the Gambrinian liquid as those who have introduced it."

So, with his large copper kettle, six men and long hours, Adam Lemp was leaving his mark in 1850. 4,000 barrels of beer, worth $24,000 rolled out the brewery doors and into the history books of St. Louis.

Photos courtesy Falstaff Museum of Brewing and the Missouri Historical Society. Left is an illustration of Adam's brewery in 1850. The original kettle (right) can be seen today in the Missouri Historical Society in St. Louis. It was donated to them by Edwin Lemp in 1955. It is 4 1/2' feet tall, with a circumference of 18 feet, and a brewing capacity of 12 barrels (372 gallons).

Adam Lemp was a pioneer in many ways and has been attributed with being the first man to manufacture lager beer in America. He was employed in Germany in a brewery before coming to America, in 1836, and may have brought his lager yeast with him. If he did, and he began brewing his beer as early as 1838, he would have effectively beaten Philadelphia brewer John Wagner to the punch by two years.

Whether he was first or second, he was definitely outselling every beer in St. Louis. He won first prize in 1858, at the St. Louis Fair for his lager brew. R. G. Dun Credit Reports in that same year listed Adam Lemp as "The most substantial brewer in the city - has made sufficient money to make him independent - owns valuable real estate." He was dubbed the "father of modern brewing in St. Louis." Meanwhile, Lemp Hall grew and was improved upon during the 1850's, until it became the largest in St. Louis. Part of its popularity was due to the fact no hard liquor was sold…only Lemp beer. Beer was seen as a lighter sin of the imbiber, as it was usually consumed in moderation. His business flourished, and it was time to bring his family over from Germany.

Lemp Hall c. 1850
Photo courtesy of the St. Louis Library

Enter the Heir

Wilheim Jacob Lemp left Germany and boarded a steamer in Liverpool, England, March 27, 1848, sailing to the new country he had heard so much about in letters from his father. He was twelve years of age. There is no mention of his sister coming with them at that time, though as noted earlier; she did die in St. Louis. She was married at the time William set sail for America and was many years older than he. We do know she bore two sons who were William's cousins: Charles and Martin Brauneck. Charles would later join William in the brewery business.

There were rumors that during the ten years William and Johanette's father had been away, starting a new life in America, Justine Clermont Lemp had left Adam. This is unsubstantiated.

Arcadia

William's passport does not list his mother as traveling with him. It was typical on passports to list family members also traveling with you, as is witnessed in the other Lemp family documents. If, indeed, he did travel alone, it must have been a daunting undertaking for a youth. Whether he spoke any English has not been documented. He was sailing across the ocean to a continent far different from his native Germany. Native Americans were prevalent; in fact, many Germans traveled to the heartland of America to find areas where the Native American population was not as dense. If William had not seen his father since Adam's departure to American in 1836, then he was also traveling to meet a man he did not know, as he was a newborn when Adam left. He may have felt exhilaration at this brave new adventure, but it must have been accompanied with feelings of fear and uncertainty.

Justine Clermont Lemp   Johann Adam Lemp
Photos courtesy of Lemp Mansion

Wilheim Lemp entered into American life with his usual focus. He may have changed his name to William upon entering school to reduce prejudice and merge with his new compatriots, or the name may have been given to him as he went through the immigration process upon arrival. Many immigrants found their surnames left behind on the steamers when their first and last names were often changed in the ledgers at Ellis Island. William's father may have chosen Adam over Johann for the same reason, or the powers that be selected his middle name over his first. Either way, it was time to blend in.

William went through the school system, finally graduating from the St. Louis University. His foreign accent may not have presented the issue it might have done elsewhere, as by now the city directory was packed with names peppered with German umlauts. According to an attachment on his official passport, he "became a naturalized citizen of the United States on the 21st day of February, 1857, when attaining the age of 21 years, by reason of having immigrated to the United States as the minor son of John Adam Lemp."

William Jacob Lemp in his 20's.
Photo courtesy of Christy Hawes Bond, *Gateway Families*

After completing college, William was immediately ushered into his father's brewery business where he rose to the position of foreman in short time. Working alongside Adam Lemp, he learned every aspect of the brewery trade, resulting in his promotion to plant superintendent.

Perhaps feeling his oats, and wanting to begin something of his own, he partnered with a local brewer by the name of Wilheim Stumpf. Stumpf's brewery was located at the present-day corner of Shenandoah and Lemp Avenues, not far from the present location of the Lemp caves. At the time of their partnership in the early 1860s, the location was the corner of Ann Avenue and Decatur Street. Like other brewers in the city, Stumpf was using the area's natural caves to store his beer. He added a subterranean beer garden called Stumpf's Cave that became a popular St. Louis attraction.

Everything was progressing smoothly, until a major event changed the course of the city forever. In 1861, the Civil War came to St. Louis.

According to the Lemp Family Papers, housed at the Missouri Historical Library, William J. Lemp was on the May 8, 1861 Muster Roll of the 3rd Regiment, U.S.R.C., Co. C, Tony Niederweiser, Capt.; John McNeil, Col. (Union, Mo. Infantry). On Aug. 18, 1861, he was listed on the Muster Roll of 3rd Reg., U.S. Reserve Corp, Co. C. (A muster roll is a register of the officers and men in a military unit or ship's company.)

Civil War uprising in St. Louis on what is today's Broadway and Walnut Avenues.

By September of 1864, William was put in charge of the supply division. On September 30th of that year, he proffered an invoice of the Ordinance Stores. It lists 102 Austrian R. Muskets, 102 Bayonet Scabbards, ball screws, tumbler punches and more.

On October 13, 1864, the following letter was sent to William accepting his supply invoice and ordering him to "stand charged with these stores on the books of this Office until they are duly accounted for on a Return of Ordinance Stores, covering the time from the date of their reception until the termination of the official quarters."

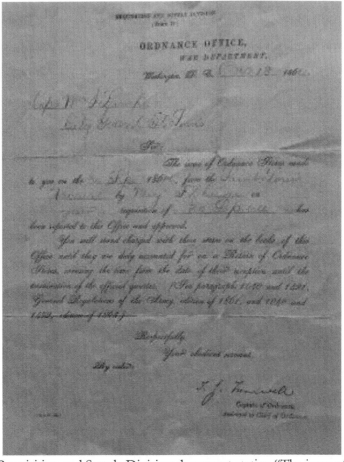

Requisition and Supply Division document stating "The issue of Ordinance Stores made to you on the 30, Sept, 1864, from the Saint Louis Arsenal by Maj. F. Deballender on your requisition of 30 Sept. 64 has been reported to this Office and approved." Capt. Wm J. Lemp is listed as the recipient of this letter.

Shortly before the above letter was received, William was made Lt. Colonel by the Head Quarters Department of the

Missouri on Oct. 5, 1864, by the command of Major General Rosecrans.

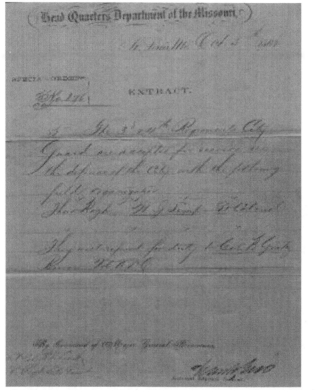

Special Orders Extract citing William J. Lemp as Lt. Colonel

It is clear from the preceding documents, that William gave several years of his life in the service of defending his newly adopted country. While he served in the local city guard, many German Americans saw active duty on the battlefields of the Civil War.

On December 3rd, 1861, while still actively involved in the Union cause, William married Julia Feickert, a woman of German descent. Petite and unassuming, she would become the heart of their future family.

One year later, August 23, 1862, Johann Adam Lemp passed away. He left a legacy for his surviving heirs and stamped his name and beer logos into the annals of brewing history. In his will, Adam split the ownership of Western Brewery between his son William, and Johanette's son, Charles Brauneck. He left them "all the equipment and stock" and a codicil stating that if either of them contested the property division, the other would inherit it all. The two men formed a partnership called William J. Lemp & Company only two months after Adam's death. Shortly thereafter, William bought out his cousin's share in the company for $3,000 in 1864, effectively dissolving the partnership. It was now full steam ahead for William, and he wasted no time in taking his father's foundation and building a brewing empire. At his side was his beloved Julia.

Chapter Two

JULIA LEMP
The Heart of Lemp Mansion

Julia Feickert Lemp
Photo courtesy of Lemp Mansion

Saint Louis, Missouri: 1878

Julia Feickert Lemp descended the main staircase of her lovely new home. Her parents had kindly given up the master bedrooms they had inhabited when the house was first built in

1868, and moved into the spacious room at the top of the stairs. They were now in their sixties, and as Julia's brood had grown, the two families had merged beneath one roof. The children had taken the double rooms across from the master suite, causing the second floor of the mansion to be constantly brimming with activity.

Julia stopped on the landing midway down the staircase to stare at the morning light sparkling on the twin glass doorways leading from outside into the main foyer. The cracked glass had been custom done; its small fractured surface sending the light into a dance of sparkling diamonds. It was one of her favorite views of the house and she often chose the front staircase over the back, winding steps just to look at the doors below. From this vantage point she could also see into the formal Lady's Parlor; the foyer chandelier hanging just within view.

She continued her descent, her long silk day dress sweeping the carpeted runner. The tight corset she wore was already beginning to bind and she found herself missing the days of her pregnancy when a woman was finally freed from the whalebone contraption meant to cinch each lady's waist of the 19th century into an impossible 18-inch hourglass. She smiled. In truth, she was enjoying the reprieve from back-to-back pregnancies that had produced four sons almost a year apart since 1867. Her youngest daughter Hilda had been born three years ago, giving her a chance to catch her breath. Annie, her thirteen-year-old daughter, was a great help with the younger ones, when she wasn't complaining about how they were the bane of her existence. She stopped to consider that the little boy she had lost during childbirth on July 4th in 1862, would be sixteen now. Imagine that. The wave of sadness abated, but only slightly.

At the bottom of the staircase she turned left into the double parlor and found her housemaid, Mary Burchers, *dusting the plethora of art pieces tastefully set about the 36-foot-long room. Each trip to Europe the family embarked upon, would net new paintings, bronzes, statues and objects d'art that could be seen adorning every wall and marble table top.*

The twin fireplaces, with their rich African mahogany wood, gleamed in the light filtering in through the sheers of the tall windows adorning the west-facing wall. Expensively upholstered couches and chairs in tufted red velvet or striped satins were clustered into convenient vignettes throughout the room, welcoming guests to sit and share the news of the day. Twin gasoliers hung from the 12-foot high ceiling, dripping with cut crystal prisms that threw light from the giant mirrors atop the fireplaces. The Aubusson rug with its floral pattern of greens and reds was the perfect complement to the soft hues of sage vines embossed on the William Morris wallpaper that covered the walls from dado to picture rail. Gold guilt sparkled along the frieze work and cornices.

Typical parlor in the 1800s.

But it was the magnificent ceiling that caused their many guests to stop and stare in awe. A giant oval depicting a blue sky studded with voluminous clouds dominated the center. A thin powder blue ribbon was painted to hem in its circumference before being tied into a stately bow at one end. Surrounding the glimpse of sky were panels of soft pink, small rose buds, embroidered in oils, adorning each, while a running section of soft mint green offset each component. Tiny pin-striping and scrollwork were painstakingly detailed until the overall splendor of it was hard to take in all at once. Julia knew her husband was less than thrilled with the mural, declaring it too "frilly" and ostentatious. It was an ongoing war, but so far, she had prevailed in keeping it.

She crossed to Mary, giving her directions for the day. After the parlor was polished, she was to move into the dining room and do a linen check.

Ceiling mural in Lemp Mansion Parlor
Photo courtesy of Ron Bueker

Once a month, when company wasn't expected, she liked to go through the inventory of dishes, tablecloths and napkins. She reminded the 19-year-old maid that the carpet sweeper was to be run over the rugs in all the rooms today. She also mentioned her evening gown she would like retrieved from the cedar closet in the attic, as they were expecting a business acquaintance of William's for dinner that evening. She reminded Mary that once the noon meal was over, to put out the French linen tablecloth with the red rosettes and two candelabras for the dinner service. The silver compote with the ivy design was to be placed in the center of the table for the fruit display. She complimented the girl on her work, placed a maternal hand on her shoulder, and made her way out into the hallway near the closed door to the library.

The subtle smell of cherry laurel water wafted out of William Lemp's personal bathroom as Julia passed near it on her way to the back staircase. The door was partly ajar and she knew the barber had come and gone, and her husband was already at the brewery. She peeked in to see wet towels hastily draped over the arm of his personal barber chair that sat near the diamond-paned window by the fireplace.

William Lemp's personal barber chair.
Photo courtesy of private collection.

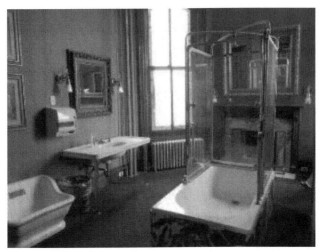

William Lemp's personal bathroom on the first floor of Lemp Mansion. Photo courtesy of Rebecca F. Pittman

She loved the feeling of dampness in the air and the pungent smell of soaps. The massive glass-enclosed marble tub William had imported from a hotel in Italy dominated the room. It was a great source of pride for him, as it was the only one of its kind to be found in this part of the country. Many a visiting friend or business acquaintance had been offered the use of William's bathroom after their tête-à-têtes in the library next to it, as his surreptitious way of showing off his prize acquisition. Other than that, the household knew it was off-limits, unless permission was granted. A smaller bathroom at the end of the hall on that floor, near the storage vault, was for everyday use.

Julia walked to the winding stairs leading to the basement. She thought of the new addition of the spiral design that replaced the old stairs to the 2nd floor and attic. The old staircase had risen up to the upper floors at a knee breaking 45-degree angle. By winding the stairs in a graceful curve, not only could one get a vertigo-enhancing glimpse of the tunnel-like drop from the attic to the basement through its center, but it made it easier to traverse— something the often-

pregnant Julia, and older Feickerts, dearly appreciated. It had been added during the expansion of the house and the old floor joist openings could still be seen in the brick wall between the first and second floor landings, noting where the floor and a wall had been removed to make way for the new stairs.

Her daughter Annie intercepted her as she reached the basement level. She was anxious to hear if she would be allowed to buy a new dress from Worth of Paris. Julia was training the young woman in the social skills necessary to prepare for her "season" when at sixteen she would be presented to society. They had covered etiquette, calling cards, table manners, polite conversation, and even the cumbersome steps to the quadrille; a dance always in demand at any high-profile ball or wedding.

Julia was not surprised that her young daughter was now entrenched in the world of fashion, as the hemlines, bustles, and crinolines seemed to change with each year's trip to England, Paris, and New York City. William was always generous in his clothes allowance for the family, but the new Princess Gown* with the cuirass bodice would not come cheap—not if Charles Frederick Worth of England was designing it.

His fashions were the rage of Paris and he had draped the royal frames of dignitaries such as Napoleon III's wife, Empress Eugénie. The notion was, if you were wearing a Worth, everyone could guess just how much you were worth!
Julia kissed the cheek of her petite, lovely daughter and promised to put forth the request. She encouraged Annie to work on her French and elocution, and then made her excuses as she must corral the cook to go over the needs for the dinner this evening, and the regular grocery list. She entered the kitchen as the sounds of squeals came from the staircase, where Willie and Louis were chasing her daughter with a disembodied chicken foot from the outside pantry.

*The Princess Gown is on the left. There is no clear distinction
separating the waist from the bodice, such as the dress on the right.
The Princess Gown offered the women of the late 1880s a garment
that not only showed off their figure to perfection, but also, was void of
bustles or crinolines. (Crinolines were a rigid skirt-shaped bell of
steel designed to hold the folds of a skirt out to a desired look.)

*Mathilda Bressler put down the ladling spoon with which
she had been stirring a large copper pot of stew and smiled at
the mistress of the house. At 21-years-old, she was the oldest
of the female staff, and enjoyed taking care of the meals for
the Lemp household. She knew she had it better than most of
her constituents who rarely saw a nice beef joint. There was
always a turkey or pheasant from the game larder in the
wood shed. The kitchen larder was filled with fresh
vegetables, the store room with canned goods, and the zinc-
lined ice box was never without a full supply of dairy
products. She wiped her hands on her crisply starched apron
and turned to the small table at the side of the room where the*

food ledgers were kept. This was a daily meeting with the "Missis" and she was prepared.

For the next hour, the two went over the necessary staples that would need to be picked up. The canned goods, such as baked beans, Hills Brothers Coffee, Eagles Brand Milk, and peaches could be purchased from the local grocer, along with Heinz vinegar, Welch's Grape Juice, Quaker Mills Rolled Oats, and pickled products. The fresh fruit and vegetables could be picked up from the Soulard street market, a few blocks over, and the butcher could be counted on to know the Lemp's cuts and portions. The ice and milk wagons came regularly, though most often the brewery supplied the house with ice.

Mathilda often bragged to the neighboring servants about the perks of working at the Lemp's, including hot and cold running water sent over through the brewery pipes. This house did not need to fetch and carry water. Every modern appliance that appeared on the market found its way into Mathilda Bresslers' kitchen. The other cooks in the area tired of her trumpeting each new addition, including the spotless linoleum floor laid just last year, while the others were making due with wood. The gas-fitted range with its sleek black cast-iron surface was a source of pride for Mathilda. Her meals came out more-evenly cooked than with the old, sooty, coal-heated ones.

Emma Trautwein entered from the scullery, the front of her apron wet from scrubbing pots, pans and dishes. She was a quiet young girl of 15, who dealt with the more odious chores of the household. To her fell the morning lighting of the fires in the female's rooms, when the massive mansion's hallways were freezing. She scrubbed, plucked fowl, gutted fish, peeled, scoured and scrubbed. Her only dalliance was a quick gab with the young Beauvais's maid across the street as she passed their doorway on the way to market. She would allow herself a few moments of gossip before she hurried on her way to the shops.

Julia smiled at the girl, as Emma took a hot, wet rag to the giant wooden table that held court in the center of the kitchen. Here all the meals were prepared. It was the hub of the kitchen. Copper pots, pans, and ladles gleamed in the light from the windows flanking the fireplace, where now the stove resided. Hooks, nooks, and shelves on every wall cradled every size of cooking utensil on the market. Dried herbs hung upside down in tied bunches from nails, while the everyday white china shone from their racks in the pantry. The more expensive formal dinnerware was housed in special cupboards, sometimes locked with the keys Mrs. Lemp kept on her person. A tall cabinet with felt-lined shelves housed silver candelabras, serving spoons, candle sticks, compotes, dessert dishes, rare crystal goblets, fluted champagne glasses, wine glasses, and cut crystal serving dishes. To handle the clean-up of these pieces required tender care; a copper-lined sink in the scullery was used, as its side had more "give" than zinc or stone.

Typical late 1800s kitchen centered around a center work table
with shelves laden with pots and pans.

Frederick Wachter stepped into the kitchen to let Mrs. Lemp know that Mrs. Herr had stopped by to see her and he had shown her to the Lady's Parlor. The cook poured out two steaming cups of tea and arranged them on a platter with some biscuits and small linen napkins. She handed this to the butler, after asking Mrs. Lemp if that would be satisfactory for her guest's visit. After reminding the cook that Mr. Lemp would be home for lunch—and the cook reminding her that they were running low on Mason jars—Julia Lemp followed the houseman up the back stairs to greet Mrs. Herr.

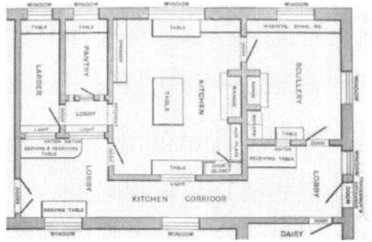

The photo shows a typical kitchen layout with scullery, larder & pantry separate from the main kitchen. Scullery maids often stood on slatted wooden crates so their feet wouldn't be encased in water that continually sloshed on the floors.

Behind Every Man...

Julia A. Feickert was the daughter of Jacob and Elizabeth Hoster Feickert. She was born in St. Louis, Missouri on July 26, 1841. Her parents were both born in Germany and were among the wave of Germans who came to Missouri in the 1830s, hoping to better their lives and take advantage of this "land of plenty." The Gilded Age was an era of rapid economic growth, primarily in the North and West. American wages, especially for skilled workers, were much higher than in Europe, which attracted millions of immigrants. It was the era of the Industrial Revolution, and the United States shone as bright as Lady Liberty's torch.

In 1837, Jacob Feickert purchased property on 92 2nd Street, where he began a long list of entrepreneurial pursuits. His original business was listed in the city directory as a "bakery." In 1845, it fell under the name of "flour store." In 1850, the census shows him as owning a "coffee house." He went into partnership with his brother-in-law Frederick Jacoby in 1851, forming a new business called Jacoby & Company at the corner of 43 Market and 2nd Streets. In 1854, the business name was changed to Jacoby and Feickert. Finally, the 1870 census shows Jacob Feickert, age 50, as a saloon keeper.

Jacob and Julia Feickert, Julia Lemp's mother and father, and the first owners of Lemp Mansion.
Photo courtesy of Christy Bond, *Gateway Families*

The death of Fredrick Jacoby, Jacob Feickert's brother-in-law and business partner, was the first funeral to be held in Lemp Mansion. He died in 1876, leaving Jacob as his administrator. The business inventory showed mainly cigars and spirits on the ledgers. His funeral was probably held in the double parlor at the mansion, as were so many to come.

Jacob Feickert is the first name on the title to Lemp Mansion, but it is probable that William Lemp, his son-in-law, put forth most of the money to buy the land from Henry S. Reed in 1866, and build the stately Italianate home in 1868. William's net worth in the 1870 census was $235,000 in real estate holdings, and $100,000 in personal property. Jacob, on the other hand, showed only $2,500 in real estate and $1,000 in personal assets. When Jacob and Elizabeth Feickert died, only 16 days apart from each other, on January 5, 1892, and January 21, 1982, respectively, William Lemp administered their estate. Three lots were listed as Jacob's real estate assets: his store at 414 2nd Street, Lemp Mansion at 3322 13th Street (earlier named Carondolet Avenue), and a burial plot in Block Number 70 in Bellefontaine Cemetery, in St. Louis.

On February 4th, 1892, Julia Lemp signed over the rights of administration of her parents' estate to her husband William. Jacob's probate records show that William handled all the responsibilities connected with Jacob's death, including paying Eberle and Keyes, Undertaking Company, $135 for "25 Carriages & Hearse," and $365 for a "State Casket, Coffin lined & Cedar Box." Julia further signed two other documents stating she had received from her father and mother's estate, via William J. Lemp as administrator, the sums of $10,820, and $250. Lemp Mansion was listed on Jacob Feickert's inventory as such:

"A parcel of ground in city block 1539 fronting 153 feet ...on the east line of Thirteenth Street (later 2nd Carondolet Avenue) by a depth of 150 feet running eastwards to the alley, and consisting of lots number Seven, Eight, Nine, Ten, Eleven and Twelve of William Wibte's subdivision, and a portion of fractional block number Fifty-two of the St. Louis Commons. Improvements: A two-story brick mansion with basement and attic...containing twenty-one rooms; also, a two-story brick stable in the rear, a wood shed and a laundry."

Jacob's total inventory consisted of the following: He had $150 on him with an additional $991.00 in deposits in the German Savings Institution, stocks, U.S. registered 4% bonds in the amount of $10,000, and two Promissory Notes totaling $21,000, held against William Lemp. Interest was waived on the note, with William owing $13,000 "in consideration of the maker's defraying all the household expense of Mr. and Mrs. Feickert from December 1st, 1889."

Julia Lemp seemed to remain in the background during the tumultuous years of the Lemp dynasty. Only a scattering of newspaper articles find her in the society pages of the prominent publications of the day. Yet based on the cultural climate of the 19th century, the expectations of the wealthy in the Gilded Age, and her obvious devotion to her family, it is certain that Julia hosted and planned many society parties, dinners, receptions, and other events demanded by St. Louis echelons for the wife of a multi-millionaire.

By the time her pregnancy dresses were packed away permanently, she had given birth to nine children, eight of whom survived. Being the mother of three daughters, during a time when wealthy families were held to certain standards in their homes, lifestyles and fashions, must have been formidable. It fell to her to make sure the girls were ready to take on American society, displaying all the etiquette, carriage, and bearing dictated by the era's creed. In those days, education was still a boy's ticket to advancement in the world, whereas women depended on landing a good husband; preferably one with breeding, money, and an admirable standing in the community. As the Lemp's wealth grew over the years, so did the expectations placed on the family's heirs.

For Julia Lemp, while her husband grew a brewing empire, not only did she oversee the machinations of running, decorating, and maintaining a beautiful home befitting his status, but also raised eight children to fulfil their individual roles, and go forth in life and prosper.

During the Victorian era in America, wealthy women were also expected to "give back" to the community by means of hosting sewing circles and other soirees dedicated to raising funds for the poor. They championed functions that underscored civic events of the day and were expected to present themselves in a manner befitting their station in life. Even the clothes they wore in public were critiqued and remarked upon. There were outfits designed strictly for boating expeditions; walking about town; morning, afternoon and evening frocks; as well as ball gowns that were expected to reflect the latest in European fashion. Her stationary, responses to invitations, calling cards, table settings and manners were all on display. The image of a wealthy married woman reclining on her chaise lounge, eating delicacies, and reading the latest Jane Austen novel was one not based upon reality. It is a certainty, Mrs. William J. Lemp was the woman behind the man, quietly handling her station in life without need for the lime light.

Chapter Three

The Building of an Empire

St. Louis, Missouri: 1892

The Cherokee/Minnehaha cave tunnel, leading from Lemp Mansion to the brewery elevator at the corner of Cherokee and DeMenil, was cold, with a faint mist appearing sporadically, depending on the depth of the frequent turns. William Lemp had used this secret underground walkway to his offices on the days he wanted privacy. Above him rode cable cars, horses and carriages, accompanied by the hectic wave of pedestrian life in 19th century St. Louis. The cobblestone and macadamized streets were slick, muddy, and not without the aroma of horse manure. In 1880, it was estimated the 2,280 horses and mules, used to pull the 496 streetcars, deposited 23 tons of manure on the city streets every day.

William walked briskly along the uneven stone floor, his mind filled with the details of the hours that lay ahead. The 55-degree temperature of the cave barely registered. He passed the recessed area the family used as a make-shift concrete-lined swimming pool—a reservoir once used for the lagering of beer before refrigeration rendered it unnecessary. The hot water from the brewery was used to keep it heated. Two hundred feet ahead lay the underground theatre he had constructed to entertain his family and guests, with its crude floodlights and man-made scenery. There was a spiral staircase leading from that area to the surface near Cherokee Street. On days when he wasn't as distracted as he was this morning, he would often slow his pace, recalling the parties here, almost hearing the strains of an orchestra's music echoing in the corridors from one of their balls held in the nearly-empty lagering caverns.

Lemp cave tunnels and caverns. The one on the left was later used as a ballroom by the Lemp family.
Photos courtesy Terry Gambill with Ghosts and Haunts.

Swimming pool in the cave

Taking the elevator, he rose to the surface inside the brewery. The pungent smell of brewing yeast assaulted his nostrils, as he entered the Brew House, to the sound of cheers. A broad smile broke out beneath his trimmed beard. He was 56-years-old, but it was not a birthday the men were celebrating. Today, November 1, 1892, Western Brewery would be incorporated under the name The William J. Lemp Brewing Company.

He made his way to his office amid congratulatory slaps on the back, handshakes and nods. Waiting for him inside the room marked with his name plate, were his sons Louis and William, Jr. (Billy). The company secretary, Henry Vahlkamp, was there as well, smiling broadly. An attorney stood waiting, the needed paperwork laid out across the modest desk. Next to the line indicated for the new president, William signed his name with a bold hand. By the words, Vice-President, Billy signed William J. Lemp, Jr., making his customary sweep of the letter "J." Louis F. Lemp signed next to the title of Superintendent, and Henry Vahlkamp proudly placed his John Hancock near Secretary. All of the stock was owned by the family, making it a closed corporation. With the attorney's witnessing signature, it was official. The moment was celebrated with the clinking of glasses. Within the chilled mugs swirled the amber liquid that made this moment, and their fortunes possible— Lemp Beer.

As the others left his office, to join in the celebration heard throughout the massive buildings, William turned to look out the tall, arched window at what he had created. In only 27 years, since the brewery's first brick was laid in 1865, his company had taken over three city blocks, producing 300,000 barrels annually, with total sales in excess of $3 million. Just since 1878, they had added an addition to the Brew House, a second Stock House, a Bottling Plant addition, a Boiler House, Wash House & Keg House, Condenser House, and a Locomotive House, with an addition following in the same year. This year, a Machine Shop and Ice Plant had gone up.

Besides the brick and mortar, he was utilizing the railway system that had extended his reach worldwide. With 125 of his own refrigerated cars, Lemp Beer was now reaching ports as far away as Paris, Berlin, South America, Hawaii, Shanghai, Australia, London, and Calcutta. Lemp Beer had already won silver medals in such exhibitions as the Centennial Exposition in Philadelphia, and the Paris Exposition of 1878. Even with Anhueser-Busch nipping at his heels, William Lemp saw nothing but prosperity ahead. In another year or two, his son Frederick would be ready to move into a corporate position at the brewery. It was full steam ahead.

William spent the remainder of the day overseeing the new buildings going up and talking with his house foremen. The ringing sounds of metal being beaten into infrastructure were a common cacophony at the plant, while the smell of brewing barley, yeast, and hops was just as pervasive.

He stopped in each of the brewery departments, checking ledgers, sampling, and asking questions. He surveyed the cooling rooms, wash house, dining hall, and massive malt and barley house. It was three stories tall with three underground cellars; some still used for lagering. Each malting season, 125,000 bushels of malt were prepared. The kiln area was on the other side of the partition separating the 142' x 106' room. William surveyed the crop. He loved running his hands through the bushels of barley, relishing the quality the Canadian grain brought to his beer. He did the same with the hops in the Hop House, bursting the small pine cone-shaped heads to release the soft herb-like aroma; knowing their bitterness would be unleashed during the brewing process. Each building had its own unique aroma. It clung to his clothes and perfumed his beard with the sweet unmistakable smell of brewing beer.

William stopped a foreman to ask about a batch of wort, testing the overseer's knowledge of the giant vats,

51

temperatures, and operations. It was well-known among the men, that when Mr. Lemp was on the premises, he would be asking questions to keep them on their toes. But it was in a jovial, good-spirited comradery with his workmen that he gave these daily tests. It was also common to see him ditch his waistcoat, roll up his sleeves, and help in the various departments, side by side with the men in his payroll.

At the end of the day, William, Billy and Louis stepped out of their offices at the corner of Cherokee and 13th Streets and turned north toward home. Henry Vahlkamp had been invited for a celebratory dinner at the Lemp home and he hurriedly locked the office door. William glanced to his left at his mother-in-law's house. The lights were on in the front parlor. They crossed the street, dodging several carriages, and passed the DeMenil Mansion on their right. Up ahead, the lights were blazing in the windows of 3322 Thirteenth Street, highlighting a soft snow that had just begun to fall. With eager steps, the three Lemp men—William, (56), Billy (25), and Louis (22)—strode confidently home.

On the Home Front

The years between 1878 and 1892, had seen comparable changes at the Lemp home, not just the brewery. In 1884, an extensive radiator system had been implemented in every room of the house; including the front entry in the hallway. No more would the family and staff awake to a freezing home or dread going out into the hallways where the fireplaces' warmth did not reach. The house servants were no doubt thrilled to be spared the early morning routine of lighting the fires in 15 rooms of the house, including the servant's rooms in the attic. (The radiators are still used today at Lemp Mansion and this author can testify to their efficiency.)

St. Louis itself was evolving. Just a street over from Lemp Mansion, on 7th Street, the trolley cars were running on electricity as of 1891. The lilting clang of the bell could be heard through the Lemp home's open windows in the summer time. The trolley line ran all the way into downtown St. Louis. Horse and buggies were still the prevalent way to travel, and bicycles remained in vogue, with each year turning out the latest style.

In 1889, gas street lights were installed in St. Louis. It was the task of the town lamp lighter to go about each evening and light the lamps. Oil lamps were still commonly used in homes, supplemented with candlelight. The "chimney and wick" could be found adorning tables throughout even the wealthiest homes. Electricity for residences was still over a decade away. Eads Bridge had opened in 1874, giving St. Louis a direct passageway across the mighty Mississippi.

Eads Bridge during construction.
Photo courtesy Missouri Legends.

Woman walking on the frozen Mississippi in 1905, possibly Elsa
Lemp. Photo courtesy St. Louis Public Library.

Babies at Lemp Mansion

Besides keeping up with all the new contraptions the
Industrial Revolution rolled out in the Gilded Age, Mrs. Lemp
did her part to contribute to the growth of the Lemp Empire.
Two more additions had been added to the family. Edwin Lemp
was born on August 28, 1880, followed three years later by Elsa
Lemp on February 8, 1883.

Childbirth, in the 19th century, was fairly archaic by today's
standards. The men of the family stayed their distance as
midwives and doctors went through the rituals associated with
delivering a human life. If you were a middle-class woman, or
upper-middle class, you could afford to hire a doctor to come
into your home. Women also gave birth in private maternity
hospitals, but the fear of unsanitary conditions prevailed during
the 1800s. Puerperal sepsis—blood poisoning caused by
bacteria entering the vagina or uterus, often via hands or
medical equipment, during or after birth—was the main cause

of maternal death. It was nicknamed "childbed fever" and was a major concern. As late as 1921, New Zealand had the second highest maternal mortality rate in the western world. Many doctors, who had no concept of sterilization or contagion, would transmit diseases from woman to woman with their own bare hands. Wealthy women often chose to have the baby delivered at home where the environment was more within her control.

The pregnant women of the Gilded Age were put through unpleasant rigors in preparation for childbirth. The abdomen, thighs and external "lady" parts were first scrubbed with warm sterile water and soap, then rubbed dry, to be followed by a bath of a dichloride solution containing Lysol. She was shaved, and the procedure started again. But wait…it gets better.

According to John Gunn's 1861 *Gunn's New Domestic Physician*, "The parts of generation during labor should always be well oiled or greased with lard, as it greatly assists and mitigates the suffering, and lubricates the parts of passage." (Gunn)

After the hapless woman has been Lysoled and greased, she is put in clothing that can be removed after childbirth with as little hassle as possible. This usually consisted of a waist shirt, petticoat, stockings and bed slippers. This way, the petticoat and stockings could be taken off over the feet, while the waist shirt was removed over her head. During labor, she was given something to help with the pain—towels.

According to Gunn's helpful book: "A towel, sheet, or some conventional article, should be tied to the bed post, so that at each pain the woman may pull it, as it assists her very much in her efforts, and she derives great benefit and comfort from the support." Pain during childbirth had been ordained as divine and ordered by God, according to the Bible. In 1853, Queen Victoria was chloroformed during the birth of Prince Leopold, and a new era of pain control was born. After the Queen's acquiescence to drugs, women took a skeptical look at the Biblical dictates and lined up for their Murphy's inhalers.

Murphy's inhaler was a pain relief device used in childbirth from 1848. Invented by Dr. Edward William Murphy, chloroform could be dropped on the cotton ball in the chamber at the end. The woman in labor could place it up to her mouth and inhale as needed.

Once the child was born, a new set of rules kicked in. Postpartum care involved holding very still for a prolonged period of time. Physicians of the day were terrified "important things" might fall out of a lady if she moved around too much. Women were told they could have no visitors for a fortnight, to keep the new mother from becoming overly fatigued or agitated by local gossip. A five-minute interview was granted the husband. Only after five or six days, was she allowed to be propped up in bed for an hour at a time. On the tenth to fourteenth day, she is allowed to sit in a chair for an hour at a time, and finally she is permitted to stand or walk after three weeks. During the third and fourth week, she is instructed to lie down or recline on a sofa most of the time. She should wear a wrapper to keep her body unrestricted. Stairs were forbidden until the end of the fourth week, and finally she was allowed to escape the house for a walk or drive, at the end of the fifth week. Shopping and visiting was postponed for "some time" longer."

Bathing involved soaking in a solution of warm milk and water. If there was a great deal of swelling, an emollient poultice of bread and milk, or linseed meal, was applied. In extreme cases of throbbing in the generative organs, leeches were deemed necessary.

Gunn did give the long-suffering new mother a final pat on the head: "That women generally endure pain and sickness with more fortitude and patience than men, is evident. Looking forward with the pleasing hope of being the mother of a tender offspring, upon which she can lavish her affection and tenderness, sustains her in fulfilling the conditional requirements of Nature. Few men could be induced, for any consideration, to suffer in a similar manner." (Gunn)

Maternity Evening Dress 19th Century. Courtesy Musee Gailleria

Julia Lemp "suffered" through nine pregnancies. Many families of the 19th century produced ten children, or more. The sad outcome, was that New York City saw over 12,000 homeless children being taken into shelters during the mid-1870s. This was due to a number of factors, including back-to-back depressions. The number of still births during this time was also a sad reality.

Elsa Justine Lemp's birth in 1883, marked the last of Julia's confinements. Mrs. Lemp was 42-years-old at that time, and helping her husband with a burgeoning beer industry.

In 1892, many things had changed in the Lemp household, besides the addition of two children. Julia's beloved parents, Jacob and Elizabeth Feickert died sixteen days apart in January of that year. They had lived with the Lemp family in the giant room at the top of the stairs for over 16 years. Jacob was 77 at the time of his death and his wife Elizabeth was 74. It was no doubt a terrible blow for Julia to lose both her parents in one month. Scarcely had the flowers been removed from the parlor, and the undertaker paid for her father's death, before she was arranging the blooms that would stand guard near her mother's casket in the same room. It was the third funeral to be held beneath the magnificent mural of clouds and sky that adorned the double parlor ceiling. Plants and flowers from the atrium, just through the twin folding doors of the parlor, were brought in to give the room a feeling of life and beauty. No doubt, her mother had guided her and helped tremendously in the rearing of eight children. The Feickerts lived to see their oldest granddaughter, Annie, married in 1886.

In 1892, William was now 56, and Julia 50. The children were growing and leaving the nest. Billy was now 25. He had attended Washington University and taken technical courses at the United Brewers Academy in New York City, graduating in 1885. Before that he had traveled to France and Southampton, at the age of 22, aboard the *Vanderbilt*. The passenger list has him as a "merchant." The steamer arrived in New York on September 13, 1858.

He had lived temporarily across the street at 3333 13th Street, as a boarder in 1891, (no doubt due to the lack of space at home, and a need to have some privacy of his own). He returned to live at Lemp Mansion from 1892 until just before his marriage in 1899, to Lillian Handlan.

Louis, the second eldest son, was 22, living at home and helping run the newly incorporated William J. Lemp Brewing Company, in the capacity of Superintendent. He was already enthralled with horses and racing. He had gone to Germany to train under some of the leading brewers, sending home to his father a copious handwritten 159-page review of the entire process of brewing beer. He was ranked as one of the leading brewmasters in America.

Charles Lemp was only a year younger than Louis. At 21, he was a focused young man who already had his eye on finance and politics. He rose to 2nd Vice-President and Treasurer of the brewery. He also came in handy later, as his signature appears as the notary public on many of his family's passport applications.

Frederick Lemp was born in 1873, and was 19 in 1892. Handsome and charming, he was favored by his father to one day run the brewery business. Fate had other plans.

Hilda Lemp was born in 1875. At 17-years-of-age, she had already been presented to society the year before. Looking every bit the stereotype of a sturdy German woman, she appears to be happy for the moment, living at home and preparing for the day she would walk down the aisle. That day came in 1897, when she married into another brewery dynasty—the Pabst family.

Edwin was now 12, and Elsa, 9. By all accounts, they were very close, well into their adult years. Elsa's sisters were much older, and while they cared for her with a maternal instinct, it was her brothers she followed on equestrian pursuits and outdoor adventures. Only eight years later, the 1900 census would show only Edwin and Elsa still living at home.

Anna Lemp, or "Annie" as she was most often called, was the oldest Lemp offspring. She was a grown young woman of 27 in 1892, and was already married and running a home of her own.

Chapter Four

Anna Laura Lemp
To the Manor Born

"Annie" Lemp age 3.
Photo courtesy of Lemp Mansion Museum.

St. Louis, Missouri: 1886

Anna Laura Lemp was born May 27, 1865, in St. Louis, Missouri. The oldest daughter of William and Julia, she was ten years older than her sister Hilda, and eighteen years Elsa's senior. Her world at home during her growing years was one of younger brothers, no doubt teasing her, yet giving the invaluable introduction to the world of boys and men. She later married (twice) and bore a son of her own.

Annie and Hilda in 1885: their final days as two single women.
Photo courtesy of Lemp Mansion

Annie was a beautiful young woman, presented to St. Louis society only "two seasons" before she married. At the age of 21, she walked down the aisle for the first time, marrying Heinrich Julius Meyer, on April 28, 1886.

Annie Lemp: possibly her entry into society or engagement photo.
Photo courtesy of Lemp Mansion

The perfume from the exotic flowers, decorating the first floor of 3322 Thirteenth Street, scented the staircase and upper floors as the bridal party excitedly prepared for the day. This was the first wedding of the Lemp children and the excitement was high. Annie looked into the tall Cheval mirror with anticipation as one of the maids helped her step into the expensive French gown.

"It was made of a heavy faille francois, with a very long train, bouffante at the back and finished with a heavy cord at the bottom. From the sides, it fell away in graceful folds, displaying a petticoat covered with deep flounces of rich pointe d'Alencon lace. The corsage was cut square at the

throat and filled with the same rich lace. Demi-sleeves, trimmed with the lace, were met by long white gloves. At her throat was a collar edged with small pearls and filled in with filmy costly lace, caught at the throat with a bar-pin set with large diamonds. The veil fell in folds down to the hem of the long train and was caught in the hair with large diamond pins to match the solitaire diamond earrings." **–Sprague Scrapbook**

Typical gown of a wealthy 19th century bride.

Across the hall her mother was undergoing the same transformation, no less impressive, as the family jewels were put on full display. "Mrs. W. J. Lemp wore a rich velvet reception gown of black gros-grain en traine, with rich trimmings of cut jet passementerie, to which was attached innumerable pendants, flashing in the light with each movement. Her corsage was cut montant, with demi-sleeves, and garniture of lace, with superb diamonds. At her waist was a bouquet of Marechal Neil roses."—

Sprague Scrapbook

Billy, acting as usher for the ceremony, was likewise putting the finishing touches on his ensemble. He and his father would be decked out in the finest fashions of the Gilded Age. This would include black trousers, white shirt, waist coat of fine brocade, cravat (tie), black frock coat and polished shoes. Diamond tie pins and cuff links would have been in style, as would gold insignia pieces. A black top hat finished the effect.

Frederick Wachter, today acting as butler in full livery, announced the arrival of the wedding carriages, each sporting flowers on the railings and horse appointments. It was time to go to the Church; only minutes away in Soulard.

A 1900s diamond ring

The local newspapers were effusive in their description of the nuptials:

"On Wednesday, at 2 p.m., at the Evangelical Lutheran Trinity Church, the marriage of Miss Anna Laura Lemp to Mr. Henry Julius Meyer was solemnized. The whole service was conducted in German and according to the simple rites of the Lutheran Church. Miss Lemp is the daughter of Mr. Wm. J. Lemp, the wealthy brewer. She made her entrée into society two seasons ago, and her reign as belle and beauty was brief but brilliant, as she was not only admired for her beauty, form and figure, but also for her amiability and winning manners. The fair young bride is petite and graceful, with golden brown hair laying in loose curls upon her brow, from beneath which shine the tender blue eyes, veiled by dark lashes. The delicate bloom of her cheeks was not paled by the ordeal, but remained the same.

"Mr. Meyer is the son of H. J. (Conrad Friedrich) Meyer, of the firm Meyers Brothers, and is a handsome and distinguished young man. (His father had just returned after spending two years in Denver, setting up a branch house for his wholesale druggist business. Author's note.)

The Wedding March rang out joyfully, as the bridal procession marched up the aisle. First came the ushers leading the way. They were Messrs. William Lemp, the brother of the bride, Mr. Fred Meyer, brother of the groom, Mr. Will Orthewein, and Mr. Con Mothey. They were followed by Mr. and Mrs. C. F. Meyer, the parents of the groom. Then came Mrs. Lemp upon the arm of the groom, and close behind them, the bride, escorted by her father.

"After the ceremony, the bridal party and guests proceeded at once to the residence of the bride's parents. The handsome homestead had been elaborately decorated with the rarest flowers and glossy foliage plants. One end of the salon was transformed into a bower from which was suspended the marriage bell, made of pure white roses and carnations. An orchestra was in attendance, rendering charming selections of music all the while. Tony Faust had carte blanche and served a delightful menu in  courses. The guests were seated, and toasts were freely drunk in the lighter Rhine wines, followed by champagne in abundance. The presents were not on display, but were costly and magnificent. The reception was very small and quiet, with only the nearest relatives and friends being invited to the house. Everything was elegant, refined, and unostentatious."

Besides the immediate family, there were 70 guests, including Ex-Mayor and Mrs. Henry Overstolz, Mr. and Mrs. Adolphus Busch, and their daughter, along with Captains and Colonels.

Wedding illustration from late 1800s and illustration on the previous page, courtesy of Eon Images.

"The happy pair left on the 8 o'clock train for Milwaukee, and from thence to Fort Wayne, Indiana (the groom's home town). They have engaged passage on the German steamer *Fulda*, which sails on the 12th of May. They intend making an extended tour of Europe, visiting France, Germany, England, Switzerland and many other points of interest in the old world, remaining abroad six months. When they return, they will spend the winter with the bride's parents, Mr. and Mrs. William J. Lemp."

The "pomp" was over, but the "circumstance" was just beginning. The Lemp-Meyer marriage was fraught with similar difficulties that would later plague the married bliss of both Billy

Lemp, and Elsa Lemp Wright. While the newspaper reports of the troubled couple were nowhere near as notorious as the William Lemp, Jr-Lillian Handlan divorce, they were scintillating nevertheless.

On March 16, 1893, *The Saint Louis Post-Dispatch* announced in bold print:

Mr. W. J. Lemp's Daughter

Depositions Being Taken in Her Behalf at Colorado Springs Colorado Springs, Colo., March 16. "Since Sunday, W. J. Lemp, a millionaire St. Louis brewer, and a friend of the family have been occupying rooms on North Colorado Avenue in an unostentatious dwelling in the fashionable part of the city. Their business here is to probe into the Meyer divorce case, which is now in a St. Louis court. "Last winter and spring, Mrs. Annie L. Meyer, a daughter of Mr. Lemp, began to decline in health. She was taken to Manitou Springs last summer by her family, and several weeks were passed at the Barker House. During their stay, Mrs. Meyer improved considerably. Henry E. Meyer, her husband, joined the party in August. Many friends were made by them. One of the parties was Mr. Konta, a thorough gentleman, whose name has been used most unpleasantly in the attempt to ascribe improper conduct to Mrs. Meyer.

"Last fall, after their return to St. Louis, the cause of the lady's ill health became apparent. Henry complained to his mother-in-law that Annie was growing cold toward him. Annie admitted to them that there was trouble which she had resolved to keep an unhappy wife's secret. Then she told of a threat made by her husband and her treatment at his hands. The application for divorce followed."

Henry visited Colorado Springs again in December, in the hope of gathering evidence against his wife and his proclamation that he had cause for "jealousy in the attentions of gentlemen." He brought back with him two depositions he had obtained from Will Cunningham, clerk at the Barker House, and John Woody, a prominent livery stable man, with what he hoped were sufficient insinuations. However, the facts fell short and his cross-bill for impropriety against his wife did not hold up.

The paper continued with the reporter's explanation for William Lemp's visit to the Springs: "The visit of Mr. Lemp was to take depositions of the citizens of Manitou Springs and residents there during the summer of 1892. The taking of testimony commenced in the office of Attorney Lunt, in Bank Block today."

Among the "citizens" served were a chambermaid from the Barker House, a Mansion House bowling alley/billiard hall attendant and others. They all testified to "the perfect lady-like demeanor" of Mrs. Meyer. James Markey, another attendant at the bowling alley did say he "had personal dislike and thought one gentleman too familiar." Judge Harrison was present with Mr. Meyer as his attorney.

Alexander Konta. Photo courtesy of Lemp Mansion

Almost a month later, the *St. Louis Post-Dispatch* ran a story indicating that Henry Meyer had paid a gentleman from Manitou to come to St. Louis and bare false testimony against Annie Lemp Meyer and her association with Alexander Konta. Will Cunningham, the clerk and porter at the Barker House, admitted to having "his expenses paid" to "tourist" in St. Louis. He confessed to going into the court house in Independence, Missouri to file his deposition, and that he "just swore to anything." He then went on to say he "was afraid to meet Mr. Lemp, afraid he would get after him with a club." Meyer had others approached to bear false depositions. In the end, the testimonies in favor of Mrs. Meyer and Mr. Konta won out. One such witness, was S. M. Fargo, wife of a member of the firm of Wells, Fargo, and Company, Chicago, who stated in her deposition that she "was continuously in the party last summer, and could testify to the lady-like conduct of Mrs. Meyer, and gentlemanly conduct of Mr. Konta. She had heard gossip, but no comments that the two were too much together."

Barker House, Manitou Springs, Colorado. 1890

The Meyers were divorced and Annie married Alexander Konta in 1895, two years after all the hullabaloo in Manitou Springs. (Manitou Springs is a small hamlet skirting Colorado Springs, Colorado, that was known for its curative waters, clean mountain air and resort getaways.) The Meyer divorce was obviously something the Lemp family was not hoping for when the beautiful wedding, heralded by St. Louis society pages only 9 years earlier, made headlines. Henry had run to Julia to shout his case, while William had to journey to Colorado Springs twice in a month's time to try and put out the fires. The only joyful outcome of the Meyer-Lemp union was a little boy born November 13, 1887: Geoffrey.

Geoffrey Meyer Konta
Photo courtesy of Lemp Mansion

New York City in the Gilded Age

Mark Twain and Charles Dudley Warner first penned the term "Gilded Age." It was their satirical description of the years after the Civil War when fortunes were flaunted on a ridiculous scale, while corruption pervaded national politics, law enforcement, and government agencies. Corporate buccaneers and Robber Barons held sway, while thousands lived in squalor.

These two authors saw a society veiled by a thin coating of gold. Nowhere in America was this bombastic use of wealth more apparent than within the marbled mansions of New York City, and the summer "cottages" of Newport, Rhode Island in the late 1800's.

When Annie Lemp later married Alexander Konta, she became ensconced in this city of excess, upon moving to New York City with her husband, shortly before 1910. The 1900 census shows the Konta's still living in St. Louis with one son, Geoffrey Konta, age 12. Jo Heitman is listed as living with them as a "watchman." By 1910, they are living in Manhattan at 45 Exchange Place. They have another address at Hempstead, Long Island.

Geoffrey Konta as a young man.-- Lemp Mansion

An interesting fact:
On a May 24, 1894, a passport for Annie Lemp, lists the son traveling with her as "Edwin," giving him the same birth date as Geoffrey, her only son. Her divorce was final by then from Henry Meyer. Was she hiding her son from someone? His name later appears as Konta. Was he adopted after the Konta-Lemp marriage?

45 Exchange Place, Manhattan in 1900

Konta residence at Hempstead, Long Island. --Lemp Mansion

45 Exchange Place was in the heart of the financial district of
New York City; Wall Street was only minutes away. Alexander

was a noted stock broker and may have selected the address to facilitate his dealings with the market. He was also a well-known playwright and banker, and he took great interest in politics and foreign affairs of the day. He was embroiled for a time in a lengthy trial concerning German ownership of a Washington newspaper and its sympathies with anti-Prohibition zealots. Konta's wife embodied both a German and a brewery legacy, making him a key target. An inflammatory letter involving him added fuel to the fire, but he was later cleared of involvement. The fact that his son Geoffrey later went on to become an attorney for the great William Randolph Hearst (a newspaper magnate that was very prominent in the New York newspaper business during the Gilded Age) was not lost on those who were not convinced of Alexander's innocence in the affair.

Foreign dignitaries were listed among Konta's friends. He created a replica of Jerusalem for the 1904 World's Fair in St. Louis, partly due to his friendships with the Turkish rulers of Palestine and Jerusalem. It covered 10 acres and had 300 buildings, replicating in minute detail the glory of the Holy Land. As his wife, Annie would have been ensconced in the upper crust of the great city and involved in hosting dinners and events befitting the couple's status.

The New York Times ran the following article on the society page on January 17, 1913:

"A dinner was given last night by Alexander Konta in the Louis XVI room of the St. Regis. The guests included Captain Rostrom*, formerly of the *Carpathia*, Miss Margaret Wilson, daughter of President-elect Woodrow Wilson, Mrs. S. MacDonald Sheridan, Mr. and Mrs. David Crompton, Captain and Mme. Gadski Tauscher, Miss Tauscher, Mr. Fisher, and Mr. and Mrs. Geoffrey Konta." The guest list is impressive and shows Konta's reach: from political ties to foreign dignitaries, along with the cream of New York high society.

*Captain Arthur Rostrom was the captain of the *Carpathia*, the only ship to reach the stricken *Titanic* and rescue the survivors still bobbing about in the waves in lifeboats on that frigid April morning in 1912. One of the survivors was John Jacob Astor's pregnant wife. Mr. Astor's body was found ten days later, on April 22nd. He was listed as Corpse no. 124 of the 306 bodies held afloat by their life jackets floating in the Atlantic that day. He was listed as follows: Age 50, with light-colored hair and moustache, attired in a blue serge suit, a belt with a gold buckle, and a brown shirt with the monogram *JJA* on the collar. A diamond ring circled one of his fingers; diamond studded cuff links still clasped the shirt at his wrists; and a gold watch was found in one of his pockets. In his wallet was $2,400 in US dollars (over $51,000 by today's standards), and £225 (roughly $62,000 in the 21st century). His estimated wealth was $87 million, over $1.8 billion today.

Ironically, Elsa Lemp Wright had tried to purchase passage on the Titanic, but changed her mind when she was told there were no more first-class tickets available.

Anna Lemp Konta in New York Society
Courtesy of the Missouri Historical Society

By 1913, when the Konta's dinner party was hosted, the Gilded Age had entered its death throes. Though during the late 1800s and early 1900s, when Annie Lemp Konta was first introduced to this high-rolling elite society, it was the talk—and scandal—of the American continent. From dinner parties where guests sat dining upon horseback at indoor dining tables laden with every delicacy known to man, to horse races where the bids equaled the national debt, it was a time of unabashed spending. Names such as Carnegie, Vanderbilt, Rockefeller, Whitney, and Gould were symbols of industrial triumphs netting them millions, and of excessive greed and ostentatious displays of wealth. Yachts, thoroughbred horses, marbled mansions, sumptuous summer retreats, and unlimited European travel were in constant display, as these dynasty heads spent money like water in an effort to outdo each other. Their wives, jewels adorning their ample bosoms, and wearing the latest fashions from Paris, vied for attention on the avenues of New York. They thought nothing of spending millions on a party that would last one evening. The Gilded Age became a mad race to see who could grab the biggest headlines for the most jaw-dropping parties.

Caroline Astor dominated this era with her highly coveted 400 Club. It was rumored the Club got its name from the number of people who could fit into Mrs. Astor's ballroom. She took the old money society to a new level; doggedly keeping the Noveau Riche from entering her circles, until Cornelia Bradley-Martin hosted the event that put New York society on its ear.

On February 10, 1897, the Bradley-Martins hosted a costumed ball taking excess to an entirely new level. Mrs. Astor arrived wearing over $4.6 million dollars in diamonds and other jewels, causing one reporter from the **New York World** to exclaim "It was perfectly astonishing how Mrs. Astor managed to find a place for so many jewels; they covered her like a cuirass." (A cuirass is a piece of armor consisting of a breastplate and backplate fastened together.) Cornelia's jewelry weighed in at a mere $2.3 million in today's dollars.

The evening's twenty-eight-course formal dinner included lobster, caviar-stuffed oysters, terrapin, duck, and roast English suckling pig. 4,000 bottles of 1884 Moet et Chandon, with a corkage fee alone of $138,000 in today's money, flowed, offering each guest over a quart of the amber liquid each. All total, the one-night affair had cost the Bradley-Martins $8.9 million in today's measure. When the millionaires of the Gilded Age began wrapping their cigars in hundred-dollar bills, stamped with gold initials, it was the final nail in the era's coffin. The outcry of the scandalized country was heard far and wide.

Into this atmosphere of excess and shallow indulgence stepped a young woman from St. Louis who had been raised in a family where hard work was heralded, and making society headlines was not the ultimate goal. Anna Lemp Konta was not content to ride on her influential husband's coattails, or to spend her days in idle pursuits involving the latest couture or visits to Newport. She contributed to society through two published books that were praised for their depth, tenacity and breadth.

According to the New York branch of the **St. Louis Post-Dispatch**, dated December 19, 1909: "Mrs. Alexander Konta, daughter of the late William J. Lemp of St. Louis, has written a book. It is not a society novel. It is called *"A History of French Literature,"* and it lives up to its ambitious title. The work has been praised by literary experts as one destined to become a text book. Indeed, before the book was published it was subjected to the scrutiny of professors at Harvard, Yale, and Columbia, all of whom acknowledged it to be a masterpiece.

"When Mrs. Konta, known to St. Louisans as Miss Annie Lemp, became interested in French literature and decided to write its history, she decided to do the drudgery of the work herself. She bought a typewriter, learned to operate it, and then she began. She labored continuously for 10 years. Her husband says that she was often busy into the night."

New York Branch of *St. Louis Post-Dispatch* Dec. 19, 1909

After her book on French literature, she penned a piece called *A Plea for Moderation: Based Upon Observations of an American Woman in a Belligerent Country.* It was published in 1915, and was about World War I: 1914-1918. It was 24-pages long and met with mixed reviews. It was from the viewpoint of a German-American at a time when America was entangled in a war against Germany. It was later touted for his timeliness and courage.

Anna Lemp Konta was a woman of substance and fire. She traveled extensively, devouring the cultures she studied. Her youngest sister Elsa was a constant guest at the Konta home, attending parties and galas, and thoroughly enjoying New York City in the Gilded Age. Elsa was visiting Annie when news reached them that their father had just committed suicide in their home in St. Louis.

Annie Lemp Konta passed away on August 19, 1939, at the age of 74.

Annie in 1900, with Elsa, in a novelty photo.
Photo courtesy of Lemp Mansion

Chapter Five

Hilda Lemp
A Marriage of Brewing Dynasties

Hilda Lemp's Engagement Photo
Photo courtesy Lemp Mansion

St. Louis: March 5, 1897-

Hilda "Mae" Thusnelda Lemp was born November 20, 1875, in St. Louis, Missouri. She was the second oldest daughter and ranked 6th in line of the living Lemp children. Known for her beautiful blond hair and striking blue-grey eyes, she was a sought-after beauty in her day. In fact, one young man in particular would simply not go away.

Hilda Lemp paced her mother's bedroom; her long evening gown sweeping the Oriental rugs as she absent-mindedly picked up a perfume bottle from the dressing table and smelled its stopper before striding nervously over to stare at a rare French painting adorning the wall near the fireplace. No amount of cajoling from her sympathetic mother could quiet her.

Typical Victorian bedroom for a wealthy woman in the 19th century
Photo courtesy of CR3AT.com.

Directly below them in her father's library, Hilda's fiancée was pleading with William Lemp, Sr. to have the marriage date set...the sooner the better. This was not the young man's first attempt to convince the wealthy brewery owner to give his consent to a wedding date sooner than the coming fall. Gustav Gottlieb Pabst found Mr. Lemp unmoved as the two gentlemen puffed on imported cigars in the luxurious library of Lemp mansion; its walls covered with treasures brought back from the multi-millionaire's travels around the world. The giant Lemp Brewery logo adorning the wall opposite the fireplace did not escape the notice of the heir to the mighty Pabst beer dynasty. Both men continued to state their cases as Hilda Lemp paced in the room above. As far as Mr. Lemp was concerned, there was no need to hurry the wedding date. It could wait until Hilda's return from their annual spring European vacation. The fact they would be away for three months only added to Gustav's anxiety.

Typical library in the 1800s.

No doubt, William Lemp was still stinging from the whirlwind marriage and divorce of his oldest daughter Annie to Henry Meyer. Eleven years earlier, she had made headlines over some scandal that sent William running to Colorado Springs to curtail a potential nightmare for the family. When Annie married Alexander Konta—one side of the divorce triangle—only two years after the Meyer marriage was over, it added fuel to the gossip that had only barely begun to die down.

Now here he sat with an anxious young man who had just undergone a major scandal of his own, when his previous tumultuous marriage set Milwaukee newspaper headlines ablaze. Despite the fact that Gustav was the son of William's dear friend, Captain Frederick Pabst, Mr. Lemp was probably hoping to give the proposed marriage to his daughter a little more time in order to let the inflammatory tales of the first Gustav Pabst marriage, to stage actress Margaret Mather, die down.

Hilda watched from the window at the end of the upstairs hallway as a perturbed Gustav Pabst strode down the stone steps of Lemp Mansion and climbed hurriedly into his waiting carriage. He needed time to cool off. She watched as the Phaeton took off at a fast clip. Obviously, the marriage would go forth in the fall as her father had planned, and she would travel with her family to Europe first, also as planned.

Phaeton, a sporty carriage of the 1800s.
Photo courtesy of KristenKoster.com

The Saint Louis Post-Dispatch, ever vigilant in its timely reporting, caught up with William Lemp Wednesday morning, following the impromptu meeting with the anxious Gustav Pabst:

"Mr. Pabst's visit at this time was a great surprise to me," William told the reporter. "I do not know that he expected the wedding to be arranged for at once. It cannot take place until after our trip to Europe. We shall leave in two or three weeks, and be away three months. When we return, it will be time enough to arrange the details. Of course, the wedding will take place; the engagement has already been announced."

Indeed, the **Omaha Daily Bee** had run the announcement earlier that year:

"Society circles of Milwaukee, Chicago and St. Louis are just now deeply interested in the announcement of an engagement between Colonel Gustav G. Pabst of Milwaukee and Miss Hilda Lemp of St. Louis. In the two cities named it is almost the sole topic of conversation among society folk and in Chicago, where the families of the contracting parties have many friends. A few years ago, Colonel Pabst was married to Margaret Mather, the celebrated actress, but the union proved uncongenial and the couple was divorced."

That the "union proved uncongenial" was a kind way to put it. It had been a major embarrassment to the Pabst family, as papers from Milwaukee to Salt Lake City carried the story with gleeful prose:

Rock Island Argus (Rock Island, Ill.) Oct. 03, 1895. " Mr. and Mrs. Gustav Pabst, formerly Margaret Mather, the actress, created a sensation near their home at Twenty-ninth and Cedar streets yesterday. Numerous residents in the vicinity were eye-witnesses to an altercation which began in a buggy in which the couple were riding and which ended at the corner of Twenty-fourth and State streets, where Pabst wrenched the whip from his wife's hand as the latter struck her husband full in the face.

"Mr. and Mrs. Pabst were driving along Twenty-seventh street about noon when suddenly, just as they were about to turn into Cedar street toward their home, Mrs. Pabst grabbed the whip from the socket and doubling it, struck Mr. Pabst full in the face. Mr. Pabst jumped out of the buggy and started down the street. The woman drove the horse to a post, hitched it, and followed her husband, overtaking him a block away, where she struck him four times in the face. Mr. Pabst then wrenched the whip from her hand and threw it away, but Mrs. Pabst resented this by striking her husband full in the face with her fist.

"Then Mr. Pabst moved on at a rapid pace, the woman following, both entering their home on Cedar Street."

Margaret Mather during a performance at The Broadway in NY.

The article goes on to say that since their marriage in Kenosha in 1892, Mrs. Pabst retired from the stage. Their marriage was kept secret for several months. During the 1800s, a stage actress was considered a lowly station in life, akin to a prostitute. It is rumored the Pabst family was not happy about the union. Gustav had become enamored with Margaret Mather after seeing her perform on stage and followed her throughout the country, grabbing a box seat at each of her performances. She finally caved to his advances and they married. But Gustav found that actresses don't mind attention, even on a ritzy avenue in Milwaukee.

Gustav's father hurried over, much like William Lemp did for his child, to put out the fire before it caused a family scandal. Within minutes, Gustav and Margaret were denying (despite myriad witnesses) that the incident ever happened. "At midnight, last night Captain Frederick Pabst, and his son Gustav, called at all of the newspaper offices and denied emphatically that there was any truth to the horse-whipping story," quoted the *Rock Island Argus*. Colonel Gustave Pabst said, "My wife did not strike me. There was no altercation and there is absolutely no truth in the story." Alas, it was front page fodder despite the powerful family's denials.

Colonel Gustav G. Pabst and his father Captain Frederick Pabst
Photo courtesy of the Pabst Mansion

Friends were questioned but none could give any reason for the altercation. Mr. Pabst was unable to be found for comment. It seems the public still embraced him as the *St. Louis Post-Dispatch* lauded: "Col. Pabst is wealthy, and his experience with a theatrical wife has not affected his standing in Milwaukee society. He is still considered a good catch."

Margaret sued for divorce on the grounds of incompatibility and won a $40,000 alimony settlement and her freedom in 1895. *The Salt Lake Herald* ran an article in December of that year, stating: "Mrs. Gustav Pabst, better known as Margaret Mather, did not continue her journey beyond this city. She is now ill at St. Joseph's hospital, where since Friday; she has been unable to see even her Chicago relatives. She is said to be suffering from nervous prostration, said to have been brought on by her recent domestic troubles."

Margaret Mather returned to the stage, to mixed reviews. She was said to be suffering from a chronic illness. She died onstage while performing in Charleston, West Virginia, in 1898, only one year after Gustav married Hilda. She was buried in the white gown from her *Juliet* portrayal from a previous play. She is interred in the Elmwood Cemetery in Detroit.

Brewery Trust Formed by Cupid

GUSTAV PABST ANXIOUS TO HASTEN THE WEDDING

MR. LEMP SAYS "BIDE AWHILE"

The Pabst-Mather scandal was soon replaced with new headlines as the *St. Louis Post-Dispatch* leaked news of Gustav's new love interest the morning after Colonel Pabst's visit to St. Louis. "Colonel Gustav G. Pabst of Milwaukee surprised millionaire brewer William J. Lemp by dropping in on him at Lemp Mansion Tuesday night....The indefinite nature of the wedding plans have set the gossips to speculating again. They wanted to know just when the long-expected event would take place, but nobody at the Lemp Mansion could or would enlighten them.

"Colonel Pabst is still in the dark, although those who claim to know, say he came all the way from the city of yellow bricks to find out when he could claim the fair daughter of the house of Lemp for his own....Colonel Pabst will remain in the city a few days and then return to Milwaukee and "bide a wee."

"Miss Hilda Lemp is a beautiful and accomplished girl and a universal favorite in South End society," the article continued. "She is 22 years old. Col. Pabst is rich, debonair and 30. He is a son of Capt. Frederick Pabst, owner of the Pabst Brewing Company... While in St. Louis he will be a guest of the Lemp family. He was seen out driving with William Lemp, Jr. Wednesday morning."

Hilda Lemp on the wings of the "aeroplane" that would deliver Falstaff beer far and wide.
Photo courtesy of Donald Roussin at **beerhistory.com**

Gustav Pabst returned home to Milwaukee without obtaining an answer as to when he could marry William Lemp's lovely daughter. The family set sail for England, as planned. It is witnessed by a passport application made by Mr. Lemp on April 26, 1897. It lists himself at 61 years of age, traveling with his wife Julia, daughters Hilda and Elsa, and son Edwin. Charles Lemp's signature is above the title of Notary Public. Mr. Lemp may have won the battle, but he had underestimated his future son-in-law's tenacity, as two stubborn Germans locked horns.

The bold headlines adorning the *St. Louis Post-Dispatch* a month later showed the victor of the Lemp-Pabst marriage debate:

WILL WED IN LONDON
COL. PABST COULDN'T WAIT FOR MISS LEMP TO RETURN TO ST. LOUIS

FOLLOWED HER OVER THE SEA

"Miss Hilda Lemp and Col. Gustav G. Pabst will be married in London next Monday…The wedding was to have been celebrated in St. Louis this fall, but, for the second time in his career, Col. Pabst's ardor will hasten his entrance into the married state.

"Impatient of delay he followed his fiancée across the Atlantic and urged his case so eloquently that the union of the two great beermaking houses of Lemp and Pabst will be rattled in "deah old Lunnon." (An affectionate eponym for "dear old London.")

"St. Louis people who had been looking forward to a brilliant wedding here were surprised and disappointed when they learned that the union of the two great brewery families would not take place here."

The wedding was hastily put together while the Lemp's were still vacationing in London. A telegram from Milwaukee announced the wedding of Hilda and Gustav would come off in England "next Monday," instead of late in the fall, in St. Louis. "Mr. and Mrs. Lemp will be present at the wedding," it reported. As to William Lemp putting his foot down, the debate ended, in effect, Pabst-1 Lemp-0.

Hilda Lemp and Gustav Pabst Wedding Announcement

The **Sprague Scrapbook** was replete with its usual sumptuous description of the quiet wedding.

"The wedding will take place in a picturesque chapel in Ventnor on the Isle of Wight where will be performed the marriage of Miss Hilda T. Lemp, second daughter of Mr. and Mrs. William J. Lemp of St. Louis, and Colonel Gustav G. Pabst of Milwaukee, Wis.

"The Isle of Wight, where the ceremony will be performed, is an ideal spot for a wedding. It lies in the English Channel just off the mainland and a short distance from Southampton. English Ivy grows luxuriously all over the place. Flowers bloom as seen nowhere else. Handsome homes, many belonging to theatrical celebrities, are seen on every side, surrounded by English box and hawthorn. There could indeed be no more fitting place for mating and yesterday's pair of lovers are not the first to so discover.

"The affair was very quiet and simple. Only those members of both families who are in Europe were present. Tasteful arrangements of flowers filled the church with festoons of ivy about the walls. An effort was made to preserve the same decorations as those which filled the chapel two years ago, for Miss Annie Lemp, the bride's older sister, who was married to Mr. Alexander Konta, in St. Louis. Those who are familiar with the bride's beautiful blond hair and rose-colored complexion may imagine what a stunning picture she presented in her bridal dress of white satin brocade, a creation from Charles Frederick Worth. Her bridesmaid was Miss Elsa Lemp, a younger sister. She was escorted down the aisle by her father where he dutifully gave her away.

Hilda Lemp in her wedding dress by Worth.
Photo courtesy of Lemp Mansion

Other newspaper accounts went on to say the couple was married in the Bible Christian Church, which was very handsomely decorated for the occasion. The Rev. J. C. Pye officiated. Edwin Lemp was the best man. After the ceremony, there was a wedding luncheon at the Royal Marine Hotel. The guests included Mr. and Mrs. William J. Lemp, Mr. and Mrs. Alexander Konta, Master Edwin Lemp and Miss Elsa Lemp, and Mr. and Mrs. Nunnemacher of Milwaukee, sister and brother-in-law of the groom, who were married early in the summer and who are now on their wedding journey.

After the luncheon the newlyweds left for London, and then a lengthy trip through Europe and the East. The Lemps (no doubt still reeling from the hurried festivities), along with Annie Lemp Konta, sailed from Southampton for America on the initial trip of the *Laiser Wilheim der Grosse*, the North German Lloyd Company's magnificent new steamer.

Hilda Lemp Pabst on her wedding day
Photo courtesy of Pabst Mansion, Milwaukee, Wisconsin

> Luckily, for Hilda's hurried trousseau, the House of
> Worth, the most-desired fashion designer of his day, had a
> store in London, from where he originated. Paris carried
> his jaw-dropping designs and he was sought after by
> celebrities, royalty and dignitaries of the day.

The marriage of Hilda Lemp to Gustav Pabst on September 14, 1897, was not the first union of "beer brewery heir meets beer brewery heir" in the Pabst family. Only recently, Gustav's younger brother Frederick had married Miss Uhlein, daughter of August Uhlein, the head of the Schlitz brewery. The Lemp-Pabst marriage helped unite the interests of three of the largest breweries in the United States. One has to wonder which lager was offered most often at family get-togethers.

Three generations of Fredericks: Capt. Frederick Pabst with his son Frederick, and grandson Frederick. Photo courtesy of Pabst Mansion

From all accounts, the Lemp-Pabst marriage was a happy one. They loved to entertain family and friends. Hilda loved to barbeque at their family farm. Recipes made with beer were tested in the Pabst kitchen and served lovingly to their growing family. They had three sons: Gustav Gottlieb Pabst Jr., born May 1899, William Frederick, born in 1902, and Edwin Lemp Pabst, born Dec. of 1908. William and Julia lived to hold two of the three young members of Hilda's legacy.

The christening of one of Hilda's sons as Edwin Lemp Pabst must have meant a great deal to Edwin. It shows her affection for a brother who was always there for his family, as we will later learn. One of Hilda's granddaughters was given the name Elsa Lemp Pabst. Born in 1936, it was a lovely tribute to a woman who died much too young in 1920. Little Elsa was devoted to her grandparents. She is seen here riding with her grandfather, Gustav Pabst, on one of his prize horses at the family farm.

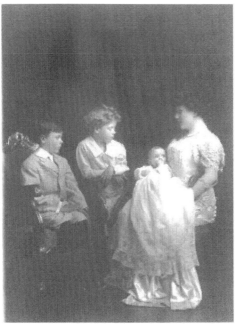

Hilda with her three young sons William, Gustav & Edwin.
Photo courtesy of Pabst Mansion, Milwaukee, Wisconsin

93

Col. Gustav Pabst with his granddaughter, Elsa.
Photo courtesy of Pabst Mansion.

The 1900 census of Milwaukee, Wisconsin shows Gustav (33), Hilda (24), and Gustav Jr. (1). They have three servants, Frederick Rukert (23), Minne Hasse (27), and Anna Schneider (30).

While the Pabst mansion they created is an imposing structure, sitting majestically on a bluff overlooking Lake Michigan, by all accounts the newly married couple led a quiet life. The home boasted 4 bedrooms, 6 full baths and one half-bath. It is listed at $1,450,000 in today's real estate market. Gustav's sister Marie lived just to the north in what is known as the Goodrich House. The home was designed by the same firm, Ferry & Clas that designed Captain Frederick Pabst's palatial mansion on Grand Avenue, in Milwaukee. Hilda and Gustav's home is made of a limestone ashlar façade, trimmed with wrought bronze grilles. The columns were cut from single blocks of stone after Mrs. Hilda Pabst was said to be disappointed with the original sectioned columns.

Hilda "Mae" Thusnelda Lemp was an unostentatious person. She lived a life devoted to her family and died in Wisconsin on July 8, 1951.

Hilda and Gustav Pabst's home at 2230 N. Terrace Ave, Milwaukee

Interior views of the Gustav Pabst mansion

Gustav Pabst was the second owner of the Pabst Brewery, after his father Captain Frederick Pabst. He was the first Pabst to be educated as a Master Brewer. Fascinated with aviation, as many were in those inspired first days of air travel, he was on the Aero Club's Public Safety Committee with Orville Wright. Gustav was also known for his importation of upland game birds from around the world. He raised prized cattle, horses and hunting dogs. A family man and gentleman farmer, Gustav Pabst was also the most outspoken proponent of the repeal of Prohibition, and was urged by other brewery owners of the time to take the cause to Washington D.C.

"The aim of civilization is to make men better and stronger by the exercise of willpower, not imposing arbitrary rules upon them. Temperance is civilization and intelligence. Prohibition is tyranny."

Gustav Pabst penned that message and took it to President Woodrow Wilson. Several years later the 18th Amendment prohibiting the sale of alcohol was repealed in the United States.

Gustav Pabst

Chapter Six

Elsa Justine Lemp
An Unfinished Life

Elsa Justine Lemp in August, 1883 (6 months old)
Photo courtesy of Lemp Mansion

Saint Louis, Missouri: 1900

Elsa Justine Lemp bounced into the world on February 8, 1883. She was the last born into the Lemp household and was a full 18 years younger than her oldest sister Anna. Hilda, her only other sister, was 8 years her senior. Elsa was far closer in age to her brother Edwin, who was only 3 years older.

According to the 1900 census, only Elsa and Edwin were still living at Lemp Mansion with their parents William (63) and Julia (55). Elsa was 17 and Edwin 20 (although the census has them as 16 and 17). Elsa's sisters were both married: Annie for the second time in 1895, and Hilda in 1897. Her brothers Billy, Louis and Frederick had all married the previous year in 1899 in a whirlwind of flowers, cake icing and "I Do's"—Louis in the Spring, Frederick in August, and Billy in October. The children of Lemp Mansion were departing faster than animals deserting the open door of the Ark. Julia Lemp was still finding rice in her furs.

The large house seemed oddly quiet. The Feickerts had passed away in 1892, and many of the servants had married and moved on to create lives of their own. In the 19th century, the only servants allowed to be married were the head butler. Thus, the servant turnover was high as young people entered and left service as their marital status, or employment opportunities, changed. It was not necessarily a reflection on their happiness with a household if they moved on after a short time.

In 1900, Minnie Harteustein now captained the kitchen at Lemp Mansion, instead of their beloved Mathilda Bressler, while Minnie Casper and Eva Wetzel carried out the daily servant's responsibilities—largely cleaning and helping with the arduous task of helping the Lemp women dress in the layered fashions of the 1900s.

Eva Wetzel tugged on the corset lacings as Elsa Lemp held fast to the post of her four-poster bed, her face a twisted spasm of pain. She had endured the changing fashions of the Victorian era with the same stoic indulgence as her mother and sisters, but the corsets were the bane of every female. If they weren't plumping up your breast and thrusting them forward, as they did in the Pigeon look, they were bending your spine into an unnatural S-shape that caused your fanny to protrude to the likeness of a female baboon. The designers, seemingly with the intent to cause as much pain to the internal organs as possible, were forever changing the corset's infrastructure from iron-to-steel-to-whalebone in ever-evolving contraptions to minimize the female waistline and enhance the bosom and bottom.

Trussed like a thanksgiving turkey, Elsa stepped into the petticoat, and floor-length dark skirt. At least bustles were gone and a girl could sit down without major adjustments to her backside. She buttoned up her high-colored pastel shirt while Eva helped tuck it in at the waist and encircle it with a flattering belt. Perhaps she could skip the stockings, just for now, until it was time to go out. Like every woman of her generation, she looked forward to the late afternoon when ladies, who staying in for a time, could slip out of the corset and lounge in their tea gowns.

1900s corset

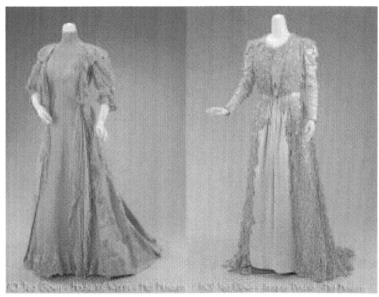

Tea gowns from 1900s.
Photo courtesy of glamourdaze.com

Minnie Harteustein drew in her breath while she continued to press the bread dough into compliance as she mixed the butter, eggs and flour in a large bowl. The hurried, thudding steps she could hear descending the stairs to the basement could only be Miss Lemp again, checking on the preparations for her tea party for that afternoon. She could understand the young lady's excitement at hosting her first tea since being presented to society a few days earlier, but honestly, the girl had changed the menu four times.

Elsa Lemp exploded into the kitchen, her face beaming. In her hands was a lady's magazine, opened to a dog-eared page. Elsa came around the giant kitchen table that was covered with flour, various pastry ingredients, and bowls of rising dough for the scones she had requested. Minnie held pressed lips into a thin line as the young lady thrust the opened magazine beneath the cook's nose. As Minnie feared, the page boasted a large photo of intricately decorated mini-

cakes, all looking as if they had come from the palace of Louis IV.

Reigning in her impatience, she told the optimistic Miss Lemp that the scones were already underway, and there wouldn't be time to create the intricate cakes pictured in the photo. The cook pointed to the various ingredients scattered about the table: finely grated orange rind and dried cranberries for the Cranberry Orange Scones; grated lemon rind and freshly washed blueberries for the Lemon-Blueberry Scones; and finally, almond extract and dried cherries for the Cherry-Almond Scones. There were also chopped bits of chocolate for a special pastry that would be topped with drizzled frosting. Various teas were steeping in copper pots on the cast-iron range and their sweet aroma filled the sunny kitchen.

The protruding lower lip Ms. Harteustein had come to expect from Elsa Lemp during her pouting moments was in full evidence. The cook knew, as well as she knew how to prepare cherry tarts, that she would not win this argument. She took the magazine from the girl and studied what she would need to do to recreate the delicacies smiling at her from the page. Elsa hugged her and danced from the room.

1900s cook

When Julia Lemp entered the kitchen a few moments later, she walked into a shower of flour, powdered sugar and words unbecoming a lady of the Lemp household. The cook reminded her, respectfully, that servants were not considered "ladies," and then apologized for the earthy language. She told Mrs. Lemp that the young Elsa had changed the menu, and formality of the occasion, several times. First, it was to be a simple tea party, less formal—a "kettle drum," the girl had called it. Simple sandwiches of cucumber or tomato, along with tea, lemonade and a few simple biscuits. The cook told the lady of the house that Minnie, the 25year-old maid, had barely returned from buying milk from the milk truck, the cucumbers and tomatoes from the produce stand over on Soulard, and more sugar and butter from the grocers, when Miss Elsa had stopped by to say it would be a formal tea after all— with the fine china, linens, meat sandwiches (cut into petit fours), buns, rolls, scones, fruit displays, ices, tea, chocolate, lemonade and coffee. Now, the scones are being replaced by, or added to, small cakes she found in a lady's magazine, and Minnie has dashed off to the butcher for the select meats for the sandwiches.

While Mrs. Lemp was trying to mollify the rattled cook, Elsa darted into the milieu once more, announcing she had changed her mind.

Her cousins were coming and she wanted to put together an informal grouping of blankets on the back yard where the guests could dine "a la picnic." The cakes wouldn't be needed after all, nor the meat sandwiches. Cucumber and tomato (on small bread squares) would be fine...and scones.

Elsa w/2 of her cousins having a picnic. Elsa is on r. in the striped
shirt. Photo courtesy of Lemp Mansion

1900 was a whirlwind year for Elsa Lemp. Her father had
taken her on a trip to Paris on April 20th, along with her mother.
It was a special trip just for her. The family took spring trips to
Europe almost every year since her father had turned over the
reins of the brewery to Billy and Louis. But this trip, Hilda
wasn't with them as she usually was, and Frederick hadn't joined
them since 1894. It was the first time Edwin had not been
along. Her father was 64 years of age now, and he spoiled his
youngest daughter. They would visit the House of Worth in
Paris, and there she would pick out her season's wardrobe.

Elsa Lemp, probably in her "season," being presented to society. 1900.
Photo courtesy of Lemp Mansion

Early 1900s fashions. Courtesy glamourdaze.com

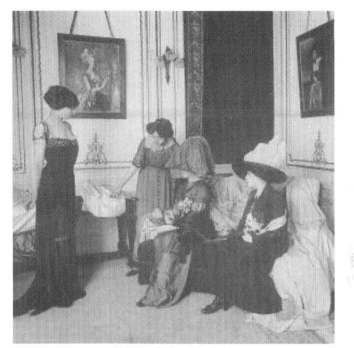

House of Worth in Paris.
Photo courtesy of glamourdaze.com

As 1900 dawned, the world looked forward to a bright new shining century. Automobiles were making their appearance; businesses were installing telephones (although it would be awhile yet for residential streets to become wired for the new contrivance). In 1887, trains had begun transporting people farther and farther from their doorsteps, necessitating the opening of St. Louis's Union Station in 1894. Electric trolley cars were replacing cable cars in 1901, while elevators began appearing in 1890, and were swooping happy shoppers to the heights of modern-day skyscrapers in downtown St. Louis. One such imposing edifice was the Wainwright Building, a 10-story red brick office building at 709 Chestnut Street. It was among the first skyscrapers in the world and became the prototype for buildings to come. Barr's Department store was another cloud-scraping structure that would open in 1911, offering everything the modern woman could ask for, including the latest in fashions. These were not the couture's created in upscale Parisian boutiques however. And if you were a wealthy socialite, only the House of Worth would do.

Elsa and the Belle Epoch

The *Belle Epoch* ushered in the 1900s, with a swirl of silk gowns beaded to perfection, with figure-enhancing lines. *Belle Epoch* means Age of Opulence, and indeed it was—if your purses could handle the price tags. Millionaires' daughters from around the world headed to Paris for their twice-a-year pilgrimage. Fancy Parisian boutiques were crammed with eager young debutantes, their weary mothers in tow, who were also ready to indulge in the latest fashions themselves.

1906 - EVENING DRESS - 1912

Photo courtesy of Glamourdaze.com

During the months of Spring and September, the sidewalks of Paris were teeming with the crème of the crop. The rue

Halevy, rue de la Paix, la rue Auber, Place Vendome, and rue Taitbout sported the best in fashion salons. The wealthy were welcomed with cushioned chairs, refreshments, and the latest catalogues from which to choose this year's must-have fashions. If you were a returning customer, you were given your own *vendeuse*—a woman who would take care of you personally as you chose your wardrobe for the coming season. She would know all your secrets, both those pertaining to your form, and often, much more. These fashion houses depended on their wealthy clientele. You were measured, and those statistics kept on file, along with your color preference, favorite designer and upcoming social events. Models wearing the latest in European fashions were paraded before you, as you sipped on expensive beverages and flipped past pages of alluring gowns. The latest designs from the greats, such as Poiret, Worth, Callot Soeurs, Jeanne Pacquin, and Madeleine Cheruit graced the copies of *Les Modes*.

House of Redfern—Galerie-de-Vente—Paris 1910
Photo courtesy of Glamourdaze.com

In one spring shopping trip, a young girl would select day dresses, tea gowns, boating attire, evening gowns, sportswear (bloomers were being worn by women who were happily bicycling everywhere), lingerie, car coats, walking suits, and jaw-dropping costume gowns for upcoming balls. Fancy corsets, shoes and hats were all on display.

An ad from 1900 with a lady in bloomers.

Once the purchases were made, the measurements taken, and the bill proffered, the exhausted shoppers would step from the frenzied shops and go out to see the sights. It started all over again in the fall. The parcels would be dutifully packed with the hand-stitched outfits, the sleeves carefully packed with tissue paper to maintain their shape, and shipped to New York City, where they would then continue on to their destination.

This was also a time to see, and be seen, on the fashionable avenues of France. More than one pretty heiress came to the "City of Lights" to purchase finery, only to find herself smitten with local royalty. In fact, these introductions between

America's wealthy and Europe's titled were far from coincidental.

They called them the "Dollar Princesses."

During the Gilded Age, the ultimate goal of many a New York hostess was to usher their eligible daughters to Europe during "the season" in the hopes of capturing a royal title with their opulent pocket books. As Geoffrey Beard noted, "With declining rents and a fall in the value of property, many English peers needed their capital regenerated." By the turn of the century more than five hundred Gilded Age American heiresses had "joined hands" with European royalty, usually for titles and convenience, although sometimes cupid played a part. Some wealthy American parents even resorted to bribes to obtain a royal invitation for their daughter to a ball or event where the Prince of Wales, or other notables, might be attending. Adorned with diamond tiaras and jewel-studded stomachers, these wealthy young women from the Continent strolled the tree-lined boulevards of Paris in hopes of bagging a royal catch.

One such marriage, on December 21, 1895, was between Miss Clara Hazel Busch, daughter of the famous brewery owner Adolphus Busch, and Count Paul von Gontard of Germany. As one paper reported, "The wedding is an international event, the most notable of its kind socially that has ever taken place in St. Louis." 2,000 invitations went out, two floors of the gorgeous Southern Hotel were retained for months for guests from Europe, New York, Milwaukee, Chicago and pretty much every prominent city in America. It was reported the affair cost Adolphus $100,000 (the equivalent of $2.9 million in today's economy). Besides over $50,000 in bridal gifts from the adoring guests, Adolphus chipped in an additional $100,000 estate in Germany as part of his daughter's dowry. And privy to this spectacle of wealth and privilege was one Miss Hilda Lemp, who was one of the bridesmaids. One has to wonder if Hilda looked at her own simple ceremony a few years later and compared the two.

Indeed, London and Paris offered the young rich debutantes of the Gilded Age much more than fashion and some vacation time. The two cities were on every heiress's travel radar during that all-important spring season each year.

Elsa Lemp circa 1910
Photo courtesy *St. Louis Post-Dispatch* Newspaper

Fashions may have been on Elsa Lemp's radar but they were far from her only obsession. She grew up around five brothers who loved everything the outdoors represented. They were into fishing and hunting, horseback riding, motor cars, golf, travel, and any seductive new device coming off the assembly line. As a young woman, Elsa was said to be independent, feisty and quite accomplished at a number of endeavors herself.

The Lemps owned box seats at the Olympic, the popular theater in downtown St. Louis. Their names filled almost every society column reporting on the latest play or concert presented at the venue. *The St. Louis Republic* wrote on May 14, 1901:

Society People See The Play

"That society following, which has long found Mr. Goodwin's comedy rules to its liking, evinced curiosity and interest in his Shakespearean venture by appearing in the Olympic last night. Men who came without ladies lined the walls, and no small number of pretty girls in pretty light dresses, hung over the railing during the entire performance. Enthusiasm over the play was pronounced, with much applause as the result.

"Mr. and Mrs. William J. Lemp and Miss Elsa Lemp sat in the front circle and near Mr. and Mrs. Shapleigh Boyd."

Another evening found the Lemps enjoying Mrs. Campbell's play "The Joy of Living." The article sites that Mr. and Mrs. William J. Lemp attended, along with their daughter Mrs. Gustav Pabst of Milwaukee, formerly Miss Hilda Lemp, Miss Elsa Lemp, and Edwin Lemp.

Horse competitions found the Lemps in the Lemp Box as noted on Nov. 1901: "In the Lemp Box were Mr. and Mrs. William J. Lemp, Jr., Mr. and Mrs. Gustav Pabst of Milwaukee, Miss Elsa Lemp and Mrs. William J. Lemp, Sr. who wore black satin and duchesse lace. Mrs. Pabst was in watermelon-pink crepe, trimmed in much shirring, while Mrs. Lemp, Jr. wore gray crepe and white chiffon, with a white-plumed hat." The evening before William and Julia were both in the Lemp Box along with Elsa, Louis, and a J.W. Kearney. Elsa and Edwin were often at the Olympic together, as well as traveling abroad.

The St. Louis Republic mentioned Edwin's return, after traveling to New York City with Elsa in August, 1905: "Mr. Edwin A. Lemp returned last night from a three weeks' visit in New York and the Jersey coast. Miss Elsa Lemp will remain East the remainder of the summer." This trip was no doubt to visit Annie Lemp Konta. It was a year and 6 months after their father's tragic death. The Lemps were seen often at social functions, weddings, concerts and area entertainments. There is no mention of Charles attending these events with them. Louis is mentioned only in the horse riding venues.

1904 and 1906 spelled the end of innocence for Elsa. On Feb. 13, 1904, her father, William J. Lemp shot himself in his upstairs' bedroom. That same year, her mother, Julia, began suffering with health issues and was finally admitted to a sanitarium in Rochester, Missouri. According to an article in the *St. Louis Republic* dated December 6, 1904, a group of wealthy young women were going on a grand tour of Europe and beyond. "They expect to go first to London and Paris, and later to spend two months in Southern Italy," the *Republic* stated. "This will be followed by an extended tour of Egypt and the Nile, with Turkey and Greece to follow. The trip is expected to take about fourteen or fifteen months…Miss Elsa Lemp is considering the trip but is also doubtful, because of the illness of Mrs. William J. Lemp, who is now in a sanitarium in Rochester, Missouri."

Julia struggled with the diagnosis of cancer she received only a month later in 1905. An elevator was put in at Lemp Mansion in 1904, when her weakened condition first began to manifest. The grand staircase was taken out and an open lift installed that ran from basement to attic, in the 4 stories of the home, in hopes of making the many floors more easily managed.

Julia Lemp finally succumbed to cancer on April 16, 1906. Her entire family gathered in her room on the 2nd floor of Lemp

Mansion to pay their last respects to the woman who had always been "the heart of the home."

(More about William and the brewery's progress will be presented next, as we go into the men of the Lemp family.)

When Elsa finally rallied, finding herself now the wealthiest single woman in St. Louis, after her mother and father's wills were read, her brothers and sisters took her under their wing. She visited Annie often in New York City, enjoying "the season," that ran after November when the summer "cottage" people returned to their mansions and threw outlandish parties. It was Hilda's home in Milwaukee that hosted her wedding, Charles and Billy who witnessed her passports, Louis who taught her how to sit a saddle, and dear Edwin who stayed by her side and took her in after their mother passed away. She had always been close to her family.

A rare photo of the 3 sisters. (l. to r.) Elsa, Annie and Hilda.
Photo courtesy of Lemp Mansion

Billy signed Elsa's passport application in 1907. William and Julia were dead, and Billy stepped up as witness for Elsa due to her age. He lists the William J. Brewing Company as his address, and states he has known her for 24 years.

Elsa's passport of 1907 w/Billy's signature at the bottom.

At a petite 5' 2" tall, the pretty blond with the blue eyes, small chin and oval face was anything but demur. Elsa would have pedaled off happily on the latest bicycle, was known in her later years to own several expensive automobiles and drove them herself. She could work a billiard table, and was ringside for most of the competitive horse events. For good reason...her horse often won.

ODDS FISH.
A magnificent specimen of the walk, trot and canter horse; owned and ridden by Miss Elsa Lemp of St. Louis. He won the championship in his class at Saratoga last year, and is one of the best of his kind ever foaled.

Odds Fish, Elsa's prize quarter horse, often beat out her brother's horses; something I'm sure was the subject of much good-natured ribbing at the family table. As the caption with the above photo states, Odds Fish won the championship for his class in Saratoga, Florida. It also lists Elsa as the rider. If you look closely, you can see the ubiquitous Italianate brick window openings of the Lemp Brewery in the photograph. The Lemps kept renowned stables at the brewery in what was once the Cooling House. There will be more about the stable and their show horses when we talk about Louis Lemp.

Elsa Lemp, possibly her engagement photo. 1910.
Photo courtesy of Lemp Mansion

Elsa Lemp Is To Wed in Milwaukee April 12
Special Train Will Carry St. Louisans to Nuptials at Pabst Home

St. Louis Post-Dispatch, March 9, 1910:

"The marriage of Thomas H. Wright and Miss Elsa Lemp will take place April 12 in Milwaukee at the home of Col. And Mrs. Gustave Pabst, it became known Wednesday.

"A special train will carry the family and friends from St. Louis to Milwaukee. It is to be an orchid wedding, but not ostentatious."

And so, the world was made aware that the richest girl in St. Louis was getting married. While the news made headlines across the country, it was for more than just romantic sentimentality. There was the money angle as well. Upon her marriage, Elsa would receive $100,000 of her inheritance. ($100,000 in 1910, is the equivalent of $2.5 million today.)

MISS LEMP TO BE BRIDE TODAY
GETS $100,000

St. Louis Post-Dispatch, April 12, 1910:

"One hundred thousand dollars, Miss Elsa Lemp's wedding portion of her more than $1,000,000 inheritance from the $10,000,000 Lemp estate, becomes payable to her at the hour of her marriage to Thomas H. Wright in Milwaukee Tuesday afternoon.

"The will of the bride's mother, Mrs. Julia Lemp, bequeathed to her one-seventh of the estate, to be hers absolutely at the age of 30, but with the provision that she should receive $100,000 on her wedding day.

"The executors of the estate are the bride's brothers, oldest of who is William J. Lemp, Jr.

"Dispatches from Milwaukee Tuesday stated that the wedding is to take place at the home of Gustav Pabst and is to be a family affair, attended only by near relatives.

To Be A Quiet Wedding

"Mrs. Hilda Lemp Pabst will act as hostess for the few wedding guests. The other members of the immediate family are in Milwaukee. The Rev. Paul B. Jenkins, of Immanuel Presbyterian Church, Milwaukee, was selected to perform the ceremony.

"No "showers" for the bride or stag parties for the bridegroom preceded the event. Miss Lemp's preference having been for a ceremony unmarked by display.

"Edwin Lemp, it was stated, would give his sister away. She has made her home with him in the West End for several seasons, while other members of the family have lived on the South side.

"Thomas H. Wright, the bridegroom, is a well-known business man and clubman.""

Thomas H. Wright
Photo courtesy of Lemp Mansion

ELSA LEMP IS MARRIED
Thomas H. Wright, St. Louis, and Bride Leave on Honeymoon.

Sprague Scrapbook, April 12, 1910:

"A wedding of wide interest in Milwaukee and St. Louis society took place this afternoon at 5:30 o'clock, when the marriage of Miss Elsa Lemp to Thomas H. Wright, St. Louis, was quietly celebrated in the home of the bride's sister, Mrs. Gustave Pabst, 416 Terrace Avenue.

"The Rev. Paul B. Jenkins read the service in the presence of a few friends and relatives in the drawing room of the beautiful Pabst home. The bride was unattended. Her brother, Edwin A. Lemp, of St. Louis, gave her away.

"The bride wore a handsome gown of white satin with a court train and with trimmings of rose point lace. She carried a shower bouquet of orchids and lilies of the valley. Her tulle veil was caught up with orange blossoms. The house was simply decorated. In the drawing room, Australian ferns and white orchids were used and in the dinner room pink roses and lilies of the valley.

"Mr. and Mrs. Wright left to-night for a wedding trip. They will reside in St. Louis.

"Among the out-of-town guests were: Mrs. Alex Konta, New York, a sister of the bride; Mr. and Mrs. Thurston Wright, Pittsburg; Misses Julia Maffitt and Stella Schnaider; Messrs. And Mesdames George Welch Simmons and Charles Parsons Pettus (Thomas's sisters and their husbands); the bridegroom's mother, Mrs. Richard B. Wright, and the bride's three brothers, William J., Charles and Edwin A. Lemp, all of St. Louis."

That Edwin was chosen to give Elsa away, and that she had been living with him since the death of her mother at the St. Regis Apartments in St. Louis, was no surprise. As stated earlier, they were very close in age and spent a great amount of time in each other's company. Her brother Louis is not mentioned.

The Topeka State Journal reported that Elsa Lemp "is a blonde of unaffected manner, and has been greatly admired since she entered society several seasons ago."

Once again, St. Louisans had been cheated of a Lemp marriage. Not only was Elsa Lemp well known in society, but her new bridegroom was recognized as belonging to the upper-class as well.

Thomas Henry Wright was born in St. Louis, January 6, 1877. He was the son of Richard Beck Wright and the former Virginia Belle McCampbell. He graduated from Smith Academy in St. Louis, in 1899, and attended Washington University. He was associated with Moore Brass Company as Vice President, which became the National Bearing Company, and later a division of the American Brake Shoe Company. At the time of his marriage to Elsa, he was living, along with his mother, with his sister, Mrs. Charles Parsons Pettus, at 33 Westmoreland Place. Their marriage certificate states his age as 33, Elsa was 27.

They traveled often during their 19-year marriage. Edwin accompanied them at times, along with friends.

Elsa and Thomas traveling aboard an ocean liner in 1911.
The passenger list shows their address as 48 Portland Place,
St. Louis. Elsa is third from right on the bottom row, Thomas is fifth
from right, and Edwin (squatting) is at the far left on bottom row.

Gated entrance to Portland Place neighborhood.

When they returned from their honeymoon, Elsa bought a palatial home in the trendy, and wealthy, Central West End of St. Louis. There were street names in St. Louis synonymous with money and elegance, and Portland Place was one such area. A gated community with heavily landscaped homes, pristine lawns, and stately manors, 48 Portland Place fit right in.

48 Portland Place, St. Louis, Mo

Built in 1905, 48 Portland Place is a 9,618-square foot red brick mansion with Tudor split timber detailing. It boasts 6 full baths and 2 half baths. The massive dining room features tiger oak paneling. Elsa plunked down $80,000 for it ($2.3 in today's dollars), and the happy newlyweds moved in.

Over at 3322 South Thirteenth Street, Charles and a couple of servants were the only ones living in Lemp Mansion. After Julia Lemp's death in 1906, Elsa moved in with Edwin at his beautiful apartment in the St. Regis Apartment complex. Only 48 apartments comprised the massive red-and-white brick edifice; each almost 3,000 feet in spatial luxury.

St. Regis Apartments, St. Louis CWE

Foyer Entrance of St. Regis Apartments, St. Louis CWE

The St. Regis sat near Forest Park in the Central West End (CWE). From that time forward, Elsa's residences would revolve around the area; walking distance from the massive park that housed the St. Louis World's Fair in 1904. St. Regis Apartments, Portland Place, and Hortense Place (where she would later live…and die) were all within minutes of each other.

Trip to Egypt. Top row, l. to r. Elsa's maid (in broad straw hat), Elsa (in hat with plume), Thomas Wright (in bowler). Photo—Lemp Mansion

From all accounts, the marriage between Thomas, or "Tom" as his family called him, was not a harmonious one. Thomas moved up the ranks from salesman to Vice-President at the More-Jones Brass and Metal Company in St. Louis. Yet, it was noted, that it was Elsa's money that purchased not only Portland Place, but the mansion in which they would live on Hortense Place. There was also gossip that she paid for her own wedding ring and bridal gown from Worth of Paris. While one might expect the dress as a personal purchase, the ring raised a few eyebrows. Some wondered if she had anything to do with Thomas Wright's sudden advancement at More-Jones.

Reports of a stormy relationship soon surfaced. An independent, wealthy, head-strong heiress, and a popular businessman and clubman, may not have been the perfect match. When Elsa became pregnant, three years after the marriage, it may have felt that perhaps a happy family could be made of the union. No doubt the news was met with happiness in both families. But just as her mother had before her, Elsa lost her first (and only) child. Patricia Lemp Wright was still-born on August 18, 1914.

It may have been at this time, that Elsa began to succumb to what her generation called "spells." Melancholy, depression, nerves…it came with many names and was usually handled with drug store remedies; often Laudanum. Innumerable Victorian women were prescribed the drug Laudanum for relief of menstrual cramps and vague aches, including irritability, nervousness, and mood swings. Since its primary ingredient was Opium, it was later  regulated under a physician's care, but originally it was sold without a prescription at your local druggist.

Based on the myriad complaints Elsa put forth in 1918, in her divorce filing, it appears the marriage to Thomas Wright may not have been her best choice. This was a woman who had lost a brother to a sudden heart attack, a father to suicide, a mother to cancer (only a few years prior to her wedding), and had delivered a dead child. With a husband's dismissal of her needs and emotions, she may have teetered dangerously near the edge, as she grappled for some form of firm foundation under her feet. To someone of this mind-set and life experiences, as well as an unstable genetic make-up, the cold indifference of the man she married was too much.

Elsa filed for divorce on February 1, 1919. The grounds upon which the decree was granted were based on her husband's reported indignities. Elsa alleged in her petition that her husband had "destroyed her peace and happiness by his conduct," and "had long ceased to love her," that "he treated her with indifference in the presence of her family and friends in their home." He absented himself from home "in order to be away from her," she charged, and "had abandoned her." All these things she stated had "caused her great mental anguish," and had caused an impairment of her health.

The allegation of abandonment, however, was not the ground of the decree, as desertion must cover a period of one year to be cause for divorce, whereas Mr. and Mrs. Wright had been separated only since December 20, 1918.

After the separation, it was said that Mrs. Wright continued living in her home at 48 Portland Place, and Mr. Wright had been living alternately with his sisters, Mrs. Pettus and Mrs. Simmons. He later took an apartment at the Westmoreland Apartments, 5330 Pershing Avenue, of which he still held the lease for several more years. At the divorce trial, Dr. Frank R. Fry testified that Mrs. Wright had been suffering the three previous years from a mental and physical breakdown, which, he said, he attributed to her domestic troubles. The judge ruled in her favor after only an hour of deliberation. Most cases took up to three weeks to be delegated, but Judge Falkenhainer of the Circuit Court expedited her cause.

The fact that her doctor mentioned she had been suffering for the prior three years gives one pause. She lost her child four years before the separation. Post-partum depression may have played some part in it, and was perhaps the precipitating factor of Thomas leaving her alone so often—if she was having emotional issues he could not deal with. It may have all been a downhill roller coaster after the death of their little girl. People dealing with any kind of mental aberration, including depressive episodes, will lash out in rage, suffer from panic attacks, and become irrational, exhibiting expansive mood swings. Sometime, during the 13-month separation, after the divorce had been filed, Elsa traveled to New York City to get away. She may have stayed with Annie. During this time, she changed the will she had made as a married woman, and erased Thomas from it. Under this will, he would inherit nothing upon her death.

Perhaps it was the common, irrational bond of a co-dependent relationship, where two parties are drawn together, even when the combination is lethal, that caused Elsa to open her door to Thomas Wright when he followed her to New York City, one year later. Whatever transpired, they were reunited, and remarried in that same city on March 8, 1920. Twelve days later, she was dead by a gunshot wound through her heart.

13 HORTENSE PLACE

13 Hortense Place today is a magnificent 114-year old Georgian Colonial on a private, elegant street in the Central West End, built in 1901. It is four levels, with polished floors throughout the entrance level. Off the entrance vestibule is a formal and informal lounge, and dining room. It sports a masterpiece gourmet kitchen with a separate butler's pantry connecting it to the dining room. A sunroom and breakfast room are also on the first floor. A beautiful polished timber staircase leads to the second floor which contains the master bedroom suite with an adjoining marble bathroom. Across the hallway are several guest rooms. There are five bedrooms and

5.5 baths, culminating in 6,736 square feet. A reflection pool and lush landscaping can be found behind the home. The sunroom's roof affords a private balcony through the door of the 2nd floor master suite.

13 Hortense Place, St. Louis, Mo

Back of 13 Hortense Place. Sunroom is at the left.

Perhaps, based on not only what happened at this address, but others, it is not surprising to find that the street itself has reports of hauntings from different homes there. Hortense Place was named after the daughter of the neighborhood's developer, Jacob Goldman, a cotton magnate and banker. His imposing house is only two homes down from 13 Hortense Place and its façade is something that has to be seen to be believed. Nicknamed "The Castle," it is 10,000 square feet with a limestone façade. It was designed for Jacob Goldman in 1900, by William Levy. Guests and servants at the home reported hearing a little girl's voice crying "Daddy," on a regular basis. Jacob's daughter died early in childhood before the house was built, and it is believed it is her voice calling out from the grave.

9 Hortense Place. "The Castle" built in 1900.

During the 1900s, séances were all the rage. It was *the* form of entertainment and many wealthy people gathered around velvet draped tables, their faces highlighted in eerie candlelight, as the latest medium intoned questions to the spirit world. The Lambert Mansion, at #2 Hortense Place, hosted many such séances deep into the night. The children of the Carney house across the street from #2 began reporting a specter in their house that would walk through a wall at the top of the main staircase. It was later discovered a door had been there at one time but was boarded over.

Not far from Hortense Place, the playwright Tennessee Williams penned his epic story about his mentally fragile sister, Rose, in his great work, *The Glass Menagerie.*

It was into this enclave of mansions, money, and ghostly goings-on, that Elsa Lemp Wright purchased her second home, just before her marriage to Thomas. Once again, they moved in their fine furnishings, hung expensive paintings and draperies, lined the butler's pantry with fine china, wine glasses and crystal wedding gifts, and tried to start over. The house, with its sunroom that mirrored the atrium at her beloved childhood home at Lemp Mansion, was square in shape rather than the round design at Lemp, but she probably filled it with plants and birds to remind her of happier days. The balcony atop it was just like the one from home, as well. Perhaps here she could be happy and outrun the ghosts that lingered in the corners of her mind.

The entrance to Hortense Place. #13 is not shown.
Photo by Rebecca F. Pittman

MRS. THOMAS H. WRIGHT KILLS HERSELF

It was this headline on the afternoon of March 20, 1920, that alerted the world the wealthiest woman in St. Louis was dead. Immediate comparisons to her father's suicide by gunshot filled the newspaper columns. The story was rehashed in every major paper across the county, many with glaring inconsistencies and errors. After obtaining the coroner's report, newspaper interviews, police investigation records, and attending medical doctor's summation, the author compiled the various testimonies, and report it here for your consideration:

The first floor of 13 Hortense Place was filled with flowers and cards from Elsa and Thomas's friends and family, wishing them bliss and happiness the second time around. The honeymoon had only lasted 8 days. They returned on a Wednesday. That Friday, Elsa attended a concert at the Olympic where friends said she "looked healthy and happy," as she chatted with acquaintances at her box. Thomas had declined to go, begging off due to some business demanding his attention at work. Elsa went unaccompanied. Later in the afternoon, upon arriving home, she peeked in at the kitchen, between 5 and 6 p.m., to talk to Elizabeth Bender, the cook, for a moment. Bender testified Mrs. Wright was happy and nothing appeared to be wrong. Yet by 7:00, only one hour later, the testimony changes. Ms. Bender and a maid state that Mrs. Wright looks "very nervous." Thomas Wright said his wife "scarcely ate anything." He further testifies that she was "up all night with indigestion and nausea," a condition with which she often suffered, according to himself and the servants.

Elsa and Thomas' master bedroom at 13 Hortense Place from a recent house listing photograph. You can see the bathroom through the open door. To the left of the fireplace are steps up to the door leading to the sunroom balcony. The open door to the right of the bed leads to the hallway.

In the preceding photograph, the fireplace, radiator, and layout are original to the room; the furnishings and art are not. While "closets" in the 1900s, were typically armoires or free-standing wardrobes, upper-class families did have walk-in versions, so the mirrored door leading to a closet may be authentic to the house. If not, it was more likely there were two wardrobes; one for him and one for her. (Thomas's testimony says "I went to get a change of underwear from *a* closet." If there was only one closet, you would expect him to say "*the* closet." "A" seems to indicate more than one. A photo of the bathroom on page 131 shows it is small, allowing for a walk-in closet next to it.)

Because of witness's testimony, we know a couch was also in the room, probably under the front facing window just behind this camera view, and a book case was next to it. Thomas Wright testified his wardrobe was on the same side of the room as the bathroom door only in the other corner. Twin beds had a night table placed between them where a .32-caliber revolver was kept in the drawer. The beds were where the one in the photo is pictured, as it's the only place in the room where a fireplace, doors and windows don't preclude it. A chandelier was probably hung from the ceiling, and by 1920, it was no doubt electric, as electricity was in use by 1914.

Typical "closet" or wardrobe, 1900s.   Elsa's bathroom today.

Hortense Place formal dining room today.

Main entry at 13 Hortense Place

Staircase on the left goes to second floor. The door you can see is a guest room. Right is the stairway from attic looking down.

13 Hortense Place. The master bedroom is the 2nd floor window on the right beneath the dormer. The sun room, or atrium, is at the right of the photo with roof access from bedroom.
– Photo by Rebecca F. Pittman

Colt Pocket Positive Revolver • Caliber: .32 Police • 1935

THE TESTIMONY:
The Police

Inquest held at #13 Hortense Place. March 20, 1920, 2:00 P.M., on the body of Elsa Lemp Wright.

Questioning and Examination conducted by Wm. Dever, Deputy Coroner.

Sergeant Michael Burke being first duly sworn testified:

Q. You made an investigation on the shooting of Mrs. Elsa Wright?

A. Yes sir. I found she was lying in bed with a bullet wound in the breast, just about here (indicating).   Q. The left breast?

A. Yes sir.

Q. Alright, what else?

A. That is all. The revolver was lying in the room with two cartridges in it, one with a bullet and one empty one in the barrel. Q. Was there any sign of any struggle in the room?

A. No sir.

Q. She was lying in bed?

A. Yes sir, peaceably.

Q. Fully dressed or in her night clothes?

A. In her night clothes.

Q. Do you know where the revolver was found?

A. No sir.

Q. Did you ask?

A. Why, I didn't, the Coroner handed it to the officer.

Q. Do you know where the revolver fell?

A. No sir.

Q. Do you know who it belonged to?

A. No sir.

Q. Do you know whether or not there was a note found?

A. No sir, I don't.

Q. Did you interview any of the family in regard to this?

A. Yes sir, a servant and some gentleman that was around at the time I came in. One of the maids stated she heard a shot and ran into the room, and the lady was still alive and gasping when she came in.

Q. Did she say to you whether or not the lady made a statement?

A. She was talking to the officer at the time.

Q. That is all you know about it?

A. Yes sir, that is all.

Officer August Klein being duly sworn testified:

Q. What did you get from your investigation in regard to the shooting of Mrs. Elsa Wright?

A. I was called here this morning and the lady was lying in bed.

Q. What time?

A. About, oh, I guess it was 11:20 when I got here. I spoke to several here and talked to Mr. Thomas Wright. Q. What did he say to you?

A. He stated that last night they retired about nine o'clock; that his wife wasn't feeling very well, and she got up several times during the night nauseating; that about 8 o'clock this morning he got up and asked her how she was feeling, and she said "all right," and he left her and went into the bath room to take a bath. He turned on the water and about five minutes later he heard a muffled report. He went into his wife's room and asked her if she was all right and she didn't answer, but apparently looked at him. He then went towards the bed and saw the revolver lying beside of her. He then rang the bell and called for Mrs. Wright's maids who responded, Martha Westin and Kate Ruekert. They came and went into the room. I asked them later on where the revolver was when they first saw it. They said it was lying on a couch just about ten feet from the bed. They didn't know who placed it there.

Q. Who told you that?

A. The maids. They said they didn't place it there.

Q. Did you ask Mr. Wright about it?

A. Later on I asked Mr. Wright how the revolver got from the bed to the couch, and said he didn't know; he apparently had picked the revolver up and placed it there. Q. Did he say he did?

A. He didn't say; he didn't know whether he did or not.

Q. He didn't tell you that?

A. No sir.

Q. Did he tell you what time the shot was fired?

A. He said he arose about 8 o'clock, and this happened five minutes later.

Q. About five minutes after eight?

A. Yes sir.

Q. That is all you know about it?

A. That is all I know.

The Servants

Martha Westin being duly sworn: Q. Your address?

A. Right here at 13 Hortense Place.

Q. You were employed as a maid by Mrs. Wright?

A. Yes sir.

Q. Tell us what you know about the shooting that occurred here this morning?

A. Well, the first thing I heard was Mr. Wright screaming and calling my name.

Q. What time was that?

A. It was about quarter to nine, just about quarter to nine.

Q. You went to him?

A. No sir, he told me to call up the doctor, and I started.

Q. Did he tell you what was the matter?

A. I asked him, and he said it was something so terrible he couldn't tell me.

Q. Did you hear the shot fired?

A. No sir.

Q. Had you been in Mrs. Wright's room just previous to this trouble, or this shooting?

A. No sir, not this morning.

Q. Had you talked to her this morning at all?

A. No sir.

Q. Did you hear any loud talking in here?

A. No sir.

Q. Where was Mr. Wright when he notified you that something had happened, when you heard him screaming? A. I met him in the hall.

Q. Where were you at that time?

A. I was in the back hall.

Q. On the second floor?

A. Yes sir.

Q. You heard no shot fired?

A. No sir.

Q. What time did you say that was?

A. About a quarter to nine, I think; I am not quite sure, but just about that.

Q. When you finally went into the room, how long after was that?

A. Well, that was, I think about quarter to nine when I went into the room.

Q. And she was then where?

A. She was in bed, she was still living when I went in there.

Q. Did she say anything to you?

A. No sir, she had her eyes partly closed.

Q. Did you see the gun?

A. No sir, I did not.

Q. Did you at any time see the gun up there in that room?

A. Yes sir.

Q. Where did you see this gun?

A. The first time before she was separated from Mr. Wright she had it in the closet.

Q. I mean this morning.

A. I didn't see it before one of the other maids called my attention to it, that it was laying on the couch. Q. How far away from the bed?

A. About six or seven feet away from the bed, and the couch was over there by the book case.

Q. Did Mrs. Wright ever complain to you of being ill?

A. Yes sir, often did.

Q. Did she ever say to you that she would take her life?

A. No sir.

Q. Have you ever heard anyone threaten her life?

A. No sir, never.

Elizabeth Bender being duly sworn: Q. Where do you live?

A. I just live here.

Q. You are employed here in what capacity?

A. Cook.

Q. Tell us what you know about the shooting that occurred this morning?

A. I know nothing, Mister.

Q. When did you first hear that Mrs. Wright had been shot, or had shot herself?

A. The girls told me.

Q. What time?

A. I can't tell you the right time.

Q. Did they come in all excited and tell you that something had occurred upstairs?

A. I was in the kitchen and they came in all excited and told me.

Q. What did they say to you?

A. They said something awful happened, and I says, "What is it?", and they said, "Mrs. Wright is dead," and I says, "Dead?", and they said, "She shot herself."

Q. Did they say someone shot her or that she shot herself?

A. No sir, we didn't know what to think.

Q. Did you hear any noise in her room this morning?

A. No sir.

Q. Did you hear any loud argument or talking?

A. I didn't.

Q. Do you know whether Mrs. Wright has been ill, or was ill last night?

A. No sir. She was in the kitchen and gave me the bill of fare and seemed perfectly happy. Q. Last night?

A. Yes sir.

Q. What time was that?

A. Between five and six.

Minnie Stover being duly sworn: Q. Your address?

A. 13 Hortense Place.

Q. You are employed here as a maid?

A. Yes sir, downstairs maid.

Q. Tell us what you know about what happened this morning?

A. I am very sorry to be in anything like this because I can't tell you anything about it because I hadn't any conversation with the people, either one of them.

Q. How did you find out something had occurred in the house this morning?

A. Well, I was engaged down here, and Mr. Wright came out in the hall and he seemed to be much excited, and I knew something had happened, of course I didn't know what it was, and I heard him call the maid.

Q. What time was that?

A. I think about 8:30.

Q. Had you seen Mr. Wright before that time this morning?

A. No sir.

Q. What did he say when he called the maid?

A. In fact I didn't pay any attention to him; I heard him call Martha.

Q. Did he seem to be excited?

A. Yes sir, very much so.

Q. He came out of the door of his room upstairs?

A. I think so, I can't tell you exactly.

Q. Had you heard any noise like a shot upstairs?

A. No sir. I never heard anything, not a sound of anything.

Q. Did you run upstairs then to see what the trouble was?

A. No sir.

Q. Did you at any time go upstairs this morning?

A. No sir.

Q. When was the last time you saw Mrs. Wright alive?

A. Not since last evening at the table.

Q. What time was that?

A. Seven o'clock.

Q. What were her spirits at that time?

A. She seemed very nervous.

Q. Did she complain, did you hear?

A. No sir, she was a very sweet little lady at all times around the house. I couldn't say anything to the contrary.

Q. Did you hear any loud words or argument up in the room this morning?

A. No sir.

Q. Did you hear any last night?

A. No sir.

Kate Ruekert being duly sworn testified: Q. You live right here, do you?

A. Yes sir.

Q. You are employed here in what capacity?

A. Upstairs maid.

Q. Tell us what occurred upstairs this morning?

A. The first I heard of it was Mr. Wright called me.

Q. What time was that?

A. I think that was about quarter to nine, I am not sure of the time, but it was close to nine. Q. What did he say?

A. I couldn't repeat the words; I was excited, but I heard him call for Martha.

Q. And then what did you do?

A. I went into the sewing room and then he told me to go in, that Mrs. Wright needed me and to stay with her.

Q. When you got in there what did you find?

A. She was laying in the bed, she wasn't struggling or anything, and she took one long breath, and I took hold of her arm and tried to rub her, I thought there was still life in her, and I tried to rub her and with that Martha came in, and she took two long breaths after Martha came in.

Q. Was she lying in the bed in her night clothes?

A. Yes sir.

Q. Was she covered, or the covers thrown back?

A. Just one hand was uncovered while she was lying in bed.

Q. Laying just the way she was laying if she went to sleep?

A. Yes sir.

Q. And where was the gun when you came into the room?

A. It was on the couch there in the room, about ten or fifteen minutes then I noticed the gun up on the couch. Q. Do you know how it got on the couch?

A. No sir.

Q. Did you at any time hear a shot upstairs?

A. No sir.

Q. Did you hear any loud words in the room?

A. No sir.

Q. Would you have heard them if there had been any?

A. I don't know, I never did hear a word between them two, no quarreling or anything.

Q. Just before Mr. Wright came out and called for Martha, didn't you hear a noise in the room? A. No sir.

Q. Where was Mr. Wright, was he in the room where Mrs. Wright was?

A. He was either in her room or in the bath room. I can't say what place he was.

Q. Had you seen Mr. Wright before this morning?

A. No sir.

Q. Before he came out?

A. No sir.

Q. Was he full dressed at that time?

A. No sir.

Q. In his bath robe?

A. He was in a night shirt; that was all.

Thomas Wright, the husband

Thomas Wright (Rel) being duly sworn testified: Q. What is your occupation?

A. Vice-president, More-Jones Brass and Metal Company.

Q. Tell us what you know about the shooting that occurred in Mrs.

Wright's room this morning.

A. You mean from last night or this morning?

Q. Just what occurred this morning?

A. Mrs. Wright didn't sleep very well, and as I got ready to get up I asked if she was going to get up, and she said she thought she would stay in bed an hour or so, and I said I thought that would be wise, and then I went to the bath room. Q. That is on that floor?

A. Yes sir, cata-cornered. I started to draw the water, and then I realized that I hadn't taken my clean underclothes, so I went out into the room and into a closet which is at the same side with the other corner of the room, and got this underwear and went back into the bath room, and of course shut the door. I heard a quick, but very slight sharp noise, it wasn't a thud or dull noise, it was a sharp noise, and I opened the door. I thought maybe Mrs. Wright had fallen. When first I opened the door, she was apparently looking right at me, and I said, "Did you call, did you throw something against the door to call me?" And by that time, I had advanced to practically the middle of the room, and then I saw the revolver on the bed. Q. Was the revolver clutched in her hand?

A. No sir.

Q. What did you do with it then?

A. I must have taken it unconsciously and laid it on the couch.

Q. Did she speak to you after that?

A. I spoke to her, and I think she tried to speak to me, I thought at first she had spoken, I thought she said something, but she evidently didn't say anything.

Q. Did Mrs. Wright ever tell you that she was going to take her life?

A. No, she never told me that at all.

Q. Did she complain last night of feeling bad?

A. She said she felt tired. She complained of being sick at her stomach. She ate practically no dinner, and she was sick at her stomach slightly.

Q. Who did this gun belong to?

A. I judge it belonged to her. It didn't belong to me. I didn't even know she had one in the house.

Q. You have never seen this gun?

A. No sir, I have never seen it before; I didn't know anything about it.

Q. Did she do any writing last night?

A. None at all.

Q. Did she seem to be in good spirits?

A. Very; she complained of being sick at the stomach, but otherwise in very good health.

Q. Can you assign any reason to this?

A. I cannot.

End of Inquest

DEPARTMENT OF POLICE
City of St. Louis Eleventh District

Letter to Col. Martin O'Brien, Chief of Police, from the Captain of the Commanding District: (No words or punctuation have been altered in any testimony or documents. Author)

Sir:

About 11:00 this A.M., this office was notified through the Chief's office that there had been a suicide at #13 Hortense Place. Sergt. Burke and Officer Klein of this district were notified who learned that about 8:05 o'clock this A.M., Mrs. Elsa Wright, 37 years old, married, born in MO., residing with her husband Thomas H. Wright at #13 Hortense Place, had committed suicide by shooting herself in the heart with a .32 caliber, Police Positive, Colt Revolver, #87398, while lying in bed in her bedroom on the second floor at the above number. Mr. Wright stated that about 9:00 o'clock last P.M., they retired, they occupying twin beds, same being separated by a small night table, and that at that time Mrs. Wright was not feeling well, and that several times during the night she got up to nauseate. Mr. Wright stated that about 8:00 o'clock this A.M., he got up and asked Mrs. Wright how she was feeling and she replied that she was feeling alright and that he then kissed her and then went into the bathroom and turned on the water to take a bath and about 5 minutes later he heard a muffled report in his wife's room and that he went into same and asked her if she was feeling alright and that she did not answer, but seemed to look at him. He stated that he then went to the bed and saw a revolver lying beside his wife. He then rang a bell and called for the maids, Martha Weston and Kate Ruekert who responded and went into the room. Dr. M. B. Clopton, offices in the Humboldt Building, located at Grand and Washington Avenues was called and pronounced Mrs. Wright dead. Miss Weston and Miss Ruekert stated that when they first saw the revolver it was lying on a couch about 10 feet from the bed. Miss Weston stated that the revolver was the property of Mrs. Wright and that she kept same in a drawer in the night table which stands between the beds.

Mr. Wright stated that he did not know that Mrs. Wright owned a revolver and stated that he could not give any reason for Mrs. Wright killing herself. He stated that they were happy and that they had just returned home from New York on the 17th, instant. He stated that he could not account for the revolver being on the couch, stating that he had evidently picked same from off the bed and placed it on the couch but does not remember doing so. He stated the reason the Police Dept. was not notified sooner was because he was bewildered and did not know what to do and that he called Dr. Clopton who notified the Coroner.

Coroner Vitt was called to the house and gave them permission to leave the body at the house. An inquest will be held at 2:00 o'clock this P.M.

The revolver when turned over to Officer Klein had one empty and one loaded cartridge in same. The revolver and cartridges were brought to this station and held as evidence.

The within named constitute the witnesses who have been notified to appear at the inquest which will be held at the home at #13 Hortense Place at 2:00 o'clock this P.M.

Signed: Captain, Commanding District

Letter from Dr. Malvern B. Clopton, Humboldt Building, St. Louis, to Dr. Rudolph S. Vitt, Coroner City of St. Louis. March 22, 1920.

Re: Death of Mrs. Thomas H. Wright Dear Sir:

I was called March 20th by the telephone about 8:30 a.m. by Mr. Thomas H. Wright to come immediately to his house, 13 Hortense Place, that something terrible had happened. I went directly and found Mrs. Wright in bed dead from a pistol wound. There was a powder marked wound of entrance between the 4th and 5th costal cartilages on the left side at the edge of the sternum. There was an exit in the posterior axillary line between the 8th and 9th rib on the same side. The bullet was lying in the night dress. There was practically no external bleeding, no hemorrhage from the mouth. The left side of the chest was dull throughout probably from hemorrhage. Death had probably occurred immediately after the wounding. A .32 caliber revolver was lying on the couch close by her. There were two shells in the revolver; one of them had been exploded.

Mr. Wright was overcome with grief but told me in detail what had happened. They had retired rather early the night before as Mrs. Wright was feeling upset. It was at the time of her menstrual period and she had not felt well enough to eat much dinner and had been nauseated several times during the night. In the morning when Mr. Wright had prepared to dress he had spoken to his wife and she told him that she was feeling better. He had gone to the bathroom adjoining the room in which they had slept. He heard a noise which he thought was made by Mrs. Wright to attract his attention, but as the water was running in the tub, he did not recognize it as a report of a pistol. He went into the room to see if she wanted anything and spoke to her. She did not make an articulate reply and only moved her arm to her head and then ceased breathing. He noticed a revolver lying on her bed and picked it up and put it on a couch close by. He called the servants into the room, and he asked them to send for a doctor immediately. There was some difficulty in making the telephone connections so that he got me over the telephone himself. There was no disorder in the room. No evidence that Mrs. Wright had moved after she was shot, as she was lying in bed so that the wound of exit was directly over the only spot of blood. She was still warm, without any evidence of rigor mortis. The bed clothes were in no way disarranged. As soon as I had learned these facts and made an examination I looked about the room for any note or writing of any sort, and found none. Mr. Wright told me that he had not seen the revolver before, and I learned later it was the property of Mrs. Wright. Previous to her marriage she had kept it in the drawer of a small table beside the bed.

I have never treated Mrs. Wright, but I have known her for some time. She, at times, had been under the care of Dr. Frank R. Fry for nervousness in which she had periods of marked depression. From all that I could learn she had been most happy since her remarriage to Mr. Wright, and the only way that I can account for her having taken her life was that during the depression attending her illness, she had a sudden impulse and had reached for the nearby weapon. Mr. Wright had been out of the room but a few minutes when the shot was fired. If there is any further information I can give you I will be glad to do so.

Yours respectfully,
Dr. M. B. Clopton

Six names of the male jurors were signed at the bottom of the official inquest ruling of suicide from hemorrhage, due to gunshot wound of the chest, self-inflicted. The time of death was listed as 8:45.

The jurors' names were signed to a blank Coroner's statement. The verdict was entered later, something even the newspaper reporters found fishy. The **Post-Dispatch** said this:

"The fact that the members of the coroner's jury, whose names were attached to the verdict in the inquest held at the Wright home Saturday afternoon, did not hear the evidence, has caused comment. Deputy Coroner Dever swore in the six men, they viewed the body of Mrs. Wright, signed a blank verdict and were dismissed. Dever heard the testimony and filled in the verdict of suicide.

"Coroner Vitt today said there was nothing unusual in the procedure, which was followed in all cases where suicide appeared self-evident.

"Section 2935 of the Revised Statutes of Missouri, 1909, relating to the conduct of the coroner's office and coroner's jurors says:

"'The jury, having viewed the body, heard the evidence and made all the inquiry in their power, shall draw up and deliver to the coroner their verdict on the death under consideration, in writing, under their hand, and same shall be signed by the coroner.'"

Other papers felt the need to mention the suspicious behavior of the blank coroner's verdict as well.

LAWYERING UP

Sometime that morning, Thomas Wright called for his attorney, who was called a "friend of the family." We do know that by 11:15 a.m., before the police arrived, Samuel Fordyce was already fielding questions from reporters and shielding Mr. Wright from the spotlight. It was Fordyce who gave the papers their first details of the tragic morning. Thomas Wright told the attorney that he called him at the same time he called for Dr. Clopton, making it 8:30 a.m.

Thomas also called his two sisters who lived in St. Louis, Mrs. Charles Parsons Pettus of 33 Westmoreland Place, and Mrs. George W. Simmons of Hanley Road. They hurried to Hortense Place. Not only was an attorney called by 8:30 a.m.

but the coroner received notice of Mrs. Wright's death about 11 o'clock through Circuit Attorney McDaniel, Circuit Judge Garasche, and Circuit Clerk Goldstein, who called at his office at the request of the family. Through them, it was arranged to hold the inquest at the Wright residence.

When William Lemp, Sr. died, they did hold the inquest the same day at his residence at Lemp Mansion. However, the jury did not sign a blank coroner's report. Charles' and Billy's inquests were held the following day at the Coroner's Court. The hurried inquest, blank verdict, lack of follow-up questions, and the late notification of the coroner and the police, is enough to raise eyebrows. In fact, if a freak automobile accident hadn't occurred, there is no telling when they would have been brought in:

Edwin Lemp Auto, on Way to Wright Home, Injures Woman

St. Louis Post-Dispatch: March 20, 1920:

"Edwin A. Lemp, brother of Mrs. Elsa Lemp Wright, while driving hurriedly to the Wright residence, accompanied by Associate City Counselor William Killoren, about 11 a.m. today, ran down and seriously injured Mrs. Lucille Hern, 25 years old, at Locust Street and Jefferson Avenue. She was taken to the city hospital suffering from an injury to the back and cuts on the head and limbs.

"Killoren said later that Mrs. Hern was crossing Locust Street north to south, when the traffic officer signaled for east and west traffic to go ahead. Mrs. Hern became confused, and ran back toward the north curbing, thus coming in front of the machine, he said. After investigating the circumstances, the police reported that the accident was unavoidable.

"Lemp had gone to Killoren's office earlier to keep an engagement with him. When he arrived there, he learned from

Killoren that Mrs. Wright had ended her life, where upon the two started for the Wright home."

Other reports listed Killoren as the driver, in fact one such report said the police were going to hold him for a time until it was all cleared up, but finally released him, and he and Lemp hurried to the Wright home. In another article, Edwin said, sadly, that he had planned on stopping to see his sister Elsa that day, as he had not seen her since her return from her honeymoon.

Discrepancies in the Story

The amount of information that was changed, or deleted, from Thomas Wright's account that day, and that of the servants, boggles the mind. These are things that stand out to this author:

1. Thomas stated under oath he did not know Elsa had a gun. He had never seen it. That same day, he told a police officer "This revolver is my wife's property and that each night she laid it on a table between their twin beds as a protection against burglars." Wright also told the policeman he saw a spot of blood on her chest where the wound was. The coroner said in his report the only spot of blood was on her back...there was only a powder burn on her chest. Neither of Wright's two statements above made it into the Coroner's report. They were told to reporters by the policeman who questioned him.

2. Deputy Coroner Dever told police that when he arrived in Mrs. Wright's room "the revolver was on the table between the twin beds." At what point, did it move from the couch to the table? Was it placed there during Thomas' admission to the police about where Elsa kept it to illustrate its location? Sergeant Burke said he saw the coroner hand the gun to the officer. Did he pick it up from the couch or the bedside table?

3. Sergeant's Burke first witness was "a maid who said she heard a shot and ran into the room." During the inquest, three hours after the police questioned the servants, the story has disappeared. Now, all four servants say they did not hear a shot. During the coroner's inquest, the two police officers were interviewed along with the servants. Why didn't the coroner simply say, "Which of these women told you she heard a shot and ran in?" It was never even asked.

4. Thomas Wright locked himself into the time he said he heard the shot from the gun and found his wife wounded and gasping: 8:05 a.m. The police officer asked him twice, and he stated each time it was five minutes after 8 he heard the shot and found her. Yet four witnesses, including Dr. Clopton, testified Thomas did not sound the alarm until 8:30, or later. Dr. Clopton said he got the call at 8:30. Minnie Stover said Thomas came running out into the hall at 8:30. Martha Weston and Kate Ruekert said it was closer to 8:45. What was he doing for 25 minutes in that room while his wife was gasping for her life? There's a bullet wound in her chest. There is obviously nothing he can do for her—CPR and a cold rag on her forehead are not going to help. He should have been out the door in two seconds yelling for help and getting a doctor. But he waited 25 minutes to run out into the hallway.

5. In Dr. Clopton's report, and Thomas' phrasing during interviews, it sounds as if Thomas yelled for the maids and they immediately went into the room to his wife. In reality, they did not get to go in until 8:45. He stopped Martha on the 2nd floor hallway, before she could enter the room, and told her to go and call the doctor. In fact, when she asked him what was wrong, he just said, "It was something so terrible he couldn't tell me." What was she supposed to tell the doctor? Why didn't he tell her then that Elsa had been shot? He also told the doctor Elsa "raised an arm to her forehead and stopped breathing," when he heard the shot and ran in. Yet we know she was still

The History and Haunting of Lemp Mansion

alive when the maids came in at 8:45, and tried to revive her by rubbing her arm.

6. Thomas makes a point of mentioning he went back into the bedroom, after he started running the bath water, to get some clean underclothes. During the inquest, he even says "these underclothes," as if he is holding them up as Exhibit A. Was there a reason that he needed to put himself way over by the wardrobe that was at the other end of the room from the bathroom door? The maid, who originally said she ran in after hearing a shot, was suddenly silenced. Had she seen him in a place he should not have been? Was he doing something out of place? Was Elsa in a different position from where they found her later? Perhaps the maid saw him holding the gun, precluding him from putting it back by Elsa's body to strengthen his story of suicide. Now, he had to put it somewhere else.

And more importantly, if he came back out into the bedroom after he started his bath, why didn't anyone ask him, since this would be the last time he would see her alive, "What was she doing when you came back out? Was she still in bed? Did she say anything to you? Did she look anxious or depressed? Did you see a gun?" These are the last moments of her life, and they paid more attention to what she said before he went into the bathroom than the more recent, and last, time he saw her.

7. Elsa's friends said she looked happy at the concert at the Olympic Friday afternoon. Elizabeth Bender, the cook says she seemed very happy when she stopped into the kitchen between 5 and 6 in the evening on Friday. Yet, at 7 p.m., Minnie Stover states that Elsa looks "very nervous" at the dinner table. What changed? Did something happen between her and Wright in their bedroom as they prepared for dinner?

8. The trajectory of the bullet was strange. After several reenactments, and studying diagrams, I found it would be almost impossible to be lying on your back and shoot yourself

at the angle the bullet traveled, according to Dr. Clopton's report. Her elbow would have been up above her ear level and she would have been shooting down toward her knee. The powder burn suggests the gun was held out at least 2" or more from her body. Some forensic reports state if the gun was pressed to her gown there would have been a starburst-shaped burn from the escaping gas, and her gown would be torn. The angle, to me, suggests someone grabbing her arm, jerking it upward, and the gun going off.

I asked **Detective Tom McLellan**, a retired Captain of the Fort Collins, Colorado, Police Department, where he worked as a police officer and detective for 38 years, to take a look at the case. I provided him with all the reports, newspaper clippings, and the inquest. This is his final finding, and his wording:

Points of interest:

1. A .32 caliber Police Positive Colt Revolver is a six-shot revolver and was the premier police weapon used by the U.S. police department at the time.

2. Dr. Clopton writes that he was contacted by phone about 8:30 on the morning of the shooting. I checked Google Maps and found that the Humboldt Building where Dr. Clopton had an office is located 2-4 miles from #13 Hortense Place. Assuming Dr. Clopton had a car, it would have taken him between 3-5 minutes, depending on his speed to get there (40 mph would get him there in 3 ½ minutes). Of course, we don't know what he had to do before he left the building, or how far he had to walk to get to his car. He may have even taken a taxi. At any rate, he was probably at the house by 8:45, or so.

3. Dr. Clopton found "a powder marked wound of entrance between the 4 and 5 costal cartilages on the left side at the edge of the sternum." Deputy Coroner Dever told the *Post-Dispatch* reporter that when he examined Mrs. Wright's body

he noticed powder marks on her gown. The powder marks on the gown, and especially on the entrance wound is a clear indication the weapon was very close (2-3"), or actually pressed against Mrs. Wright's body when it was fired, and is a significant indictor of suicide. Of course, some homicides are committed by firing a bullet into the victim while the barrel is pressed against the skin, but the incidence is rare.

4. Dr. Clopton wrote the bullet exited Mrs. Wright's body in the posterior axillary line (her left side) between the 8th and 9th ribs on the same side (left). While it was wise for Dr. Clopton to describe the exit wound, a trajectory through Mrs. Wright's body based on the exit wound location is not possible. Because of the bony structures in this area (sternum and ribs) it is almost certain the bullet struck one and could have exited the body in any number of locations which would not indicate a true trajectory of the bullet. In order to establish a precise trajectory a post-mortem examination would have to be conducted and this did not occur. Without trajectory, it is impossible to determine the angle of the gun to the body when it was fired.

5. Dr. Clopton writes that there was no evidence that Mrs. Wright had moved after she was shot "As she was lying in bed so that the wound of exit was directly over the only spot of blood." While this fact does not prove suicide, it also does not suggest a struggle ensued at the time of the shooting, and, as Dr. Clopton points out, is a good indicator that the body was not moved after the shooting occurred.

SUICIDE, ACCIDENT OR MURDER?

Here is **Detective McLellan's** summary of what his beliefs are in regard to the final outcome of this case:

1. SUICIDE

Considering the known facts in totality, I believe it is most likely Mrs. Wright committed suicide, but because there are so many unanswered questions regarding this case I can't be positive. The following facts indicate Mrs. Wright took her own life:

1. There is evidence to suggest Mrs. Wright suffered from depression and in the past had a mental and physical breakdown attributed to her domestic troubles.

2. Mrs. Wright died from a gunshot wound to the chest with noticeable powder marks on her nightgown and on the entry wound. This indicated the weapon was placed very near to her body or was in direct contact with her body when it was fired.

3. The handgun used to kill Mrs. Wright was a six-shot revolver but was only loaded with two rounds of ammunition. Using a partially loaded weapon is often found when people kill themselves. However, when a gun is used as a murder weapon it is usually fully loaded.

4. If Mr. Wright killed his wife and wanted it to look like a suicide he probably would not have placed the gun on the couch but would have placed it near her body.

5. Finding a weapon away from the body in a suicide happens quite often. Family members or friends who find the body sometimes move the weapon for safety reasons or because of shock, and at times, the physiological reaction by the victim after the gunshot causes them to throw the weapon away from their body.

6. During his testimony to the Deputy Coroner, Mr. Wright sobbed frequently. While this type of demeanor does not, in itself, verify that Mr. Wright was telling the truth, it does lend some credence to his story.

7. The fact that no suicide note was left at the scene is not unusual. Only 20% to 30% of suicide victims leave a suicide note. I worked many suicides during my career and notes were rarely left by victims.

8. Mr. Wright would not have called for the maid while she was still alive since Mrs. Wright may have been able to tell the maid her husband shot her.

2. ACCIDENT OR MURDER

Detective McLellan's statement continues:

I find the following facts suspicious, or in need of further investigation which, unfortunately, did not occur in 1920:

1. Absolutely everyone in this case could only estimate the time they first knew about the shooting, yet no one was ever asked how they determined what time the shooting occurred. These estimates vary from 8:05 to 8:45 that morning. A simple follow-up question by the DC (Deputy Coroner) to all witnesses, such as "How did you determine what time it was?" may have cleared up this critical discrepancy.

2. Deputy Coroner Dever had the members of the Coroner's Jury sign a blank Coroner's Verdict Report, and after viewing the scene they were dismissed. DC Dever then conducted the witness interviews alone and filled in the verdict of suicide later. He told the press this was standard procedure when a case is obviously a suicide, but I find this aspect of the case suspicious.

3. After Mrs. Wright shot herself, Thomas Wright contacted a doctor and his lawyer, but no one present at the house ever contacted the police. They were notified when a friend of the police chief called him and told him there had been a death at #13 Hortense Place.

4. During his testimony to the DC, Sergeant Michael Burke told him one of the maids (he did not name her) told him she had heard a shot and then went in to Mrs. Wright's room. When the maids and cook were questioned shortly after by Sergeant Burke, they all said they did not hear a gunshot. DC Dever knew Sergeant Burke testified earlier that one of the maids told him they heard a shot, yet he did not confront any of the maids

with the information to see if it would change their story. When Sgt. Burke testified about the maid, DC Dever neglected to ask him for the maid's name.

5. While DC Dever and Dr. Clopton said they found powder marks on Mrs. Wright's nightgown and entry wound (respectively), no one was asked, and no testimony was offered, regarding whether or not the bed covers had a hole in them or if powder burns or marks were on them. Upstairs maid Kate Ruekert testified that when she came into the room Mrs. Wright was still alive and that her body was covered, with one hand sticking out. Was Mrs. Wright shot through the covers or was she uncovered when she was shot? This is critical evidence and if there was no hole in the covers then someone placed them over her body after the shooting, but before Ruekert entered the room. Perhaps Mr. Wright covered his wife for obvious reason, but the question was never asked.

6. Wright testified that he had never seen the revolver used to shoot his wife, however, a *Post-Dispatch* reporter wrote that Wright made a direct statement to a policeman that the gun was his wife' property and that each night she laid it on a table between their twin beds as a protection against burglars.

While I believe, it is most likely that Elsa Wright committed suicide, it is possible she died as the result of an accident or murder. Without being able to contact witnesses or view evidence, it is difficult to know for sure.

Tom McLellan --Fort Collins Police Services Captain (Ret)

I want to thank Captain Tom McLellan for the extensive time he took to look at all the documents I forwarded to him. His report emailed back to me covered several pages and recited all the pertinent information from all three reports: Coroner's

Inquest, Dr. Clopton's summation, and the St. Louis Police report. I appreciate his thoroughness, fairness and expertise.

I also want to thank Dana McDonough, Custodian of Records, at the Medical Examiner's Office, City of St. Louis, for the effort she took to find these records from 1920, as well as other reports in the Lemp family deaths.

Based on everything I read, drawing diagrams of Elsa's bedroom, looking at possible bullet angles, etc., here is my humble opinion of what happened that morning on March 20, 1920. It is merely for your consideration. I (the author) don't have a forensic background:

I think Tom and Elsa began an argument the evening before, after she returned from the concert. She put on a brave face for her friends and the cook. In that era, it was customary to hide "unpleasantries" from the servants for one simple reason— servants gossip to other family's servants, and soon everyone knows your business. Elsa's and Tom's friends were in upper society, and thus, it was important to keep your game face.

At the matinee concert, she appeared happy. The cook said she was happy at 5-6 o'clock, after the matinee, when she stuck her head into the kitchen. Yet at 7:00, she appears to be "very nervous" at the dinner table and scarcely eats. Could a quiet argument have happened between the two right before dinner? Perhaps because he did not accompany her to the concert, or he may have announced he was going back into work the following morning, even though it was a Saturday, and they had just returned from their honeymoon? Elsa's complaints during her divorce and breakdown from Wright were that he was distant to her, dismissive and abandoned her. Perhaps she was already seeing the same signs she had the first time around and began to panic.

Another thought is this...the Doctor's report said she was on her menstrual cycle. She had a still birth during her marriage to

Wright. Maybe she was hoping for another chance at a child and now, directly after the honeymoon intimacy, she finds she is not pregnant. All the old demons from the previous marriage may be coming around.

Wright states twice during the testimony he arose at 8, chatted a moment with his wife, went into the bathroom and started running the water. He says he forgot underwear and came back into the room, crossed all the way over to the wardrobe, obtained them and went back into the bathroom, closing the door. Only seconds later he hears a "sharp sound," opens the door, crosses "to about the middle of the room," sees the gun and runs for help.

The problem with his story, is that 4 people (three maids and Dr. Clopton) put him as raising the alarm between 8:30 and 8:45. He had a chance to amend this previous statement (that he repeated twice to police and the coroner) that he found her shot at 8:05. Why didn't he change his story to put his timeline closer to the other witnesses?

It is my belief Thomas Wright was locked into his 8:05 timeline because that *is* when the gun went off, a maid *did* hear it and ran in, and saw him over by the couch and wardrobe with the gun in his hand. I also believe she saw Elsa in a slightly different pose than the one in which she was found.

We have only Thomas' words for what happened that morning. What if...

He did run the bath water, possibly to cover the sounds of an argument that was continuing from the night before. Elsa is "upset" (a word oddly used by Doctor Clopton in his report), emotional, tired from being up all night with menstrual discomforts and a bad stomach. She is sitting up in bed near the small night table where the gun is kept. As they continue to argue, Thomas declares he won't listen and grabs up his clothes. All the pain from the previous marriage comes flooding back: the fear of abandonment, dismissal, etc. In a flash of panic and emotion, possibly to keep him from leaving, she grabs up the gun and dramatically points it at herself, saying something to the effect, "I may as well shoot myself. You don't love me. I can't go through this again." He dives for the gun, jerking her arm up to get it away from her chest, and it goes off, entering the body at an odd downward angle. She slumps to her left side (where the Doctor notices the "dull color," "probably from a hemorrhage"), and is gasping for air.

Thomas jumps back in shock and backs away from the bed, the gun in his hand. A maid runs in and sees the scene. He hurls the gun from himself to the nearby couch and stands there in shock. As he sees the face of the maid, he realizes he has to do something, so he begs her not to tell anyone yet. He tells her Mrs. Wright has shot herself and he got the gun away from her. He says something along the lines of "Please don't tell the others yet. I'll get a doctor. I'll take care of it. We don't want to cause panic just yet." He tells her to go back to what she was doing.

Wright now has to act fast. We don't know at what point he turns off the bath tub water. But he comes back into the room, gently lays Elsa back against her pillow, pulls the covers over her, leaving only one arm out to support the suicide story. This would not have changed the exit wound stain if he simply laid her so her head was on the pillow. He can't put the gun back by her, in case the maid tells someone she saw him put it on the couch. It would look like he staged it.

But now reality is setting in. He looks at her, gasping, staring at him ("She seemed to be looking at me"). It won't look good for him if it comes out they were arguing. He can't be in the room at the time the gun went off. A maid may have heard him walking around in the room after the water was running so he concocts the story that he came into the bedroom for underwear and went back into the bathroom, shutting the door. This explains why he offered nothing new about the second time he came into the room to "get underclothes." It never happened. His placement in the bathroom now means she is alone, with a gun on the table next to her.

For 25 minutes, he watched her die. He waited until he was sure she was unable to speak and was near death, before he ran into the hall and called for Martha. Yet, he stops Martha from entering the room...buy a little more time. He sends her to call the doctor. Kate now comes to see what is happening, and for some reason, turns to go into the sewing room, with all this commotion going on. Why? Because I believe she was in the sewing room earlier that morning, possibly mending something, when she heard the shot and ran in. And I think the Coroner suspects it as well. He asks her twice during the inquest, "You did not hear a shot? You did not go in the room?" He even leads her by saying, "Didn't you hear a shot?" I believe he was incredulous that as close as she was to Elsa's room, she did not hear a .32 go off.

The sewing room was probably one of the guest rooms across the 2nd floor landing from the master suite where Elsa was shot. A .32 is a rather loud gun. When Thomas calls out for Martha at 8:30-8:45, Kate ran out into the hall. But then she inexplicably turns to go back into the sewing room. Why? Because I believe Thomas already told her earlier to go away and he would handle it. She is still obeying orders. Yet *now*, he says, "Go in and be with her." He knows now there is no chance of Elsa speaking. And indeed, when Kate went in, Elsa's eyes were half-closed and she was gasping her last. When Martha came in seconds later, she took her last two breaths, and died. It was 8:45.

The two calls Wright made, when he says the maid had trouble getting Clopton on the phone, were to a doctor and his attorney. He also called his two sisters to come and be with him. Samuel Fordyce, his attorney, also brought in three high-powered officials: A Circuit Court Judge, Circuit Court Attorney, and Circuit Court Clerk. Why so much man power for a suicide? And with all these court officials, not one of them say, "You know, maybe we should call the police?"

As to why a maid's story was changed, that she "heard a shot and ran into the room," and later reports not hearing a gun report, is the big mystery. If it was suicide, her hearing a shot and running in to find Mrs. Wright with a gun by her side, and Mr. Wright running from the bathroom would have supported that verdict. Then why did she change her story? Because, I believe, when she ran in, Mrs. Wright's body was in one position, and when she was allowed back in almost 40 minutes later, it was "peaceably" under the covers, lying on her pillow and the gun is on the couch. She had to be paid, or threatened, to change her story, in my opinion.

If Elsa was lying beneath the covers and reached to her right to the night table for the gun, while Wright was in the bathroom, why are the bed covers not disarranged? All the reports say she is lying there "peaceably", as if "going to sleep." The only thing uncovered is one hand. If you roll over to reach for something, I find it hard to believe you leave the other arm tucked under the blanket and nothing gets moved, especially in a twin-sized bed.

And finally, why did she pick that time to shoot herself? She's already told Wright she will stay in bed for a couple of hours. She knows he will probably shower, get dressed and go down to eat. Why not wait until he leaves the room? She waits until he closes the bathroom door and shoots herself. The timing is also suspicious in another way: They just came back from their honeymoon. This should be a very happy time for her, yet she chooses now to shoot herself? She didn't commit suicide when she lost a baby, or went through a breakdown before the divorce. So why now? Because, I believe, something went terribly wrong.

The questions that should have been asked were not. The inquest was short, perfunctory, and the 25-minute time lapse between 8:05 and 8:30 was never addressed. If Elsa's death was an accident, Thomas Wright is still culpable. He let her die. In a cowardly act to cover his hide, he, and I believe, his attorney, bribed servants, and did a speedy cover-up that included a signed blank coroner's inquest report. If you only look at two facts here—waiting 25 minutes to call for help and a maid's changed story of whether or not she heard a shot, you have enough reasonable doubt, that in today's judicial system would lead to a lengthy investigation and trial.

It may be too late, but there should be enough reasonable doubt to have the verdict changed from suicide to "undetermined."

FUNERAL SERVICES FOR MRS. WRIGHT TO BE HELD TOMORROW

St. Louis Post-Dispatch: March 23, 1920.

The funeral of Elsa Justine Lemp Wright was held at 13 Hortense Place, at 10:00 a.m. It was a small and private affair with only a few close friends and relatives in attendance.

Many flowers were sent to the Hortense Place home by friends, although there had been a formal request that no flowers be sent. The funeral service was conducted by the Rev. George E. Norton, rector of St. Michael's and All-Angels' Episcopal Church. He read a scripture passage and a poetic selection, followed with a prayer and a benediction. "Lead, Kindly Light" was sung by Mrs. A. I. Epstein.

The pall bearers were Julius S. Walsh Jr., Thomas S. Maffitt, J. G. Miller, James W. Garneau, Sam W. Fordyce, Jr., Alex T. Primm, and Charles Wiggins. Others attending the funeral besides relatives were Fesus J. Wade, Breckenridge Jones, E. B. Pryor, George J. Tansey, Mr. and Mrs. E. A. Faust, Mr. and Mrs. Adolphus Busch III, Jacob Renth and Henry Vahlkamp, two last named having been connected for many years with the Lemp brewery.

The family consisted of Mrs. Gustav Pabst, a sister of Mrs. Wright, and her husband. They arrived on a special train from Milwaukee. Mrs. Alexander Konta, another sister, and Louis Lemp, a brother, both of New York are expected today. Edwin and William J. Lemp, Jr., other brothers, who live here, are in the charge of the funeral arrangements. A fourth brother, Charles A. Lemp, is in Africa.

One of those waiting outside during the ceremony was Mrs. Anna Walters of 1314 South Thirteenth Street, who said she nursed the former Miss Lemp from babyhood.

Just when the gossip was beginning to abate, the next bombshell dropped.

MRS. T. H. WRIGHT DIED INTESTATE; HER WILL INVALID

St. Louis Post-Dispatch: March 23, 1920.

It was learned today that in the period when Mrs. Lemp Wright was divorced from Wright, she made a will, in which Wright was not mentioned, but since the remarriage, March 8, last, she had not made a will. Under the law, her remarriage invalidated the will which she made as a single person, the effect being that she died intestate. Her estate has an estimated value of $500,000 ($6 million in 2015).

According to the law governing the estates of those who die intestate, Wright, as the widower, will be entitled to one-half the estate and the other half will be divided among Mrs. Wright's two sisters and four brothers.

The will must be produced in the Probate Court, together with documentary proof of the second marriage, in order to legally establish the fact that Mrs. Wright died intestate.

It is the right of the widower, before all others, to administer the estate. If he waives this right, it then passes to the collateral heirs. If all the collateral heirs should waive their administration rights, the Public Administrator could take charge of the property and would get 5% of the disbursements, which also would be the fee of a private administrator. A member of the family, if appointed, could waive the fee. This is often done.

Thomas was not made the administrator. The Mercantile Trust Company filled those shoes. Perhaps Julia Lemp's dying contingency, concerning her bequests that no husbands of her daughters could be the executor of their estate upon their death, reached down from above and placed a staying hand on the shoulder of Thomas Wright.

MRS. THOMAS WRIGHT HEIRS WILL GIVE HOSPITAL $100,000

St. Louis Post-Dispatch: April 21, 1920.

A gift of $100,000 will be made to the St. Louis Children's Hospital by four brothers and two sisters of Mrs. Elsa Lemp Wright, who shot and killed herself at her home, 13 Hortense Place, March 20. The gift will be taken from their shares of Mrs. Wright's estate.

The gift will be made, it was explained, through a desire to carry out the wish expressed by Mrs. Wright in her last will, which was automatically invalidated by her remarriage to Thomas H. Wright, 12 days before her death.

This will, it is understood, was made last Oct. 15, after her divorce from Wright, and before the remarriage. It gave the bulk of her estate, since inventoried at $913,276, to her sisters, Mrs. Hilda Pabst, and Mrs. Annie L. Konta, and her brother Edwin A. Lemp, and provided a bequest of $100,000 to the

166

Children's Hospital. Moreover, it provided that if those three heirs should die before her, the shares of Mrs. Konta and Mrs. Pabst also should go to the Children's Hospital.

The contents of Mrs. Wright's first will have not been made known. The second will, made public today, provided that all her clothing, furniture and personal belongings, except jewelry, be evenly divided between the two sisters. To each of them she also bequeathed a strand of pearls. She bequeathed her automobile to Mrs. Konta. The house was bequeathed to Edwin A. Lemp, together with all other real and personal property not otherwise specifically disposed of.

Was on Hospital Board

The provision in the will relating to the $100,000 bequest to the hospital specified that it should be invested, and that the income, or such part of it as might be necessary, should be used to maintain an "Elsa Lemp Wright Room" at the hospital. This will be done.

Mrs. Wright was a member of the Board of Directors of the Children's Hospital and had during her life made a number of substantial gifts to the hospital.

Thomas H. Wright went on with his life. In 1925, he married Cora South Brown O'Fallon. From 1930 to 1947, he moved to 6 different residences, including moving with his new wife Cora back to Portland Place, right next door (at 46) from where he lived with Elsa. He retired from the National Bearing Company (formally the Moore-Jones Brass Company) in 1940, and moved with his wife to Southampton, New York, where he was active in civic affairs. He was president of the National Golf Links of America from 1939, until his death. Mr. Wright died in Southampton, May 16, 1961. He was survived by his wife. There were no children.

Lemp Brewery

Chapter Seven

All Glory Is Fleeting

"For over a thousand years, Roman conquerors returning from
the wars enjoyed the honor of a triumph—a tumultuous parade.
In the procession came trumpeters, musicians and strange
animals from conquered territories, together with carts laden
with treasure and captured armaments. The conquerors rode in
a triumphal chariot...Sometimes his children, robed in white,
stood with him in the chariot or rode the trace horses. A slave
stood behind the conqueror, holding a golden crown, and
whispering in his ear a warning—that all glory is fleeting."

--George S. Patton, Jr.

St. Louis, Missouri: 1901:

The turn of the century found most Americans looking forward to a time of change, greater possibilities and more technical advancements. Thanks to the Industrial Revolution, new contrivances were making their way in people's homes at an alarming rate. Telephones, electricity, new wonders for the laundry room, mass-produced furniture that gave every income a chance to have beautiful

interiors, and so much more. Marvels from the automotive industry, fashions that were giving women more freedom of movement with daring new styles, and even rumors that two brothers from Dayton, Ohio, were experimenting with flying. The Wright brothers actually piloted a flight in 1903, that lasted 59 seconds and covered a distance of 852 feet over a wind-swept beach in North Carolina. There was no stopping Americans now.

Leading the way in 1901, in the brewing industry, was William J. Lemp. The new century looked full of promise for him, his business and his family. He had watched his young children grow into successful adults, who, despite a few matrimonial hiccups, were thriving. He was making history with his brewery, as he continued to be on the cutting edge of technology.

Lemp Brewery had morphed and expanded, rolling over neighboring houses and streets like the *Blob* from some Sci-Fi movie. It swallowed homes and replaced them with brick edifices, stables and locomotive houses. William J. Lemp Brewery now covered 11 city blocks. Its tallest building, with

LEMP proudly stamped upon its tower, could be seen from miles around, both by land and waterway. The Mississippi riverfront was home to his shipping yards, and six switchbacks led railway cars into his compound. Over 700 men were on his payroll, with more in various branches. It was during this time that he upped his anti and purchased his own railroad company. The Western Cable Railway connected him to cities and business all over America, making him the first brewer to "go national." 600 refrigerated rail cars rolled out across the land carrying Lemp beer brands, such as Falstaff, Tip Top, Standard, Extra Pale, Tally and Culmbacher. 50 horse-drawn wagons serviced St. Louis, and within a few short years, Packard trucks would proudly haul the award-winning lager to its destination. The Lemp footprint was now seen in countries all around the world, as well as in the USA. A new branch, in Austin, Texas was prospering, along with an outlet in Hot Springs, Arkansas. He owned ice houses in several major cities.

W. J. Lemp Brewing warehouse in Austin, Texas
Photo courtesy St. Louis Public Library

William Lemp's Western Cable Railway Company,
and the Lemp Railway cars rolling past Lemp Brewery in St. Louis.

With the Lemp Brewery handling over 125,000 bottles of beer capped daily, and 500,000 barrels of beer produced annually, grossing $3.5 million in sales, it looked as if there was no stopping the great beer baron as he watched the 1800s fade into the distance. Just when the other local breweries were closing in on his success, William Lemp made headlines again. He built a pipeline between the bottling plant and his stock house. The pipe's insulation allowed the transported beer to go directly to the bottling machines without the loss of purity, flavor or quality. It set the brewing world on its head. The proud announcement from the Lemp Brewery offices made the papers and people came great distances to witness this technological wonder.

From the desk of the
William J. Lemp Brewing Company

"Our new pipeline (accepted by the Commissioner of Internal Revenue of the United States, as conforming in all its parts to the rigid requirements of the Government) is three hundred and fifty feet long, passing direct from the extensive beer cellars to the Bottling Department. The pipeline is located in a subterranean conduit, kept at the freezing point to insure the proper protection to the beers. It connects on the one side with our large two-hundred-barrel tanks in the cellars and with the filling apparatus in the bottling house on the other, thereby forcing the beer at freezing temperature direct into the bottles, thus avoiding exposure to air and light. From this it follows that whenever you draw a cork of a bottle of Lemp's beer, it is the same as from the wood....The public is cordially invited to verify our statement by a visit to our plant; guides will take pleasure in conducting visitors through all departments....We have no secrets, and shall be more than pleased to afford our friends and the public an opportunity to view and inspect the latest improvements required in the process of bottling beer."

And come they did. The towering brick structure of Anheuser-Busch could literally be seen from the windows of the upper stories at the Lemp Brewery, and it is said the Busch's, who were good friends with the Lemp's, were one of the first to congratulate him on this modern marvel. The William J. Lemp Brewery was the largest in St. Louis and now ranked 9th largest in the US.

William looked about him with pride. His dogged determination to take his father's brewing foundation to unprecedented heights had become a reality. He was a typical German: proud, stubborn and passionate. He did things with gusto, never happy to be sitting on the fence or waiting for something to transpire. He went out and dragged it home. With three of his sons helping to run things, he was now able to travel more and enjoy life with his wife Julia. They now traveled to Europe annually, often taking Elsa, Edwin, and any of the other children who were free to come along.

Lemp Park

St. Louis was known for its magical parks that sat center stage among the city's prospering neighborhoods. Lemp Park was such a place. It sat only a block from the brewery and covered 4 city blocks. The parks were called "summer gardens" and offered the community unique entertainment venues. On

March 10, 1900, Lemp Park kicked off a party that was talked about for years to come. Its pavilion for dancing was packed to the rafters, while the open-air theater saw a host of entertainers. The program for the Big Vaudeville Show listed Mlle. Maud, Queen of the Invisible Wire; Millette, "in marvelous feats of smoking drinking and juggling, while standing on his head on a Single Trapeze"; George Jennier, "America's Greatest Foot Juggler"; and the Century Comedy Four introducing the latest comic song, "Why Don't You Loosen Up?" The show concluded with a one-act "Laughable Farce" entitled "German Justice" which "will decide which is the best beer to drink." The slogan on the program declares: "Always drink 'Lemp's—St. Louis' Greatest Advertiser." The music for the ball included four waltzes and one polka of twenty-one dances.

Summer Garden Park, St. Louis 1900

CARNIVAL AT LEMP'S PARK
South St. Louis Will Have a Two Week's Jubilee

The Republic: Sunday, September 7, 1902.

"Laughter and merriment are to hold sway for two weeks, beginning September 28, in South St. Louis, with Lemp's Park as the place for amusement. There will be shows, dancing, songs, confetti, and much of what made the Midway famous, besides refreshments of both the light and heavy varieties.

"The well-known Gaskell Carnival Company has been engaged to furnish the greater proportion of the attractions, including dwarfs and giants, freaks and acrobats. Besides the standard form of entertainment, there are promised many novelties such as electric, wireless and otherwise."

St. Louis World's Fair

1901 also saw William joining forces with other great men of St. Louis, to head the biggest event ever held, not only in St. Louis, but in the world. The 1904 World's Fair was coming to St. Louis to commemorate the anniversary of the signing of the Louisiana Purchase. William was asked to sit on the board of directors, as well as join a handful of men who would be in charge of creating a massive venue at the fair to advertise beer's contribution to the Gateway City. It was a massive undertaking for the brewer, who already had his hands full with a major brewery operation, as well as sitting on the board at the First National Bank, and the German Savings Institution, along with being a member of the Mercantile Exchange, and other organizations.

Under the headlines, **BREWERS ORGANIZE TYROLEAN ALPS SHOW,** the names of Adolphus Busch, William J. Lemp and Associates Incorporated, were listed to "produce the fair attraction." The article announced that "every brand of St. Louis beer will be sold to the patrons of a big concession."

Tyrolean Alps exhibit w/fake mountains & castle.
World's Fair 1904

A "big concession" was a gross understatement. The massive area earmarked for a replica of the Tyrolean Alps sat atop a hill in Forest Park, commanding the attention of all entering "The Pike." German architects would be flown in to replicate a similar panorama they had created for Dusseldorf Exposition in Germany. The "Alps," made of a mixture of rock and staff, popularly called Paper Mache, or Plaster of Paris, rose a stunning 180'. A giant alpine castle was nestled next to the mountain range, with halls that could seat over 2,500 people. A tramway would carry the guests through the "mountains" where they could view alpine villages, where greats such as Mozart were born. The pinnacle of the attraction was to be food and every beer sold in St. Louis. served by waitresses in German attire, flown in from Germany. There were songs and dances from the homeland and a menu that would rival any upscale restaurant, as shown here:

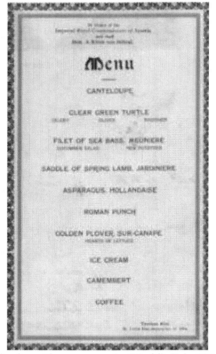

Tyrolean Alps menu at the World's Fair, 1904

By the time the Fair closed on December 1, 1904, after running since April of that year, it was reported that 20 million people had reveled in the wonders of the Louisiana Purchase Exposition. It threw St. Louis into a global spotlight. Its size and scope was never again duplicated. William, who was such a primary part in its success, would not live to see opening day.

When the William J. Lemp Brewing Company was formed in 1892, Frederick Lemp was only 19. Billy Lemp was 25 at the time and was made Vice-President, while Louis was 22 and was made Superintendent. Frederick, knowing his turn was near to have his name listed on the mast head, put his heart and soul into knowing everything he could about the brewery. He knew his father had singled him out to eventually head the plant and the young man gave countless hours of his time to understand all the machinations that made the brewery great. He was hard-working, outgoing and just as determined as his father to see Lemp beer dominate the brewing circles. Billy may have been more than happy to hand the reins to his younger brother when the time came, as he was known as a playboy and enjoyed the fun and excitement his wealth afforded him. Louis was already casting an eye at the political arena and developing a passion for horse breeding. Louis eventually gave up his seat to his younger brother Edwin. William may have realized that of his five sons, it was Frederick whose heart pumped lager beer as steadily as his own.

There are tragic historical moments, that when looked back upon, were heralded by harbingers of disaster. For William J. Lemp, one such forecast of unrest may have stared at him from the headlines of the *St. Louis Republic* the year before when it posted a full page of riot conditions brought on by a streetcar strike across the entire city: multiple bystanders shot, an attempted lynching, a crowded streetcar being stoned by a mob sympathetic to the strikers, and policemen assaulted with thrown bricks and bottles. In the end, 14 people lost their lives in the strike brought on by union action. 3,000 workers cut cables, lit bonfires, and piled boulders, rubble, and other obstructions onto streetcar tracks. Thirteenth Street, where Lemp Mansion sat, was only one street over from a major streetcar line on 7th Street where some of the action was taking place.

Another, and more poignant precursor that may have foreshadowed William Lemp's undoing, crossed his path five years earlier when twin tornadoes met above the skies of South St. Louis, only ½ mile from Lemp Mansion. On May 27, 1897, the worst tornado in St. Louis history bore down on the neighborhood known then as Soulard. It grazed the top of Eads Bridge, sparing the new structure, but tore a deadly path through the south side, flattening homes and businesses.

Reports rolled in throughout the days of bodies discovered in the ruins. Over 300 people were killed, and the damage was estimated at over $10 million.

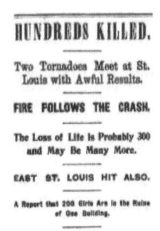

In the background of it all, creeping ever closer, like a kudzu vine waiting to choke the life out of the empire William had built, was a new dawning that would topple brewery industries and the giants that built them. The Dry Movement had already begun in the early 1800s, and was gathering steam, as its small flames were fanned by members of the Temperance Movement and other crusaders rallying against the sins of alcohol. The murmurs were there, but William, and others, failed to take them seriously.

Life had been abundant and amazing for the Lemp family. Economic depressions that had left others bereft of home and fortune in the past had never left a mark on the formidable brick structure of Lemp Mansion or the family so cozily ensconced within its walls. Hilda and Annie were married to rich husbands and living lives of prestige and opulence. Billy had married the beautiful socialite Lillian Handlan two years before, Louis was happily wed to Agnes Walsh, and Frederick had a beautiful wife, Irene Verdin, and a baby girl. Elsa and Edwin were happy and enjoying travel and all the great things the Lemp money afforded them.

Yet dark clouds above Thirteenth Street were brewing—their heavy shadows cloaking the bustling courtyards of the brewery and seeping in through the open windows of Lemp Mansion. William Lemp's twin tornadoes were about to land.

Chapter Eight

Frederick Lemp
The Heir Apparent

Frederick "Freddie" William Lemp was son number four in the Lemp household. Born on November 20, 1873, he was considered the most-handsome of the boys. With his intense gaze, stylish moustache and slender build, he cut a fashionable figure in his bachelor days. Born into a brewery dynasty, he was foreordained to learn about the ways of hops and yeast. And learn he did—with fervor.

Frederick graduated from United States Brewers Academy in New York City, but only after graduating from Smith Academy in 1890, and Washington University in St. Louis, where he received a degree in mechanical engineering. He had just been given the title of Assistant Superintendent at his father's brewery, working side by side with his brother Louis, who held the Superintendent position. He was outgoing, and always welcome in social and business circles. The 1901 St. Louis City Directory lists Frederick and his new wife Irene residing at 1601 South Grand Avenue. Married August 30, 1899, the couple were said to be very much in love. Their engagement was heralded in the **Sprague Scrapbook** with the flair and flowery prose associated with that popular publication:

The Prospective Benedict Is the Fourth Son of Brewer W. J. Lemp

"Upon the third finger of the pretty little left hand of Miss Irene Verdin of 4330 McPherson Avenue, there sparkles—nay—blazes—a solitaire diamond of such size and brilliancy that it cannot but attract the attention of the least observant. It is a stone such as one sees rarely—of a clearness and beauty that does great credit to the taste and judgment of Mr. Frederick W. Lemp, who had, it seems, the honor of selecting and presenting it to its present owner.

"Miss Verdin's engagement to Mr. Lemp comes in the nature of a great surprise to society at large, although the intimate friends of the young couple have known for some time that the betrothal existed. No public announcement was made, however, and the date for the wedding had not been definitely fixed, and the secret was to have been kept until preparations for the bridal ceremony were well under way.

"But the secret leaked out and the betrothed couple admit that the marriage will take place just as soon as they can make it convenient. "Miss Verdin's mother is now at Eureka Springs, recovering from a recent nervous attack, and Mr. Lemp's parents are traveling in California and other Western States.

Until both families come together, and the affair is discussed by them, the wedding day will not be determined upon. It will, however, be late in the spring or early in the fall, and the young couple will go to Europe to spend their honeymoon.

"Miss Verdin says the ceremony will be a very simple and quiet home affair, as her family is in deepest mourning. Her father, the late Bernard Verdin, died less than two years ago, and this was followed by the sudden death, just a month ago, of her little sister, a beautiful 10-year-old lassie who was the pet of the household.

"Miss Verdin, the eldest daughter of the family, has just passed her twentieth birthday. She is tall, with a slender, graceful figure, wavy, ash-blonde hair and gentle dark blue eyes.

Irene Verdin
Photo courtesy of Christy Bond, *Gateway Families*

"Mr. Lemp is the fourth in a family of five sons. His age is about twenty-five, and he is known as a "jolly good fellow" and is a great favorite in social and business circles. There has been some talk of one of his four brothers—"Billy," Charlie, Louis or Edwin— following his shining example in a matrimonial way, but the young men declare that this report is entirely without foundation.

""Billy," the eldest, says he "has trouble enough," Edwin, the youngest, is too young to be serious; and Charlie and Louis "haven't time."

"So, society may heap all its congratulations upon "Freddie," who is to get one of the most charming girls in the smart set."

As promised, the wedding was a small, quiet affair, held at the bride's home at 4330 McPherson Avenue in St. Louis, in August of 1899. Out of respect for the recent deaths in her family, the ceremony was played down and the couple began married life without the usual fanfare."

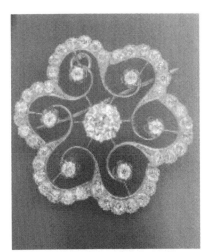 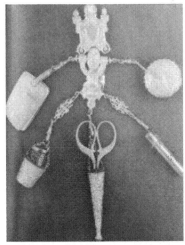

(L.) Diamond starburst pin Frederick gave Irene as an engagement present. (R.) Irene's sewing kit. Photos by Christy Hawes Bond, *Gateway Families.*

On August 29, 1900, Marion Fredericka Lemp was born and Frederick became a happy father. As he was the first of the Lemp boys to become a parent, it was no doubt celebrated with much clinking of beer steins in the Lemp Mansion rooms. Though he had not produced a male heir to the brewery empire, there was still time. But time has its own agenda, and Frederick Lemp's was about to expire.

Marion Fredericka Lemp
It was she who in later years, then married to Richard Hawes, called the
police to the Lemp Mansion when Charles Lemp was reported shot.
Photo courtesy of Christy Hawes Bond, *Gateway Families*

LEMP FUNERAL TO BE PRIVATE
St. Louis Post-Dispatch December 17, 1901

"The funeral of Frederick W. Lemp will take place at 2 o'clock Tuesday afternoon from the residence of his parents, Mr. and Mrs. William J. Lemp, Sr., 3322 South Thirteenth Street. The obsequies will be strictly private. None but members of the immediate family will be allowed to view the remains at the Lemp residence, and only the four brothers of the deceased will accompany the remains to Bellefontaine. The remains will be placed temporarily in a receiving vault. Mr. Lemp's remains arrived from California at 6 o'clock Monday evening.

"Frederick Lemp was the fourth son of the millionaire St. Louis brewer, William J. Lemp. He was 28 years old and leaves a widow, who was Miss Irene Verdin, and one child. They were with him when he died.

"Though the family desired to have the funeral as unostentatious as possible, a huge bouquet of American beauties was sent to the Lemp residence at noon by friends of the deceased. There were five dozen long-stemmed roses in the bouquet, prettily tied with pink silk ribbons."

The news that Frederick Lemp was dead stunned his family and the St. Louis community at large. Only three years after his marriage, in the summer of 1901, he began to have health problems. At first it was downplayed—he had been working long hours at the brewery, after all, and he was a new father. When the conditions worsened, it was decided he, his wife and daughter, would go out to California, as so many others had done, to get out of the polluted skies of St. Louis' factories and breathe the fresh ocean air. In October of 1901, his little family relocated to Pasadena for what they planned to be only a brief time.

Two months later, in December, William and Julia went out to the coast to visit him. William was thrilled to see his son looked much improved. After a short visit, Frederick's parents returned home. William shared the good news with the rest of the family and looked forward to having his son back at work with him once more. Julia was, no doubt, missing her new little granddaughter as well.

Only a few days after the Lemps return to St. Louis, they received the telegram that all parents dread. Frederick had suffered a sudden relapse. The dispatch from California sited the cause of his death as heart failure, precipitated by a combination of diseases. No one in the Lemp household foresaw such an event. There was no history in the family to point to this. Adam Lemp had died from liver disease, which may have been alcohol related, but this was nothing like that. How could this happen to such a vibrant young man?

The blow was tremendous. While little is said about Julia's heartbreak, or that of the other Lemp members, William's despondency was adroitly chronicled. According to Henry Vahlkamp, brewery Secretary and family friend:

"...suddenly the grief of the father was most pathetic. He broke down utterly and cried like a child. It was the first death in the family. He took it so seriously that we feared it would completely shatter his health and looked for the worst to happen."

Once again, the twin parlors at Lemp Mansion were shrouded with flowers and plants, flanking a solitary casket, as they had been for Julia's parents. It was the fourth funeral held in the stately home, with Jacob Feickert's brother being the first. Only Elsa and Edwin still lived there at the time with their parents. The hallways, that had once echoed with the sound of eight children running and laughing, now vibrated with the heart rending sobs of the young man's family. Irene Verdin Lemp remained in mourning a long time. Two years later she was spotted at a horse championship in Box 15 as a guest of Mr. and Mrs. F. W. Nolker. *The Saint Louis Republic* described her appearance:

"Mrs. Frederick Lemp, who is in half mourning, wore black lace and white silk, with a large white ostrich boa and a small black hat."

She later married again, to one Leon Bernard Langan at the New Cathedral Chapel. But happiness was not in the cards. Six months before the birth of their son, Leon Verdin Langan, she was widowed a second time when her husband died in 1908.

She moved with her two children into her mother's home and raised them. She did not marry again.

Irene Verdin Lemp with her daughter, Marion Fredericka.
Photo courtesy of Lemp Mansion

Chapter Nine

STORM CLOUDS GATHER

William Lemp, Sr. Photo Missouri History Musuem

"The time is out of joint. O cursed spite, That I was ever born to set it right." --William Shakespeare, Hamlet

St. Louis, Missouri 1904:

William struggled through the days following Frederick's death. His demeanor was greatly changed, and his family committed on his lack of focus and increasing health issues. Gone was the jovial president visiting and laughing with his workmen at the brewery. When he did appear, it was as if by rote; merely going through the actions as he walked ghost-like through the massive brick buildings, their steel girders offering some form of visible strength and support. His visits to doctors increased as his stomach maladies and insomnia began interfering with his life. His wife may have heard him throughout the night, pacing his room on the other side of the pocket doors separating their chambers, or his constant trips to his private bathroom on the first floor. He may have tiptoed past Edwin and Elsa's rooms in an effort not to wake them as he made his way down the darkened back stairs.

For his family's sake, he tried to keep things status quo. On January 8, 1903, he and Julia, along with Hilda, Elsa and Edwin attended the Crouch-Williams wedding celebration party given at the Olympic. *The Republic* dutifully lists them in attendance in the box seats.

In September, 1903, William took his wife and daughters Elsa and Annie on their customary trip to Europe, probably for the annual purchase of the next season's dresses. They sailed on the *Finland* to Cherbourg, France, returning to New York City on October 6, 1903. Perhaps in hopes that something as familiar as his annual buying trips with his family would cause him to shake off the shackles binding him, William clung to the routines that were the foundation of his life.

At home, three vaults held the family's massive art collection from past trips. Paintings, bronzes, Oriental art, carvings, sculptures, and objects d'art filled the massive 15' x 20' fireproof rooms he had installed when they first converted the mansion into their home in 1876. Whenever they traveled, the rare collection pieces were locked away.

The *Finland* Circa 1904

Throughout the dark days after Frederick's death, William clung to his family and close friends to lend him support. None was a closer friend than Captain Frederick Pabst. Though they were rival beer makers, their friendship was iron-clad and built upon years of comradery. Both men came from Germany to America at roughly 12 years of age, both were innovators in their respective cities (Pabst in Milwaukee and Lemp in St. Louis) for being the first in lager beer production. With the development of train lines connecting their two cities, and the union of their children in marriage, the two men found great pleasure and solace in each other's company. So much so, that William named Frederick after his great friend.

1904 dawned on a cold Friday morning. In only four months' time, the World's Fair would open its doors to the most-anticipated event in recent history. Across William's desk, in his library office at home, were papers stacked high with invoices, drawings, budgets and itineraries.

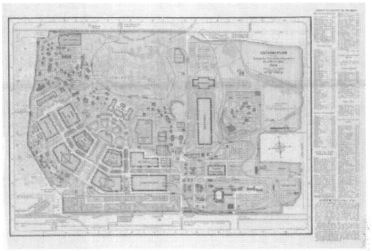

Grounds Plan for the 1904 World's Fair in St. Louis

That morning, on New Year's Day, the Lemp family was gathered in the parlor. A cozy fire was lit to give a feeling of life and warmth to the room, despite the adequate heat emanating from the radiators. Hilda and Gustav were visiting from Milwaukee, just as they had the prior year to celebrate the New Year with the Lemp family. The house was filled with sounds of laughter as 5-year-old Gustave Phillip Pabst, Jr., and two-year-old William Frederick Pabst played with balls on the large oval rug. Elsa and Edwin were curled up in matching armchairs, laughing over something trivial. Billy, Lillian and little Billy III were due over for lunch, and Julia was excited to play with the precious four-year-old and watch him with his young cousins. It was so wonderful to hear children in Lemp Mansion again. Charles and Louis were out-of-town, and Annie was celebrating the New Year in New York with Alexander and Geoffrey.

Eva Wetzel, the maid, entered the room and quietly informed Gustav that he was wanted on the phone. The young man made a joke about being "popular" and excused himself. The gaiety continued, with much talk about the upcoming fair.

It was on everyone's mind and nowhere in the city of St. Louis could you go to escape the topic.

Perhaps William felt a shadow fall across the room, darkening the happy family scene before him; perhaps not. Moments later, the conversation came to an abrupt halt as Gustav Pabst stepped through the east doorway of the room, and leaned heavily upon its frame. His face was drained of color and he looked as if his legs would give out from under him.

In hushed tones that the others could barely hear, he announced his father had just died. William's second tornado had landed.

MILLIONAIRE BREWER DEAD
The End Was Unexpected

Milwaukee, Jan. 1—"Captain Frederick Pabst, president of the Pabst Brewing company, died at his home here today of pulmonary edema, aged sixty-seven years. His death was unexpected, although his health had been failing for more than four years. During the last ten days, Captain Pabst had not left his home, owing to the severe weather, but his condition seemed to be improved and his family was not prepared for his death.

"At 8 o'clock this morning he suffered a relapse. He retained consciousness and was able to converse with his wife and children, who were summoned to his bedside. Captain Pabst seemed to realize that the end was near and talked with his family about his affairs until ten minutes before his death, when he became unconscious and passed quietly away."

Another article mentioned that Gustav Pabst was away visiting in St. Louis for New Year's Day when his father died.

Captain Pabst had been struggling with a number of ailments, including pulmonary edema, diabetes and emphysema. In 1903, while traveling to California, he suffered two strokes before returning to Milwaukee. After receiving a doctor's report that his life expectancy was less than 6 months, he stoically called his family together on Christmas day, of that same year, and gave each of them a gift of $1,000,000. He passed away only a week later.

A rare photo of William Lemp with Captain Frederick Pabst.
Photo courtesy of Lemp Mansion

William and his wife traveled by train to Milwaukee where he attended his good friend's funeral. It was a very private affair, held in the Pabst mansion's music room. An enormous crowd of mourners outside gave tribute to the Captain's popularity in Wisconsin. The parallels between the Captain's death and that of his son cannot have been lost on William. Both Fredericks were in California when their health failed, one substantially, the other fatally. Both were on the rebound and expected to recover, only to suddenly relapse and die. William held them side-by-side in his mind—a mind that was slowly becoming unhinged. A tether he counted on to hold him to a secure pier, forbidding him to drift off into a sea of darkness, was just severed.

The days following his return from Captain Pabst's funeral were ones of anxiety for William. His family and colleagues saw a fractured man, incapable of concentrating on the task at hand, so different from the razor focus and enthusiasm he typically portrayed. He drew into himself and went to the brewery sporadically, choosing to travel there through the underground cave passages to avoid people on the street. Instead of engaging the men with trivia about the brewing business, and personally handing out their paychecks, listening to grievances and rolling up his sleeves to work beside them, he merely passed quietly into the background as if hoping to disappear. His department heads commented on his nervous nature. He was unable to sit still, and was constantly jangling change in his pocket, or striking a card against a table as he looked off into space. He became erratic and those around him feared for his health.

At the time of his son Frederick's death, William's good friend and business secretary, Henry Vahlkamp, had kept vigil with him, pacing along next to the brewery owner as he walked back and forth along the sidewalk in front of Lemp Mansion, often breaking down into great sobs. Vahlkamp saw now the same broken man, only worse. There seemed to be no life left in him. His family was at a loss as to how to help him.

Hilda was dealing with enormous change in her own life as she grieved for the loss of her father-in-law and saw the burden of the great Pabst brewery handed over to her husband. And Julia—that stoic, quiet woman who avoided the society pages and took her joy from raising her family—was beginning to feel as if something was off with her own health. She was more tired than usual, and had vague aches and pains.

Julia may have felt they would weather this storm. They were made of solid German stock. Surely, things would get better.

Chapter 10

The Servant Heard a "Muffled Report"

St. Louis, Missouri: February 13, 1904:

William arose at 7 a.m. that cold February morning and slowly descended the stairs to the first floor. He could hear voices coming from the dining room; one of which was his wife, Julia. He spoke to her briefly at breakfast, where she showed concern over his appearance and his lack of appetite. Billy stopped by to walk over to the brewery with Edwin. He snatched up a few pieces of bacon and slurped down a cup of hot coffee. He asked William a few perfunctory questions about the day's business and commented on his father's haggard appearance. William said he had not slept well again and that he might be late coming in. Julia announced she was going downtown for some shopping, hinting that Valentine's Day was tomorrow.

After the others had gone, William showered in his private bathroom on the first floor, and dressed for work, but his stomach rumbled in protest. He climbed the stairs as though cement weights were attached to his ankles, walked to his back bedroom, entered and locked the door. Sitting on the edge of his bed, his heart began racing in a prolonged panic attack. Everything bore down on him in an unrelenting avalanche of pain and worry. The demands of the World's Fair were never-ending: meetings and more meetings, expecting so much from him when his mind could not seem to swim up from the dark fog that encased it. Something was wrong with Julia; he had noticed her tired expression and her breathing seemed to be more labored. What if she was really sick? He could not go on without her. No more death...no more funerals.

He was tired. So very, very tired. Demands from work— even though Billy, Edwin and Louis were handling most of it—his signature was still needed on the important things, and the brewery was outgrowing its current storehouses, requiring more and more decisions from him. His interests in the South had taken on a life of their own and the paperwork was never done. There were drawings on his desk at work for the new grain bins and the giant grain elevator tower. It was expected to be completed next year. The Fermenting House had just been built. It never ended!

He wrung his hands, feeling the sweat puddle between his palms. A new fear swam up from the depths of his mind. They had come to his home with a subpoena! He could be implicated for tampering with a witness--bribing him. If he was found guilty, it meant prison. His wife would live with the humiliation and his business would be ruined. The company he had built into a massive industry would be only the landmark of his ruined reputation. And the lawsuit from two years ago. It was breathing down his neck...hundreds of thousands of dollars!

He pressed his hands to his temples and felt the vise tighten. What good was he like this? He was too proud to watch the decline of a business that his very blood infused. He got up and paced about the room, the panic growing. Vaguely, he registered the sounds of the maids cleaning on the first and second floors. His hands were curled into fists and perspiration stained his clean white shirt. He couldn't go on like this. But what would happen to his wife and children? Could he leave them with this pain and stigma? The headlines would be sensational and morbid.

William grabbed the mantel piece, and hung on. The room seemed to be splintering around him. There was no good choice! There was only darkness! And the nights...the nights never ended as he paced the halls of his darkened mansion. He couldn't bear another of the pain-drenched nights when his stomach was coiled into spasms. The cyclone of thoughts tumbled about in his brain like morbid acrobats.

If anything, the death of his beloved son, and his dearest friend a month before, had showed him life held no guarantees. His foundation had crumbled. He was adrift. His family would be better without him. He would spare them the humiliation and financial ruin headed his way.

Grabbing up an ink pen from his small desk near the window, he scribbled a note to his family. The will he had made out two weeks before was simple and uncomplicated...and perhaps cowardly. He would leave it to Julia to handle the bequests. If left in her name, they may not be able to attach the lawsuits to it. He folded the paper with shaking hands and pressed it into a long envelope. It took several tries to get it inside. He wrote his wife's name on the front, and propped it against a stack of books on his desk. And then he walked to the window...

His wife's buggy had just made the corner at the end of Thirteenth Street. In moments, it was gone from his view. His heart twisted in pain. He looked across the street to his son Billy's house. He could see the top of the trees that shaded his grandson's play area to the south of the home. There were rumors that Billy and Lillian were having trouble. What would happen to the boy? His heart beat faster.

The giant tower with the name LEMP glowered at him...mocked him. It would stand for decades with its firm brick and fine Italianate design. He was just a man, yet he had created it. Now it felt as if the creation was destroying the creator. An image of Frankenstein flashed through his mind. His heart was pounding and his stomach clinched again. He bent over with a groan, sweat saturating his beard and hairline. With trembling hands, he reached for the desk drawer and pulled it open. The .38 revolver glistened in the dim February light coming in through the window. Tears staining his face, and his hands shaking uncontrollably, he picked it up and carried it to the bed. It was 9:30 a.m.; the day before Valentine's.

Possibly William J. Lemp's last photograph.
Photo courtesy of the St. Louis Genealogy Library.

Wealthy St. Louis brewer, who committed suicide, and his handsome
home at 3322 South Thirteenth Street. —by a *Republic* reporter.

WILLIAM J. LEMP ENDED LIFE WHILE SUFFERING FROM GRIEF AND INSOMNIA

The newspapers were already running the glaring headlines by the afternoon of the brewery owner's death in a mad race to be the first to launch the story. With amazing speed, the news spread throughout the major cities of America, and with the same alacrity, the details became skewed and confusing. Some were written with the aim to sensationalize the tragic story, while others, bore sad witness to the end of an amazing man's life. The following day, after the details had been dutifully gathered, the *St. Louis Post-Dispatch* ran the more factual account of William J. Lemp's death.

St. Louis Post-Dispatch, *February 14, 1904:*
"William J. Lemp, Sr., president of the Lemp Brewing Company, died at his home at 3322 South Thirteenth Street, at 10:30 Saturday morning, after he had shot himself through the right temple.

"Mr. Lemp arose at his wonted hour Saturday morning, ate a light breakfast and upon complaining that he did not feel well, returned to his room. He must have spent some time there in making known his last earthly wishes.

"Mr. Lemp was the only member of the family in the house at the time the shot was fired. A servant girl (Eva Wetzel) heard the muffled report from Mr. Lemp's bedroom. She tried the door, found it locked and was unable to get an answer from Mr. Lemp.

"The girl notified Henry Vahlkamp, secretary of the brewing company, at his office, by telephone, and Mr. Lemp's sons, William J. Lemp, Jr., and Edwin Lemp, went at once to the residence where they broke down the door and found their father.

"Mrs. Lemp was up town and reached home just before her husband's death.

"Hurried calls summoned the physicians of the neighborhood, but Dr. Henry J. Harnisch of 2407 South Eighteenth Street, the family physician, was the first admitted and announced that the wound was necessarily fatal. He was still breathing when Mrs. Lemp returned home (after receiving a phone call at the department store where she was shopping), and died a few minutes later without having recognized anyone. It was 10:30 a.m.

"The bullet was fired through the right temple at close range from a .38-caliber revolver. Mr. Lemp had been suffering from stomach trouble recently, in addition to nervousness...The deed was done in a moment of despondency, over ill health and the continued grief for the death of his son Frederick three years ago, aggravated by the death of his life-long friend, Captain Frederick Pabst of Milwaukee, Jan. 1, 1904.

"He became the virtual friend of the community gathered about his brewery, and thousands of persons looked to him for aid and advice. He was known to be the dispenser of much charity in a quiet manner. He did not give largely for charity through the channels that made donations public, but responded liberally by a method of his own. ...He was never ostentatious...He was reputed to be one of the wealthiest men in St. Louis.

Most of the Children Were Out of Town

"Mr. Lemp's death at this time is particularly sad to the family, as the widow and William Lemp, Jr., and Edwin Lemp, the sons who were called to the residence after the shot was fired, are the only members of the family now in St. Louis.

"Mrs. Annie Konta, the eldest daughter, is traveling in Europe. Louis Lemp, a son, is expected to land in San Francisco, on return from a business trip to Japan and other eastern countries tomorrow. Charles Lemp is absent on an extended business trip, and communicated with his home office from Chicago Friday, and his whereabouts yesterday were uncertain. Mrs. Hilda Pabst was at her home in Milwaukee, and Miss Elsa Lemp, the youngest daughter, was there as her guest."

It was learned that William had been instructed twelve years earlier by his physician, that due to his stomach condition, he was forbidden the use of stimulants of any kind. Since that time, "he drank no wine, beer, nor liquors." For a brewer, and one accustomed to travel and entertaining in his home, it must have been quite a blow.

When Henry Vahlkamp was interviewed, he estimated Mr. Lemp's worth at between $20,000,000 and $30,000,000, three times that of his dear friend Captain Pabst. Besides Lemp Brewery, he had interests in other breweries and ice plants in Galveston, Houston, Dallas, Texarkana, Paris, Temple, and San Antonio in Texas; Little Rock, Arkansas; Shreveport and Baton Rouge, Louisiana, and many other southern cities.

He was a member of the G.A.R., but of no other lodge or fraternal organization. He was affiliated with the Lutheran Church, and was formerly an active member of the Liederkranz, and other German singing societies. He carried no life insurance.

The Saint Louis Republic reported a record-breaking trip made by the Lemp children in order to be there for their mother and attend their father's funeral.

LEMP'S CHILDREN CAME ON SPECIAL
Train Having Clear Right-of-Way Covered 374 Miles in 444 Minutes

St. Louis Republic: *February 14, 1904*—A special Chicago and Alton train made up of a private parlor car and a baggage car, occupied by Mr. and Mrs. Gustav Pabst, Charles Lemp and Miss Elsa Lemp, left Milwaukee at 12:50 p.m., and arrived at the Union Station at 9 o'clock last night.

"Carriages were waiting and the party was hurriedly driven to the Lemp home.

"The special was made up in Milwaukee and had right-of-way against all trains. The eighty-eight miles between Milwaukee and Chicago were covered in an hour and ten minutes...A brief stop was made in Chicago where Charles Lemp and Miss Lemp were taken aboard, and the fast special continued over a clear track. Every train in the route and on the time of the special was sidetracked; even the Chicago and Alton fast train, known as the "Red Train" went into a siding near Joilet for the special."

Newspaper photo of Lemp Mansion during William Sr.'s funeral. The carriages are waiting at the front.

FRIENDS PAY SILENT TRIBUTE TO LEMP
Throngs Gather Around Body of Brewer Amid Profusion of Flowers

The Saint Louis Republic: February 16, 1904.

"The funeral of William J. Lemp took place yesterday at 2 o'clock. The embalmed body was placed in one of the apartments in the Lemp Mausoleum in the Bellefontaine Cemetery, and the crypt will not be sealed until after the arrival of Louis Lemp, that he may have the opportunity to view for the last time the features of his father.

"There was no religious ceremony but Dr. Max Hempel, speaker of the Free Community, made a short address at the residence at 3322 South Thirteenth Street. The greater part of his speech was a eulogy of Mr. Lemp. Dr. Hempel also made a speech at the mausoleum.

"From 11 a.m. until the body was placed in the hearse there was a line of friends passing the bier to gaze at the well-known features of the dead man. Persons of all classes were in the procession.

"All day Sunday and yesterday the Lemp Brewery and its branches all over the country were closed. At the brewery, the ice plant and Lemp Park, all flags were at half-mast.

"The room in the Lemp mansion in which the coffin lay was so filled with flowers that only the passageway for those who went to see the body was unoccupied. When the coffin was carried out it was covered with a blanket of rare orchids. It required two wagons to convey the remaining floral offerings to the cemetery.

"The internment was private, and the hearse was followed by a small number of carriages. Neither Mrs. Lemp nor her daughters went to the cemetery.

"The street in front of the house was thronged with a crowd of men, women and children, until the hearse drove away. Captain Young was in charge of the squad of police that attempted to keep the street clear.

"Doctor Frank Boogher, Deputy Coroner who conducted the inquest over the body of William J. Lemp yesterday returned a verdict of suicide. The witnesses who were examined by

Doctor Boogher were sons of Mr. Lemp and the housekeeper who heard the shot."

What the papers did not report is just another of the Lemp mysteries. Buried in the coroner's report is a rather startling sentence, and one that will remain another secret that William J. Lemp took to his grave:

"It appears that while the deceased was alone in his bedroom he secured possession of a revolver from which he fired three shots; two missed and entered the wardrobe, the third struck in the right temple and passed through the skull and brain." – Deputy Coroner

Three shots! Two "missed." Were they practice shots to get up his nerve, or make sure the gun worked. Were his hands shaking so badly that he misfired twice? The servant only reported hearing one shot. Was it the first missed shot she heard, and while she was running for help the other two went off? It is another mystery in a family saga that baffles the mind.

Julia Lemp sat stone-like in the quiet of the parlor, her face ashen, a soaked handkerchief twisted in her hands. Hadn't she just been consoling Captain Pabst's wife Maria only weeks before; telling her life would go on and to rely on the strength of her family and friends? How hollow the words sounded to her now.

Julia Lemp, & Maria Pabst, wife of Capt. Frederick Pabst

Her daughters sat nearby, their heartbreaking sobs tearing away at her soul. In contrast, the throng of people remaining in the street were eerily silent as they stared at the windows of the house and tried to imagine what was going on inside. Some pointed surreptitiously at the 2nd floor window on the left where they heard William Lemp had died. Others turned to look at the massive tower behind them bearing the dead man's name: LEMP.

Eva Wetzel entered the parlor with a silver tray overflowing with calling cards, their bottom right corners bent to signify condolences. Quietly, she asked if Mrs. Lemp would like them put in a special place for now as there was no more room for future visitors to leave their cards. Eva's face was swollen from crying. It still seemed so surreal. She heard the muffled shot over and over in her head and wondered if she could have done something to stop the horrible countdown of ticking moments that led to her employer's death. Mr. Lemp's frantic sons shouldering open the heavy oak door to get to their father, and the splintering sound of the door frame ripping apart, haunted her.

1900s calling card tray
Photo courtesy of the Molly Brown House, Denver, Co.

A horse and buggy arrived with another basket of flowers and she excused herself to go to the door. Each time she opened it, a murmur swept through the remaining bystanders outside. She accepted the bouquet. The driver doffed his hat, his eyes downcast and returned to his rig. She would place them near the dining table where an early dinner would be waiting for those returning from the crypt.

The afternoon wore on. The people inside Lemp Mansion moved about in a dream-state—reality would not make itself known for several days. Flowers, notes and callers continued to stop by the house at 3322. The workers at the William J. Lemp Brewing Company wondered what it would mean for the gigantic corporation that bore the deceased man's name.

Perhaps Billy realized the enormity of the event that had just happened, not only in terms of losing of his father, but that he was now left with the huge mantel of responsibility and power the name President would bear. The death of William J. Lemp, Sr. cast a shadow far beyond the stone steps of Lemp Mansion.

All that remained of the gossip for the local papers was the disclosure of William Lemp's will. As expected, it made headlines.

LEMP LEFT ALL TO HIS WIFE
Will of Millionaire Brewer who committed suicide, disposed of estate valued at $20,000,000

The Last Will and Testament of William J. Lemp

"I, W. J. Lemp, make, publish, and declare this, as and for my last will and testament, hereby revoking all previous wills.

"I direct the payment of my debts and closing of administration of my personal estate as quickly as the law will permit.

"I give, bequeath and devise to my wife, Julia Lemp, all my property, real, personal or mixed, wherever situated   and by whatever title held, absolutely.

"I make no gifts here to my children Annie K. Lemp, Charles A. Lemp, Hilda T. Pabst, Edwin A. Lemp, and Elsa J. Lemp, and I make no gift here to my grandchild, Marion Lemp, having perfect confidence that my wife, without any request on my part, and nonesuch is hereby made, will do best for them.

"I appoint William J. Lemp, Louis F. Lemp, and Charles A. Lemp, and Edwin A. Lemp, or any or either of them that may accept or qualify, my executors, or executor, without bond.

"In witness whereof, I have hereunto set my hand, this first day of February, 1904.

"W. J. Lemp"

William's sons, along with Henry Vahlkamp, took the will to the probate office, where Henry witnessed it. The personal inventory would need to be assessed, and debts paid, but it all seemed above board.

Julia Lemp, still reeling, must have registered several emotions at the reading of William's will. Here it was, in the finality of black ink, his words, sealing her title forever as the widow of William J. Lemp. It was left to her to handle the burden of dispersing his immense fortune, paying off any debts he may have outstanding, inventorying his possessions for the property assessment that would need to be made before the will's wishes were executed, and myriad other details that fall upon the grieving spouse left behind. It may have registered long after the will was read the importance of the date at the bottom of the handwritten page.

The "First day of February"—*not* the Thirteenth, but almost a full two weeks before he shot himself. He had known for *two weeks* that he could not handle life or its pressures any longer, and he had kept that secret from her. The pain was too much to bear.

Julia's health continued to deteriorate. She relied more and more on the elevator her sons installed to help her navigate the mansion floors more easily. The Lemp children took on as much responsibility as possible to help her through the trying days ahead.

For two years, and two months after William's death, Julia hung on. She had seen the birth of most of her grandchildren. Lemp Mansion became her sanctuary as she spent her final days within its familiar walls. Walls covered with famous paintings she and William had brought home from faraway places, photographs of her family, their faces changing throughout the years. She spent some time late in 1903, at a sanitarium, but finally returned home, her worst fears realized. As the disease ravaged her body, she clung to the people she loved, and relished the memories of the good days.

MRS. WILLIAM LEMP DEAD
Wife of Founder of Brewing Company Succumbs to Cancer

New York Daily Tribune: Tuesday, April 17.

"Mrs. William J. Lemp, widow of William J. Lemp, founder of the William J. Lemp Brewing Company, who killed himself February 13, 1904, died today from cancer. At her bedside were three daughters—Mrs. Annie Konta, of New York; Mrs. Hilda Pabst, of Milwaukee; and Miss Elsa Lemp; also, her four sons— William J. Lemp, Jr.; Louis Lemp, Edwin Lemp and Charles Lemp.

"When the will of William J. Lemp was filed, leaving everything to his widow, it was said Mrs. Lemp was the richest woman in St. Louis. Valued at $20,000,000, it is said some of the property has been turned over to the children. The bulk of the estate, however, was untouched."

Julia's will was also printed in the papers. If the Lemp children were hoping for any form of anonymity, it would not be forthcoming. The entire world now knew the size of their piggy banks.

LEMP CHILDREN SQUARE EQUALLY
Will of Brewer's Widow Disposes of Estate, Worth Over $10,000,000

St. Louis Post-Dispatch: May 25, 1906.

By the will of Mrs. Julia Lemp, widow of William J. Lemp, Sr., considered to be the richest woman in St. Louis, the Lemp estate, estimated to be worth between $10,000,000 and $12,000,000, is to be divided in equal shares among the seven children—Mrs. Annie Konta, Hilda Pabst, Elsa Lemp, Charles Lemp, William J. Lemp, Jr., Louis Lemp and Edwin Lemp. The bequests to William J. Lemp, Jr., Charles A. Lemp, and Hilda T. Pabst, are unconditional. Edwin's share is to be held in trust for him until he is 30 years old. Mrs. Annie Konta and Louis Lemp are to receive their bequests in full at once except that their shares in the brewery and in the Western Cable Railway Company are to be held in trust for them by William J. Lemp, Jr., and Charles A. Lemp, the dividends or the proceeds of sales to be used for their support.

The share of Miss Elsa Lemp is to be held in trust for her until she is 30 years old, except that $100,000 is to be paid over to her when she gets married. If she dies without issue before she is 30, her share will go to the other heirs.

The executors, William, Charles and Edwin Lemp, are empowered to fill a vacancy if one occurs, but it is stipulated that the husband of none of her daughters is to serve in that capacity.

To Mrs. Irene Lemp, widow of her son, Frederick W. Lemp, and her granddaughter, Marion, she leaves nothing, stating that she has purchased from them the part of the estate which would go to the deceased son's heirs.

To her daughters, she leaves the jewelry and household effects. To her sons and daughters collectively she bequeaths her horses, vehicles and paintings, stipulating that each heir shall have at least one painting.

She leaves the division of the property to the executors, placing "implicit faith in the kindliness which prevails among her children."

The "heart of the home" was gone. Elsa moved in with Edwin to his newly-purchased home at St. Regis Apartments in the Central West End. Lemp Mansion, the scene of so many birthdays, weddings, social affairs, celebrations, and funerals, was left in the care of one person: Charles Lemp. He remained in the home until 1910. The other children had selected the pieces of art, furnishings, and personal effects of their parents, and tried to move on with their lives. Annie maintained her home in New York and wrote her books; Hilda played the part her mother had as the woman behind the man running a powerful beer brewery; William Jr. was now saddled with the gigantic burden of not only running a massive brewery empire, but hanging on to a marriage fraught with problems. Edwin was still at the brewery, but his thoughts were elsewhere; Charles was active in the political and banking arenas; Elsa traveled and spent time with her sisters and Edwin; and Louis Lemp decided to leave St. Louis behind.

Chapter Eleven

Louis Lemp

**"No hour of life is wasted that is spent in the saddle." –
Winston Churchill**

St. Louis, Missouri: 1906

Louis Lemp was one of two sons who escaped the curse
that seemed to hang over the male heirs of the Lemp fortune.
Born on January 11, 1870, he was the second oldest of William

Lemp's sons. "Louie" studied the art of beer making under the tutelage of some of the best beer makers in the world while attending their academy in Germany. He dutifully kept notes on every stage of the brewing process, from hop selection to fermentation. His handwriting sprawled across 159 pages in an extremely comprehensive overview of the art of lager beer production. At the time of his graduation he sent the prolific diary to his father. It can be seen at the Missouri Historical Library in St. Louis.

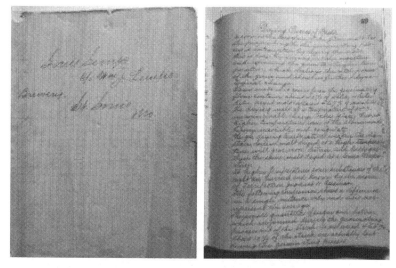

Louis Lemp's handwritten diary on the process of making beer he sent home to his father William J. Lemp while he was in Germany learning to become a brewmaster. It was 159 pages long. Missouri Historical Library.

He gave the brewery his all, rising from superintendent to second vice-president after his father's death, when Billy was forced to take over the reins of the massive corporation. He was focused and became a trustee in the United States Brewer's Association from 1903-1904, representing St. Louis.

During this time, Louis also threw his hat into the political arena. He was one of 32 men chosen for the New State Committee of Missouri. He and Dr. Spiegelhalter were named for District 10, during the Jefferson City, Missouri, caucus. His name appeared more regularly in the headlines than any of the other Lemp brothers, both due to his political aspirations, and the success of his horse breeding and racing business.

When Julia Lemp passed away in 1906, Louis turned over his keys to the brewery, selling out his shares to his brothers. It was if his duty to St. Louis, the brewery, and his family—now that his parents were gone—was over. He married Agnes Walsh (born 1887), and they would have a daughter, Louise on June 12, 1909. Louise would grow up to marry her cousin Edwin L. Pabst (son of Hilda and Gustav Pabst).

Louise Lemp, 3 months old. Photo courtesy of Lemp Mansion

Louis moved his happy little family to New York City. The 1920 census shows them living on Park Avenue: Louis is 49 at that time, Agnes is 33, and Louise is 11. He is listed as a "publisher."

But before he put St. Louis in his rear-view mirror, he made a name for himself and his horses; at first in the shadow of the Gateway Arch, but in time, throughout America.

KITTY CLYDE WON BUSCH CHAMPIONSHIP

The Republic: *Friday, August 15, 1902.*
"Louis Lemp's Kitty Clyde, a 3-year-old chestnut mare by Ben Strome-Ben Amy, won the Busch Handicap, the feature of inaugural day at Kinloch Park yesterday. Kitty Clyde beat the fast-moving Glenwood by a nose."

MR. LEMP'S HORSES WERE IN EVIDENCE

The Republic: *Sunday, July 15, 1900.*
"Mr. Louis Lemp's popular red jacket and black cap flashed to the finish line on two different occasions: Macon winning for the young St. Louis brewer in the third race, while Terra Incognita captured the best event for him."

WILL IT BE SAM PHILLIPS, WOUNDED KNEE OR STAR CHAMBER?

The St. Louis Republic: *June 16, 1900.*
"The heavy play that is sure to be made on Wounded Knee is liable to send this handsome son of Foul Shot to the post favorite. It would indeed be a popular victory if this animal shot past the post in the van. He is the property of genuine sportsmen Messrs. Lemp and Crowley who have their hearts set on the race and a victory would be more warmly welcome by them than $100,000. Wounded Knee was bred at Doctor Crowley's stock farm at Woodlands. Although yet a maiden, he rated as one of the best local 3-year-olds of the year.

"Two weeks ago, it looked as though it would be a fight between Sam Phillips and Florizar. Since that time, Doctor Cave and Wounded Knee have sprung into prominence, and their recent races have been so good that the many members of the smart set figure that they will both beat the other pair."

Louis Lemp on horseback, May 2, 1908. Photo St. Louis Library

Horses became much more to the Lemp family than a hobby or racing endeavor. Billy and Louis loved riding so much they converted the old Cooling House, once used for the brewery, into a handsome arena and began offering tutored riding lessons. Once again, the Lemps made headlines:

HORSEBACK RIDING IS NOW THE RECREATION OF THE LEMP FAMILY

The Republic: Sunday, April 5, 1903. "By exchanging his doctor for a riding master, William Lemp, Jr., familiarly called "Billy" among his friends, has solved the problem of health and good cheer.

"After trying the new medicine on himself and finding it efficacious, Mr. Lemp prescribed it for his family, his brothers and sisters, as well as his friends, so that at the present time horseback riding in a scientific way is the principal recreation of all the members of the Lemp family.

"The Academy, which was formerly used as a cooling room for the horses employed by the brewery, is one of the finest in the country, since it has been converted into a riding school. It measures 210 by 90 feet. The roof is elevated at least 100 feet above the solid wall, resting on iron braces so as to admit light and air on all sides.

"Every day the arena is covered with a fresh layer of tanbark 6 inches deep and kept in order with a rake as fine almost as a comb. Fifty horses could easily disport themselves in this vast coliseum, which is the finest in the country for size and equipment.

"As is, a dozen or more persons ride everyday under the tutelage of a special riding master, whom the Lemps have engaged for their exclusive benefit. If there are guests at the house, and they know how to mount a horse at all, they are taken to the coliseum to join in the sport.

"No matter how busy the young Lemps are, they manage to leave their desks every afternoon to put themselves under Colonel Fuch's personal charge and hygienic treatment.

"Mrs. William Lemp Jr. and little Master Lemp join the gentlemen nearly every day to take their lessons along with the elders. Having been in training for the last three months, Colonel Fuch's pupils are now experts in quadrille riding, tandem riding, vaulting, head-cutting, all sorts of rough riding, and hurdle-jumping.

"From now on the Lemp cavalcade will be a familiar sight on the boulevards of the West and South End, in the parks and on the remote country roads.

"The private stables of the Lemps contain at present ten or eleven thoroughbreds, among whom Mr. Lemp, Jr.'s Prince Albert and Louis Lemp's Claude Martin are the most noted."

LOUIS LEMP, ON CLAUDE MARTIN, ONE
OF THE FINEST THOROUGHBREDS IN THE
LEMP STABLES.

Photos and captions by *The Republic,* April 5, **1903.**

WILLIAM LEMP, JR., ON HIS FAVORITE RIDING
HORSE, PRINCE ALBERT.

The Lemps took their love of horses to the next level by sponsoring the Lemp Cup, a racing handicap competition, sponsored by the Lemp Brewing Company. All of the Lemp's could "sit a saddle," three of them competing in races all over the country: Billy, Louis and Elsa. With the stables sitting only steps from their front doors, riding became an everyday event during the warm months, and the brewery had now added another letterhead: The Lemp Riding Academy.

St. Louis Republic, Aug. 25, 1901. "Mr. Lemp's constant companion around the stables is a bulldog of forbidding countenance but amiable disposition. The little monkeys haven't got acquainted with him, and when he comes around they hunt all timber. But the old monkey's favorite diversion was to lay hold of the dog's short tail and let him be hauled around the stable.

CELEBRITIES ARRIVE ABOARD WILHELM II

The Washington Times: December 21, 1909.

New York—"The steamer *Kaiser Wilhelm II* which arrived today from German, French, and English ports, was loaded with celebrities...Among the passengers was Louis Lemp, famous St. Louis brewer.

The young politician and horse breeder made headlines wherever he went throughout his lifetime. At that time, he had only two brothers and two sisters still living, out of 8 siblings: Charles and Edwin, and Annie and Hilda. He loved New York, and also had homes in Paris. He made annual visits to St. Louis to stay close to his family and friends.

He helped finance the first St. Louis Horse Show. His partnership with Dr. Crowley, a well-known veterinarian, was a profitable one. They organized a powerful stable of show horses, headed by the famous mare May Queen, one of the most talked-of horses of her day. According to Louis this mare "could almost talk" and was a beautiful animal in action. She was unbeatable in the show ring and finally became the property of a big circus where she performed for admiring crowds for many years. Louis was an expert on appointments, such as harness and rings, and was always an important component in any horse show he entered. His horses were well known from coast-to-coast as the best in the business.

Elastic and Wounded Knee won race after race. Wounded Knee was called "the greatest horse in the winning history of the Western Turf." Elastic, a famous sprinter, established horse records all over the west.

Louis Lemp Passport Photo
Courtesy Ancestry.com

LOUIS LEMP DIES IN NEW YORK

New York Herald October 17, 1931.

"Louis Lemp, 61 years old, formerly Vice-President of the William J. Lemp Brewing Company, died early today in his apartment in New York, according to a telegram received by his brother, Edwin A. Lemp.

"Mr. Lemp, who removed from St. Louis to New York in 1906, had lived abroad much of the time in recent years. His widow and daughter, Miss Louise Lemp, are now in Paris.

"The cause of death was not stated in the telegram. Edwin Lemp said his brother had been ill for two weeks, but was not thought to be in serious condition. A sister, Mrs. Gustav Pabst, of New York and Milwaukee, took charge of the body. The place of burial has not been decided upon.

"Mr. Lemp was a son of William J. Lemp, founder of the brewery who died in 1904. After the father's death, the four sons took charge of the property, and conducted it until prohibition stopped beermaking. The Lemp plant on South Broadway, the second largest brewery in St. Louis, was turned over in part to various industrial uses.

"While still a resident of St. Louis, Mr. Lemp was an active and successful horseman, owning several horses which were winners of Horse Show prizes, and thoroughbred racers which ran at Fairground, Delmar, Kinloch and Union tracks, and at tracks outside St. Louis. Elastic, a famous sprinter, was probably the best known of his racing string. May Queen, a high school mare owned by Mr. Lemp, was shown by him in the Horse Show in the old Coliseum, Fourteenth and Locust streets, and in shows throughout the country.

"Mr. Lemp is survived by his widow and daughter, two brothers, Edwin and Charles Lemp of St. Louis, and two sisters, Mrs. Pabst, and Mrs. Alexander Konta of New York. A brother, William J. Lemp, Jr. died in 1922."

Louis lived a full life filled with successful careers, supported by loved ones. His was one of the happy stories in a family that had front row seats to tragedy and sadness. Agnes died on Oct. 27, 1938. Their ashes were placed in the Lemp Tomb at Bellefontaine Cemetery, in St. Louis, by their daughter, Louise Lemp Pabst, who died in 1977 and is also interred there.

Chapter Twelve

WILLIAM J. LEMP, JR.
The Reluctant King

Billy Lemp at 3 years of age.
Photo courtesy of Lemp Mansion Museum

Saint Louis, Missouri: November 7, 1904

William Jacob Lemp, Jr. sat at his desk at the William J. Lemp Brewing Company and looked at the stacks of

224

paperwork piled upon his desk. The stationary bearing the new letterhead with his name as President seemed even more surreal now than it did when he gave his consent to have them printed. His father had only been dead for eight months. The family was still reeling from his sudden departure. Although the brewery department heads had tried to go easy on him, there were demands to be met. The giant grain bins and elevator were scheduled to be finished next year and the punch list concerning them kept growing. A livestock shelter was needed and rumblings of the necessity of a 3rd Bottling Plant were being heard.

The World's Fair had been running since April and had finally wrapped up the prior month in October. The myriad on-going decisions concerning it, and putting out daily fires, had nearly drained him. His marriage was five years old, and his son four. The stress from the long hours at work had carried over into his home life. Contention between himself and his wife was palpable. His mother was ill, and as the oldest son, he felt a responsibility to care for her and handle the domestic needs of her home as well as his own. Louis was trying to shoulder the burden with him, and Edwin was putting in overtime himself, but for now, it felt as if the entire success of the brewery, his mother's well-being, his marriage and his other business interests were riding on his shoulders.

He had finally found a home of his own after bouncing around from one place to another: New York for college in 1885; back at Lemp Mansion at the age of 23 in 1890; boarding in a room across the street from home at 3333 13th street for two years when he turned 24 in 1891; back at Lemp in 1893, at the age of 26, to take over the room the Feickerts had used (after their death in 1892); and finally having his own home in 1896 at the age of 28, when he leased from the brewery, the two-story manor house at 3343 So. 13th street. His grandmother, Louise Bauer Lemp, had been living there *from the time it was built until her death in 1893. The home's location allowed him to stay close to his mother, and the brewery, which was only, steps away. A spiral staircase led from a secret door in his basement to the swimming pool area in the cave beneath the house, and through a tunnel to the brewery elevator.*

Billy Lemp's home (left) at 3343 So. Thirteenth St (now DeMenil Place). Photo courtesy of Shashi Palamand & DeMenil Mansion.

William "Billy" Lemp, Jr.
Photo courtesy of Lemp Mansion

William was born on August 13, 1867, in St. Louis. He was the second child, preceded by Annie, who had survived birth. The first Lemp baby, a little boy, had been still born. Billy had an intense gaze and a sharp focus on the world that was evident even in the pictures of his toddler years. He probably knew early on that his genetic make-up precluded him becoming tall. By the time he had reached maturity, he was a 5' 5" blonde with penetrating blue eyes. If Billy Lemp fixed his gaze upon someone, they knew it. They also knew he would not back down, give in, or readily forgive a slight.

Alvin Griesedieck, the son of "Papa Joe" Griesedieck, brewers themselves and great friends of the Lemps, summed Billy up by saying that Mr. Lemp was "…not unfriendly, but was by nature rather cold and crisp. He was honorable to the last degree and expected everyone with whom he came in contact to be likewise. He prided himself in the fact that his word was as good as his bond. He was known to be unrelenting toward anyone who, in his opinion, had double-crossed him or had ever lied to him. Likewise, he seldom forgave an insult, imagined or otherwise, even among members of his immediate family."

It seems Billy's tendency toward a low-tolerance level for imagined slights also included the animal kingdom. When a statement was made that he shot alley cats at night from his bedroom window, his retort was, "only the ones that were keeping me awake."

This was a man driven to succeed in any endeavor he undertook, and his name was listed on many an organization's mast head. At William Sr.'s death, he became president of the Western Cable Railway Company; Ice and Cold Storage Company; Columbia Manufacturing Company in Dallas, Texas, and Little Rock, Arkansas; Brewing and Ice Company in Ardmore, Oklahoma; Ice, Light and Power; Director of the German Savings Institute; Kiuloch Long Distance Telephone Company; St. Louis Consumer's Ice and Cold Storage; Wabash Clay Company in El Paso, Texas; Veedersburg, Indiana Member Merchants' Exchange; Business Men's League; and Democrat Masons. The clubs he belonged to included: St. Louis Mercantile, Noonday, Glen Echo, St. Louis Country, Western Rowing, Aero, Automobile, Lemp Hunting and Fishing, Liederkranz, and others. He established The Lemp Riding Academy, Lemp Cup horse racing, and crew rowing competitions. He was also the instigator for the Lemp Hunting and Fishing Club which could exhibit a less serious side:

ATE 4 POUNDS OF LIMBURGER
Winner at Lemp's Club's Contest Still Lives.

St. Louis, Mo.—"Two hundred guests of the Lemp Hunting and Fishing Club at Alton went through a trying ordeal when they attended the club's limburger cheese eating contest.

"The difference between this contest and the Salome dance is that one doesn't have to have one's eyes open to witness it.

"Joseph Uhle won by consuming four pounds of the fragrant fromage and Ed Trumble finished a bad second with two pounds to his credit. The prize was a case of beer.

"Uhle is as well as could be expected, and it is thought that fumigation will save the clubhouse for future Sunday afternoon functions."

William Jr. attended public schools and Washington University, and took technical courses in the United States Brewing Academy in New York, graduating in 1893. Upon his return to St. Louis he became submerged in his father's brewery business, starting out as Superintendent, graduating to Vice-President when the business became incorporated, and finally taking on the title of President in 1904 when his father passed away.

Billy (as his friends and family called him) was a sportsman. He and his brothers adored the outdoors, hunting, fishing, horseback riding, rowing, and motoring. If there was an adventure to be had, Billy was at the front of the line. Yet, saddled at a young age with the responsibilities of being the eldest son in a brewery empire, he had effectively had his wings clipped from an otherwise playboy mentality. His passports were few, paling in comparison to the trips his family regularly embarked upon. In fact, when William Sr. entered his 60's, he cut back on work, handed the reins to Billy, Edwin, and Louis, and began traveling extensively. Edwin often accompanied them, leaving the brunt of the work to his brothers. In all fairness to Edwin, he was easing out of the business, preferring to find some solace in the back woods of the St. Louis territory. From 1894 to 1921, Billy applied for a passport only 4 times.

Billy had a reputation as a young man who enjoyed the finer things. He had a fondness for Oriental art, good food, parties, and could "close down the bar" on occasion. He also carried a chip on his shoulder, often called "the short man syndrome." He was always up for a fight and those who knew him knew he would never back down. He could be the fun-loving "drinks are on the house" guy one minute, and turn a cold shoulder on you the next…or at worst…knock you to the floor.

Billy's passport in 1894, stated he was blonde, blue-eyed and 5' 5" tall. By the time he turned 47, his passport reported he had grown an inch and his hair had darkened to brown.

With money, comes the ever-present media attention that followed the Lemps in the same unrelenting way paparazzi does today. Billy was a newsprint favorite. He was satirized in one such publication in 1904, as a rich boy riding a hobby horse. To "ride one's hobby horse" meant to follow a favorite pastime or obsession, so the caricature could have been as innocuous as that. It could have been a tongue-in-cheek poke at a wealthy man with his toys. Horses were a huge extravagance in the 1800s and 1900s, especially thoroughbreds and racing horses.

William J. Lemp, Jr.
From "St. Louisans as We See 'Em" c. 1904

Billy made the headlines once again with a unique new twist— this time he wasn't even involved in what went down.

THIEF IMPERSONATES WILLIAM J. LEMP, JR.

St. Louis Republic. February 16, 1901.

"By representing himself as William J. Lemp, Jr., a clever thief managed to obtain a diamond sunburst worth $800 from Walsh & Phelps, Sixth and Olive streets, Thursday afternoon.

The sunburst, minus one of the largest diamonds was located late yesterday afternoon in the pawn shop of Ben Barnett & Company where it had been left as security for a loan of $175. The police have a complete description of the diamond thief, but he has not been found.

Thursday afternoon a smooth-faced young man, in a black broadcloth cutaway suit, a box overcoat and a black stiff hat, stepped into the jewelry store of Merrick, Walsh and Phelps. The clerk who observed him referred him to Mr. Walsh, one of the members of the firm.

"I would like to see the best and largest diamond sunburst in the house," said the prospective customer.

Mr. Walsh ushered him into the reception room and brought forth a tray of gems. The young man selected one, and said:

"This is all right. I will take it with me now, and you may send the bill to me at the brewery."

"What brewery?" queried Mr. Walsh.

"Why Lemp Brewery, of course. I am William J. Lemp, Jr. You certainly know me," replied the visitor.

Mr. Walsh ordered the sunburst wrapped up and transferred it to the young man.

Shortly afterwards, Mr. Walsh became suspicious, and after several unsuccessful attempts to establish telephone communication between himself and Mr. Lemp, he notified Detective Keely, McGrath and Brady of the case. William J.

Lemp said he knew nothing of the misrepresentation other than what he had learned from the police."

If the newspapers thought Billy's "twin burglar," the Lemp Hunting and Fishing Club antics, and the cartoon hobby horse were great front page entertainment, the best was yet to come, when the dashing young millionaire met Lillian Handlan of St. Louis.

Lilly Mae "Lillian" Handlan
Photo courtesy Lemp Mansion

THE LEMP-HANDLAN WEDDING

St. Louis Post-Dispatch: *Oct. 23, 1899.*

"The wedding of Miss Lillian Handlan, daughter of Mr. and Mrs. A. H. Handlan, of Lindell Boulevard, to Mr. William J. Lemp, Jr., will take place at 9 o'clock Tuesday morning at the bride's home. The ceremony will be performed by Archbishop Kain, in the presence of no guests save relatives and intimate friends. The Handlan residence, 4930 Lindell Boulevard, is to be elaborately decorated with violets and lilies of the valley, Miss Handlan's favorite flowers.

The wedding is to be organized in the French room, which is finished in pale blue and pink pastel shades, and during the ceremony the bridal couple will stand beneath a bower of palms and lilies, arranged in the triple bay window.

The reception hall and library are also to be decorated in violets, ferns and lilies, and in the dining room where the wedding breakfast is to be served immediately after the ceremony. There will be quantities of beautiful purple orchids combined with the other flowers.

There will be no attendants and Miss Handlan will be given away by her father with whom she will enter the drawing room at exactly 9 o'clock.

The wedding gown is an exquisite creation in white satin merveilleux and point lace, made princess fashion, with a long court train. The corsage is of course high at the neck, with yoke and long sleeves of rich lace and a girdle of pearls. Miss Handlan will carry a shower bouquet of white orchids and lilies of the valley tied with white tulle streamers. The wedding veil is to be held in place by some superb diamonds and pearl pins.

After the wedding breakfast Mr. Lemp and his bride will leave for New York, where they have engaged a suite at the Waldorf-Astoria. When they return, they will stop at one of the hotels until their home, at Mr. Lemp's beautiful old bachelor quarters on South Thirteenth Street, has been completely remodeled and decorated. After Christmas, they will go abroad for half a year."

The highly-anticipated wedding of the year could not have been considered dutifully reported without the ***Sprague Scrapbook,*** known for their effusive chronicling of society events. Their added narrative set the stage with a few missed details:

"...there the bride and groom stood, in the window, beneath an overhanging arch of white roses and lilies of the valley, interwoven with smilax and with a background of feathery maiden air ferns. Over their heads were two locked hearts of white roses and carnations, with "LEMP" picked out in purple violets.

"As 9 o'clock struck, Archbishop Kain...descended the steps and took his place in this room...The fair bride and her father were met at the foot of the stairs by the groom, as the organ pealed forth the bridal chorus from Lohengrin."

The article goes on to describe her dress, without much deviation from the previous article, but mentions at her high-necked collar she wore "the groom's wedding gift, a superb diamond sunburst." (This coincidence may not have been lost on Billy a few years later when a diamond sunburst broach was stolen from a jewelry store by a "Billy imposter.")

"A unique feature of this toilet, was the "something old" which the bride wore, and this was an old-fashioned pair of checked stockings, which were made sixty-eight years ago in Holland by her great-grandmother, and have been worn by her grandmother and her mother, all whose initials are marked on them.

"After the ceremony, a wedding breakfast was served...Mr. William J. Lemp, the groom's father, proposed toasts to the bride and groom. There were fifteen courses, and each guest received a souvenir: a solid silver box, with a monogram upon it, filled with wedding cake."

In attendance were all of William Jr.'s family, including Frederick. Lillian's parents, three sisters and three brothers were also present, along with Mrs. James H. Purdy, and Mr. Francis D. Purdy of Denver, Colorado.

Lilly May "Lillian" Handlan

While the other Lemp children had been married in the Lutheran faith, this was the first wedding to feature an Archbishop. Mixed religious marriages at that time were fairly rare. The young love-struck couple may have chosen to ignore the friction that impacts inter-faith marriages. They were two handsome, healthy, wealthy and independent individuals who could give as well as they got when it came to confidence and bravado. Both had grown up with every luxury and had never known want.

A perfect child was born to the royal pair a year later on September 24, 1900. The little Prince was christened William J. Lemp, III. The young family flourished in splendor and privilege; their future as shiny as the diamond sunburst William had given Lillian on their wedding day. But such fairytales are, at times, doomed to have the clock finally strike midnight.

William Lemp, III Age 6
Photo courtesy of Lemp Mansion

A portrait of Lillian Lemp with Billy III

236

LEMP SUED

On February 26, 1906, Billy was hit with a lawsuit levied at his dead father. He, Edwin, Louis, and Charles, as executors of William J. Lemp, Sr.'s estate were held responsible for an outstanding debt that none of them knew existed. It was only a few days after Julia Lemp's passing. Billy doubted his mother knew of the suit against William. It all came while he and his family were still reeling from their mother's death. It was only the beginning.

Billy and his brothers were sued for $403,000, with interest from a May 5, 1902 debt, by Richard A. Jackson, a Chicago attorney.

According to newspaper reports, "the suit grows out of the phenomenal rise in Wiggins Ferry stock. It is charged that the elder Lemp contracted to sell 303 shares at $100 each to President Wade at the Mercantile Trust Company. Jackson later acquired the claim, but when he demanded the stock, he was told Lemp, Sr. had sold it. The stock was worth $604,500 at one time. (Author's note: That amount is the equivalent of $15.9 million in 2014.)

As the contention had been going on since 1902, it may have led to William Sr.'s depressed mental state at the time of his suicide. The amount of money for which he was to be sued was a fortune.

Julia Lemp's death, troubles on the home front, a law suit...if Billy thought 1906 would be his Armageddon, he was correct.

OCTOBER 16, 1906
THE "LAVENDER LADY" MRS. WM. J. LEMP AND HUSBAND PART

Wealthy Young Brewer Who Succeeded Millionaire Father as Head of the Big Concern Leaves Wife in South Side Home for His Own Relatives at Hotel.

The newspaper headlines may not have surprised the couple's close friends, or indeed the servants who had front row seats to the marriage's theatrics, but for the rest of St. Louis, and America, the Lemp divorce was about to become the equivalent of a daily serving of a juicy soap opera. Young newspaper hawkers were descended upon by anxious crowds waiting to devour the next "inside scoop." For William J. Lemp, Jr. there was no place to hide...although he tried.

Newspaper photo of Lillian Lemp announcing the split.

On Saturday, October 13, 1906, Billy left his palatial home at 3343 South Thirteenth Street and took up temporary residence at the Washington hotel in downtown St. Louis. His brother Charles had been staying there. Their mother had died only 6 months earlier and Charles Lemp had moved back into the empty home. Billy took over the vacated rooms at the hotel.

Old postcard showing the Washington Hotel on Kingshighway and Washington Boulevards in St. Louis.

The papers highlighted the wealth of the two young people, noting that Miss Lillian Handlan was the daughter of A. H. Handlan, president of the Handlan-Buck Manufacturing Company. They outfitted trains with lamps and other things and were very successful. William couldn't have his name mentioned in print without the monikers "millionaire," "son of millionaire father who shot himself," or "heir to the big Lemp brewing business."

When a reporter from the *Post-Dispatch* cornered Billy at his offices at the brewery, he gave an unusually candid report of the situation. He told the eager correspondent that he expected Mrs. Lemp to file for divorce, and that the grounds would probably be incompatibility of temper. (When the same reporter hurried over to the Lemp residence and confronted Lillian with Billy's statement, she refused to comment, or to answer questions.)

Much was made of the fact that Lillian had stayed in Atlantic City during the summer months, returning home to find nothing had changed in her marital situation. In fact, the discord was worse.

"My wife and I have not been getting on for some time as husband and wife should," Billy told the reporter at his brewery office. "If these conditions had affected me alone, I might have continued to bear with them. But they also affected our little son, William. The child is now 6 years old, and would not be benefited by being a daily witness to the bickering of his parents.

"I had him and his welfare in mind when I left my home last Saturday. It is very detrimental to a child to live in an atmosphere such as pervaded my home of late years.

"Immediately upon leaving my home, I informed my wife's father, Mr. A. H. Handlan, of the step I have taken....I shall always do my duty by my family, and in removing myself from my wife's presence, I considered that I removed the first impediment to her happiness."

The report went on to say "While this is the first time Mr. Lemp has ever spoken of his domestic troubles, they have long been the talk of his neighbors on South Thirteenth Street. The block on which the Lemp's live is one of the most fashionable in South St. Louis. It contains the residences of the late William J. Lemp, of ex-Mayor Ziegenhein, of Gustav Cramer, and other wealthy families. The home of the younger Lemp's is on the opposite side from that of the parental residence. It is an elegant mansion in the mist of beautiful grounds.

Temper Caused Strife

Mr. E. W. Handlan, Mrs. Lemp's eldest brother, told a *Post Dispatch* reporter that he knew but little of the domestic difficulties of the Lemp's, as he had seen his sister seldom in the last three years.

"It was a matter of temper," said Mr. Handlan, "and it is hard to tell which is more to blame. Mr. Lemp is too much of a gentleman not to permit my sister to sue for the divorce, now that their differences have reached a point where the breach cannot be healed.

"Mr. Lemp has led an exemplary life and is one of the straightest men I know. There are no sensational charges on either side."

That there were "no sensational charges on either side" was, unfortunately, about to be buried beneath the onslaught of the unrelenting coverage of the most-sensational divorce trial in St. Louis history. The fact that temper played a part in the incompatibility of the couple was without question, and it was borne out by the testimony, and actions, of their servants. One such situation occurred late in September, when Lillian returned from Atlantic City. Billy was at the station to meet his family. Mrs. Lemp's display of temper, it is said, was noticeable even to the trainmen. The maid, who had been with her all summer, refused to enter the house, and took her departure then and there in plain view of the neighbors.

It was these tantalizing tidbits that prepared St. Louisans for a divorce trial that would block the streets in front of the courthouse in downtown St. Louis for over a week, sell out newspapers throughout the city before the ink dried on the headlines, and become the fodder of every noonday gossip fest within the elegant, and modest, walls of St. Louis housewives. Two young lives were about to be put beneath the brutal, unrelenting glare of the media spotlight, and their lives would never again be the same.

The trial opened on February 8, 1909 in the Courthouse on Broadway in downtown St. Louis. – Graphic design by Rebecca F. Pittman

MRS. LEMP ON THE STAND TELLS HOW HUSBAND BEAT HER

Many Times, She Declares, Millionaire Brewer Threatened Her Life With Pistol

Had Detective Trail Her, Locked Her Out Doors, Blackened Her Eye, Moved Away Furniture, and Taught Child To Be An Atheist

It was with headlines such as these posted by the *St. Louis Post-Dispatch* on February 8, 1909 that the much-anticipated trial began. People thronged the street before the courthouse and jockeyed for position to get a glimpse of the parties. Seats in the court room were at a premium, with spectators waiting in line in hopes of obtaining one. It became a fashion show for the elegant women of St. Louis, who donned their finest hats and dresses and grabbed front row seats in hopes of catching every word of the scandalous proceedings. Those who hoped to see Lillian Handlan Lemp's famous wardrobe of lavender and lace were disappointed, as Mrs. Lemp arrived on her first day of trial wearing a modest suit of black cloth with black applique at the collar and a high white neckline. According to the article:

"She sat straight up in her chair, deliberately and without apparent excitement or nervousness, raised her veil and carefully folded it upon the front brim of her hat so that her face, almost pallid in its paleness, was framed in the white lace collar beneath the chin, and the draped folds of the white veil hanging to her shoulders at each side. Her chestnut-colored hair was parted in the middle and fell in wavy rolls covering the tops of her ears. Her black-gloved hands gripped the arms of her chair as she faced her lawyer and calmly awaited the first question."—*St. Louis Post-Dispatch,* Feb. 8, 1909

Mrs. William J. Lemp, Jr., opening day of trial on Feb. 8, 1909.

St. Louis Post-Dispatch

It had been a year and four months since William moved out of their home. In that time, attorneys had prepared their cases and Judge Hitchcock braced himself for what he feared would be a major circus in his organized court room.

Representing Mrs. Lemp, was John S. Leahy, a devout Catholic. Known far and wide for his oratory skills, facial expressions, and articulation, he was a formidable presence. William Lemp hired Frederick W. Lehmann, a fellow German who sat alongside Billy on the Board of Directors for the World's State Fair, was also involved in railroads, and preferred a less "dramatic" approach to his court demeanor. He was straight forward and dogged.

The stage was now set: the parties were present, the four local newspapers were represented at the media table, Judge Hitchcock was seated at the bench, and the gavel was about to come down.

John S. Leahy and Frederick W. Lehmann prepare to do battle.

LEMP ARRIVES IN COURT

St. Louis Post-Dispatch. Feb. 8, 1909. "At 9:45 o'clock William J. Lemp, accompanied by his attorneys, Fred W. Lehmann and W. B. Thompson, entered the crowded courtroom. Mr. Lemp, dressed in a gray suit, sat down between his attorneys, and placed upon the table a large portfolio of Morocco, which he opened. It contained almost a half-bushel of legal papers, depositions, newspaper clippings and memoranda. He took from the pile a thick volume of foolscap, typewritten, and he and Mr. Lehmann, with their heads close together, bent over it and began scanning it.

"Mr. Lemp is below medium height, is not stout, and has a red face, blue eyes, and a mouth that droops at the corners. He wore a gray necktie that matched his coat and in it was a stickpin with a pearl-like sphere as large as a hazelnut."

William J. Lemp, Jr.
Photo courtesy of Lemp Mansion

Lillian Handlan Lemp, standing 4' 11", had entered the courtroom sandwiched between her mother and father, Mr. and Mrs. A. H. Handlan. The noise from the spectators turning in their seats and whispering in excitement at her entrance caused Judge Hitchcock to rap his gavel for order. Though the disappointment at her demure attire was palpable, the enthusiasm soon returned as Lillian's attorney, Mr. Leahy, called her to the stand at 10 o'clock and started things off with a bang.

The following is the testimony from the divorce trial as reported by the area newspapers.

"HE BLACKENED MY EYE"

Mr. Leahy: "Mrs. Lemp, please state an incident that took place in your bathroom in October, 1904."

Mrs. Lemp: "He was out all evening and came back at 10 o'clock. I was in the bathroom arranging my bottles in the medicine case when I heard him enter the front door. He came in the bathroom and knocked me down. I got up and he knocked me down again. Again, I got to my feet and the third time he knocked me down using vile oaths and calling me vile names. I got up after some effort and went to the telephone to call my father, but Mr. Lemp followed me, and threw my head violently back against the wall. I was very faint. He threw me down the steps and I lay awhile unconscious. When I recovered, I looked around and he was gone. I went to my room and looked in the mirror, and saw how badly my face was battered. I then went to the ice box and got a piece of raw meat and bound it on my blackened and swollen eye. Then I went into my room and locked the door. "

Mr. Leahy: "Did Mr. Lemp drink?"

Mrs. Lemp: "Yes; he drank whiskey, cocktails, all kinds of wine, and absinthe."

Mr. Leahy: "Were there times in which he did not speak to you?"

Mrs. Lemp: "Yes; sometimes he would not speak to me for 24 hours, and sometimes he would not speak to me for three months at a time."

Mr. Leahy: "Did he stay out at night?"

Mrs. Lemp: "Yes; he began in 1903 to stay out all night and he would often come home in the morning showing the effect of drink. I would not know where he had been. We occupied separate rooms and there were weeks at a time when I did not know if he was in the house or out of it. He gave me no explanation."

Mr. Leahy: "Did he take you to the World's Fair in 1904?"

Mrs. Lemp: "He took me only three or four times to the fair."

Mr. Leahy: "What company did you have in your home?"

Mrs. Lemp: "I had none at all to speak of except my son. He was my only and constant companion since his birth."

Lillian went on to say she tried to please Mr. Lemp: she found out the kind of food he liked and had it prepared for him, but he began to be irregular at his meals in 1904, and from then on, she could not depend on him at all.

October 13, 1906, after returning from a drive, Lillian found he had moved out all her furniture, ornaments, paintings and part of her clothing to his late mother's home across the street. She said she sent him Christmas presents but he never sent any to her.

GUNS AND DETECTIVES

Mr. Leahy continued his questioning to Mrs. Lemp by bringing up two topics that had the court room twittering.

"Did your husband carry a revolver?" he asked Lillian. "Yes; he was never without a revolver in his hip pocket. He would take it out on the slightest provocation. Two or three weeks after the baby was born we were driving and Mr. Lemp got in a controversy with some teams blocking the street and he drew the revolver. He would draw the revolver if our carriage was blocked by other carriages at the theater. He would draw it many times and threaten to shoot me. He slept with it under his pillow, the muzzle pointing at me.

Lillian Lemp

"We were at table," she said, telling of an incident involving their butler, Donaldson. "When the bell rang, Donaldson went to the door. It was a man delivering some hats, but Mr. Lemp thought it was someone else. Donaldson announced that "a man with hats" had come to the door. Mr. Lemp said "Damn you!" He drew a revolver and cursed the butler, and put the muzzle to his head, and threatened to kill him."

Mrs. Lemp went on to say that her husband regularly shot the neighborhood cats for sport, left the gun on the dining table for their little son to see and was constantly terrorizing her with it.

She went on to tell of general behavior exhibited by Mr. Lemp that had caused her to become "a mental and physical wreck" during those years of neglect.

"Tell what happened when you got home from a reception at your mother's in 1904," Mr. Leahy admonished.

"When I got home it was morning. I rang and rang the bell but got no answer. I went around to the rear and one of the servants let me in. I knew my husband was home. I went up to his room and he was lying there laughing at me. The bell from the front door was within a foot of his head."

She told of missing possessions of hers: jewelry, ornaments and pictures that she found out later he had given away.

When asked about the time Mr. Lemp hired a detective to follow her to Palm Beach during a vacation she took with the baby, she stated:

"I and the baby went to Palm Beach, Florida and a detective hired by my husband dogged my steps at all times. He tried to get me to flirt with him. He smiled at me and tried to pet the baby, and even engaged a room next to mine, with only a door between. I looked over the top of the door and saw him listening."

RELIGION PLAYS A PART

During Lillian's time on the stand the elephant in the room was brought to the foreground.

"What is your religion, Mrs. Lemp?" Mr. Leahy asked her.

"I'm a Roman Catholic."

"What is Mr. Lemp's religion?"

"He has no religion."

"Did he give you directions as to the religious education of your child?

"Yes; he said there was no God and he did not want his child trained up to be a Catholic."

"Did he object to the baptism of the child in the Catholic Church?"

"He did object but I had it done. I told him I was going to have it done."

"Did you speak to your child about the existence of God?"

"Yes; he would ask me what made it rain or snow and if Santa Claus made it snow. I told him God sent the rain and snow. Mr. Lemp would shrug his shoulders and sneer and say, "Don't you believe it Bill, there is no God; it's silly to believe that." I did not eat meat on Friday and tried to train my son not to eat it, but my husband made him eat it."

It was at this time in the trial that two documents were presented as evidence for each party as to the raising of William Lemp III in a religious environment. Both documents were signed on the same day by Mr. Lemp and Miss Handlan shortly before their marriage ceremony. In one, she agreed not to influence the child religiously until "it is 7 years old." The other was signed in the presence of the archbishop who married them and in it Mr. Lemp agreed to permit a child to be baptized in the Catholic Church and reared in it. These were two ante-nuptial agreements.

Mrs. Lemp claimed on the stand that when she signed the paper stating she would not interfere with any child of hers religious upbringing until it was 7, that the contents of the contract had been covered with a piece of paper and only the area she was asked to sign was visible. She had signed it, not thinking anything of it, and putting trust in her husband that things were on the up and up. Mr. Lemp's attorney argued that his signed document superseded the other as it was signed last.

And on and on, the battles went. The throngs grew larger each day as the week-long trial marched on. Finally, William J. Lemp had his time on the stand, on Saturday, February 13 (the 4-year anniversary of his father's death). He volleyed back against every accusation his wife leveled at him.

Point One: The Bathroom Assault Accusation

Mr. Lemp: "I had returned to my home from my mother's house between eight and nine o'clock at night," he recalled. "Mrs. Lemp was in her dressing room. I pulled off my coat and sat down. An argument started. She alluded to my mother and my brother and sisters, stating that I was simply their 'tool' and that they were "using" me. I told her to keep quiet; I did not want to hear that line of talk.

"I left the room and she followed me with a book or magazine, as if to strike me with it. I pushed her into the dressing room. She ran past me to the telephone. I went out, and in passing her I told her if anyone wanted me, I would be at the brewery. I went across the street to the office, and remained there about an hour, and then I returned with the night watchman. She was in her dressing room, and the door was locked. I asked her to let me in. She refused. I did not threaten to break in the door, or to enter it by force. I simply said, "Please open the door." The nurse, Rosie Sachsberger, who was in the house, suggested I go to the guest's room, and I went there and slept."

Lehmann: "Did you strike her or push her down the stairs?

Mr. Lemp: "I did not! I know of no worse crime than for a husband to strike his wife, the mother of his child."

When asked if he struck his wife, Mr. Lemp half arose from his chair, his right hand extended, and his face flushed with emotion, and nearly shouted as he declared, "I did not!"

St. Louis Post-Dispatch: Lemp Trial Feb. 13, 1909

Point Two: Guns and the Butler

Mr Lemp was asked to tell his side of the story pertaining to drawing a gun on the butler.

Mr. Lemp: "The butler was told that whenever there was someone at the door he should announce who had rung the bell. We were at dinner when I heard the front bell ring. Donaldson opened the door and called out "Hats!" My wife asked "What hats?" The butler answered "Why your hats of course," in an insolent and surly manner. I rose, offended at the manner in which he made the announcement, and the butler backed up. He went into the kitchen and I ordered him to come back. He refused. I followed him in and h backed toward a table on which the cook kept the carving knives. Then I drew my revolver, in self-defense. I covered him with the revolver and said, "You have been insolent to Mrs. Lemp, and here is your chance to apologize." Donaldson apologized to Mrs. Lemp then and there. I put up my gun and finished my meal."

Mr. Leahy: "Did you slaughter cats with your gun?"

Mr. Lemp: "I do not kill cats for pleasure. I only shoot those that disturb my sleep."

When asked if he kept a gun beneath his pillow with the muzzle pointed at his wife's head, he admitted to sleeping with a gun beneath his pillow but the muzzle was not pointed at her head. Billy said "When I was 22 years old, they made a brewmaster of me. I weighed only 120 pounds and I had to go all around through the brewery alone at all hours of the night. That is why I carried a gun...I admit that it grew to be somewhat of a habit with me. But I did not carry it always."

As for locking his wife out, his story was different. He claimed she came home late after he was already asleep, and that, the bell annunciator having already been turned off, he did not hear her ring. She went to the rear, he said, and the servants let her in.

From their marriage in 1899 "up until May 1907, I paid all my wife's bills. We quarreled in October and November, 1904. The reasons for this..." were the way she conducted the care of their home", and "her remarks about my mother." William admitted they had separate sleeping quarters and did not speak sometimes for months at a time.

William's attorney summoned one of their household servants to the stand to rebut Lillian's Lemp's claims that her husband had beat her badly and inflicted damage to her face by pushing her down the stairs.

Rosie Sachsberger, a former servant, testified that after Mrs. Lemp locked her husband out of his room, he walked the floor all night, as the guest room was not prepared for sleeping. Miss Sachsberger said that after Mrs. Lemp telephoned, she claimed her husband had choked her and thrown her down the stairs, but when she looked at Mrs. Lemp, she saw no bruises.

However, she said, Mrs. Lemp "was much excited and gritted her teeth."

The courtroom may have been a little shocked at William's candor concerning his treatment of his wife. While he maintained he had never struck her, he did not deny moving her things out of the house while she was away on a drive, having female friends over at the house while she was out-of-town, hiring a detective to spy on her, and other vagrancies. The newspapers chronicled the juicy details of William's hiring of a detective.

Point Three

LEMP ADMITS HE SENT DETECTIVE TO WATCH WIFE

Deposition of Rich Brewer Tells of Trip Sleuth Made to Florida

St. Louis Post-Dispatch: May 12, 1908:

"William J. Lemp, millionaire president of the Wm. J. Lemp Brewing Company, admitted in his examination before Special Commissioner George M. Block that he sent a detective to Palm Beach, Fla. to watch the conduct of his wife, Mrs. Lillian Handlan Lemp, there in the winter of 1904-1905.

"The depositions were filed in the Circuit Clerk's office Tuesday. Ford Thompson, whose father is one of Mr. Lemp's attorneys, attempted to suppress the depositions immediately after they were filed by taking them to his father's office.

"Chief Clerk Lewis turned down the young man's request, but Thompson was so eager to prevent the newspapers from seeing the depositions that he invoked the aid of Judge Kinsey. Kinsey told the youthful Thompson he was too busy trying a divorce suit to listen to his plea.

"In a deposition taken April 10, Mr. Lemp explained the details of the detective transaction. He said he wrote to a friend, Simon Uhlman of New York, a retired hop merchant, asking him to send out a "good, reliable detective." Uhlman sent out to Lemp's attorney, Charles F. Krone, a detective named Charles Hemstead or Hemstead. Lemp met him several times in Krone's office and Hemstead was given his instructions.

"Hemstead went to Palm Beach a week before Mrs. Lemp and made reports to Krone by letter of her conduct there. Lemp read the reports. The nature of these reports was not gone into in the depositions.

"Mr. Lemp and Krone paid Hemstead and he (Lemp) furnished the money to Krone. Asked when Krone last heard from the detective, he said about March 30 of this year."

Sent to Watch "The Madame"

The trial continued. Lemp was asked what instructions were given Hemstead.

"Well, I can only answer broadly," he replied, "by stating that this detective was sent down there to watch the Madame."

"To observe her in what respect?" he was asked.

"To see how she conducted herself," Lemp replied.

"Was he given any directions to observe her conduct with reference to any particular individual?"

"I don't remember."

"I will ask you," said one of Mrs. Lemp's attorneys, "if this was not the substance of it—that the observations he was to make of her conduct were with reference to her conduct with other men?"

"Well, that was implied, no doubt, in the instructions."

"Did you give the detective a letter of introduction to the hotel people at Palm Beach?"

"I wouldn't be absolutely positive, but I don't think I did."

"Didn't you ask them to give him a room immediately next to that occupied by Mrs. Lemp?"

"I did not," replied Mr. Lemp.

Mr. Lemp was shown an alleged picture of the detective, but could not identify it. He said Hemstead was about 40 years old.

Here, Mr. Lemp was asked for the third time, by Mrs. Lemp's attorneys, when he had last seen his brother, Louis Lemp, and where Louis Lemp is now. Witness replied that he last saw him a year and a half ago and that he now is residing in New York. The lawyers did not explain why they were so eager to learn the whereabouts of Louis Lemp and his separation from his brother.

DOMESTIC ISSUES

William Lemp testified to his dissatisfaction with his wife's capabilities when it came to maintaining their home.

"The rooms would not be properly cleaned," he claimed from the stand. "Time and again I would come home and the meals were not ready. Often she would leave the house with the boy and give the servants no instructions regarding meals for me."

Lemp stated that Lillian told him she was tired of the hassles and bother of the house and if he wasn't happy with how it was run, he could hire servants himself. This statement was made by her, after he complained she would be gone all day, leaving him with only a laundress. William had, at one point, even brought Lillian's mother and father into the dispute, telling them of their daughter's poor ability to run the house.

"Didn't you have the means to hire all the servants in that house that were needed?" inquired Leahy.

"I had the means, yes," Lemp replied.

"You were the absolute master there?"

"No, I do not consider that I was master."

Lemp underscored this point by bringing up his dislike of his sister-of-law, Vella Handlan (pictured at right), and despite the numerous times he had asked she not be constantly in their home, his wife insisted on inviting her over on a regular basis. Lemp said Vella "had shown great discourtesies" to him. When asked to  elaborate on the term "discourtesies," William stated that she would ignore him, refuse to talk to him in his own home, and give his wife advice regarding him in a negative context. He became so repulsed by the woman's presence that he would not sit down to dinner with her.

Point Four: Religion

Lillian's attorney, Mr. Leahy, went after William Lemp on the witness stand pertaining to the subject of the two ante-nuptial agreements concerning the raising of a child in the Catholic Church.

Mr. Leahy: "When did you have your first discussion with your wife regarding the ant e-nuptial contract she signed, giving you control of the religious training of your child?"

Mr. Lemp: "It was in June, 1899, about the time we became engaged."

Mr. Leahy: "And yet you waited until after you signed the contract for the Archbishop, waited t   wo days prior to the wedding, and until, at your mother's house, only your relatives were present, before you had her sign it?"

Upon the objection of William's attorney, Mr. Lehmann, as to the question being multiple questions, Mr. Leahy amended his query:

Mr. Leahy: "At the time you signed the contract in the presence of the Archbishop, providing the children were to be raised as Catholics, did you intend to keep the agreement?"

Mr. Lemp: "No, I can't say that I did."

The questioning between the two parties continued, as the attorneys for both sides hammered home their points. Lillian Handlan Lemp sat sandwiched between her two lawyers and watched William's face intently during his testimony. At times, when he refuted a point she made, she would turn to her attorney and shrug her shoulder with a wane grin. She took copious notes throughout the trial, pausing only to consider William's testimony, a pencil pressed thoughtfully against her lips.

William's demeanor on the stand was composed, calm and direct, even beneath Mr. Leahy's barrage of questions. He became emotional only when describing his disgust at any man hitting a woman, or when he talked about matters concerning his son.

The next topic was brought forward for the judge's consideration, as well as the court room spectators, newspaper reporters and the general public:

A ROSE BY ANY OTHER NAME

Mr. Leahy: "You said in your deposition that you were greatly annoyed by your wife's costumes. You said she wore high lace and lavender colors. 'The almost constant wearing of lavender,' you said, 'made her conspicuous.' You also said she wore long trains. Did this offend your taste?" the attorney asked William Lemp.

Mr. Lehmann objected and William remained silent.

Mr. Leahy: "Didn't she wear the same costumes before her marriage?"

Mr. Lemp: "I have no recollection."

Mr. Leahy: "You say you can't remember what your wife wore before her marriage?"

Mr. Lemp: "I don't remember."

Mr. Leahy: "Now wasn't it purple she wore instead of lavender?"

Mr. Lemp: "Sometimes it was purple."

Mr. Leahy: "Was it the color you objected to?"

Mr. Lemp: "It was the almost constant wearing."

Mr. Leahy: "You wanted change and variety then, did you?"

Mr. Lemp: "I didn't want her to be conspicuous by wearing the same thing all the time."

When asked if William had a hand in the newspaper headlines nicknaming

Lillian the "Lavender Lady," Billy denied it, even though a witness had seen him enter the home of the reporter the day before the first headline came out using the colorful name.

Lillian took the stand, and as expected, denied the constant wearing of lavender.

Mr. Leahy: "Did you dress to attract attention?"

Lillian: "Absolutely no."

Mr. Leahy: "Did you wear lavender to the exclusion of other colors?"

Lillian: "I don't remember ever wearing lavender in my life."

Mr. Leahy: "What were your favorite colors?"

Lillian: "Black, white, and violet, and sometimes tan and gray. My trousseau was of those colors."

Mr. Leahy: "Did your husband object to them?"

Lillian: "No, he admired my trousseau very much."

Lillian Handlan was well known throughout St. Louis for her fashions. It was said that she wore a stiff taffeta to church, waiting until everyone was already seated to make her entrance. The material would make a swooshing sound as she walked down the aisle to her pew, causing all to turn and look at her. Crowds would often see her off at the train station, where she would wave a demur gloved-hand as she entered her coach. Her livery for her carriages was reportedly all lavender, or a hue thereof. When her three sisters were presented to society, it made the social pages and Lillian's attire was duly noted.

"Assisting was Mrs. William J. Lemp, Jr., eldest daughter of the household, in a princess gown of black and white."

"SHE NEGLECTED MY MOTHER"
William's Testimony:

The subject was brought up concerning William's mother's treatment by Lillian during Julia Lemp's long illness.

Mr. Leahy: "Didn't your wife take flowers to your mother frequently during her last sickness?"

Mr. Lemp: "She visited her possibly twice a week and took flowers."

Mr. Leahy: "Don't you call that frequently?"

Mr. Lemp: "No, not when my mother was on her deathbed." William's voice broke and his eyes rimmed with tears.

Lillian's Testimony:

When asked how often she visited her sick mother-in-law, who lived across the street from the couple, Lillian replied:

"I visited Mrs. Lemp every day, and we were devoted to each other."

She refuted William's claims that she denied his mother access to William III. Lillian said she never objected to her little son visiting his grandmother.

To counterattack William's ruse to make his wife out to be coldhearted, Lillian's attorney pointed a finger at the defendant, citing cruelty not only to his wife, but to their little son, by evicting them from their home.

LITTLE LEMP HEIR OUSTED WITH MOTHER

They Must Leave the Mansion of Millionaire Brewer by Court's Order

Loses His Play-Park

St. Louis Post-Dispatch: March 24, 1908. "Little William J. Lemp III played with his pet lamb yesterday afternoon in the big wooded playground that has been his ever since he was large enough to learn to walk, wholly unconscious that he must soon give it up.

William Lemp III Age 6
Photo courtesy Lemp Mansion

"Justice Spies yesterday ordered his mother to leave the mansion and the grounds at 3343 South Thirteenth Street, which have been their home since her marriage nine years ago to William J. Lemp, Jr., the millionaire brewer. And when she goes, the boy will go with her and leave his playground.

"There is no playground in St. Louis more delightful for a boy than the one that has been provided for this boy. It contains an acre of ground that slopes gently to the south. It is covered with the smoothest and greenest of sward, kept shaved close by servants until it is like velvet under foot. There are shade trees a-plenty, and clusters of shrubs that are tents of bloom in the springtime. There is a fountain and a fish pond, and birds in cages, and monkeys that swing by their tails from trees.

"And around it all, inclosing it from prying eyes and the interference of boys and girls that are not wanted, is a board fence six feet high, so tight that there is not even a crack to peep through.

"It is nice to be a millionaire's son and have such a playground. It will be hard for the boy to leave it. But his father and mother have fallen out and are fighting each other in the divorce courts with the bitterest rancor.

"The latest move of the husband was accomplished yesterday, when he secured the order from Justice Spies ousting Mrs. Lemp from the mansion.

"In dispossessing Mrs. Lemp and her boy of the home yesterday, there was presented the legal spectacle of a man suing himself. The mansion is owned by the William J. Lemp Brewing Company. It had been occupied by William J. Lemp, Jr., president of that company, his wife and son, and servants, from the time of his marriage until he left his wife. To get his wife out, he filed suit in the name of the company against himself and family, as tenants, for possession, and for $150 rent. The same lawyer, Charles Krone, represented both plaintiff and defendant.

"Neither Mr. Lemp or Mrs. Lemp was in court, and only one witness, Henry Vahlkamp, secretary of the brewing company, was examined. His testimony consisted merely of the statement that William J. Lemp, Jr., president of the brewing company, had rented the house from the company, and that he had not paid the rent for four months.

"Judgment was entered for the plaintiff, giving the company possession of the mansion and a judgment for $150. He agreed to stay the execution for a few days, to give Mrs. Lemp an opportunity to move without being evicted by constables."

Lillian moved in with her father and mother, taking Billy III, his lamb and donkey, with her. Billy was still living at the Washington Hotel as the trial dragged on. So, on one street stood two mansions, both belonging to the Lemp's, both shrouded in yesterday's memories of happier times.

"MY DEAR PAL"

"My Dear Pal: I wish you could see what I am going through to make 'him' take me to the show tonight. Of course, the day is not over, and I may still succeed. If I fail, then I shall go anyway, with Ham and Ella. However, he does not know that.

"Tomorrow I will again take Vella to the matinee. Although I cannot be with you, to watch you at a distance or to feel your presence, is my only happiness and recreation.

"Do telephone me when' you can, as I usually answer the phone 'now.' In case I do not, you can always put up the phone again, or else say my brother wishes to speak to me.

""He" is going hunting next week, and I wish to heaven he would never return. I am completely worn out, and God alone knows how much longer I can stand this loathsome bondage.

"In this black life that curses me,
Black in night in this foul hole,
I thank whatever Gods there be,
For my unconscious soul.

"In this foul clutch of circumstances,
I have not winced or cursed aloud,
Used as a lottery ticket of chance,
My hand seeks blood with heart unmoved."

The preceding is the unsigned letter found by William J. Lemp, Jr. in his wife's dresser drawer, which he photographed in the architect's department of the brewery. He attached the copy to a deposition. Lillian Lemp claims she placed it where he would find it as a "decoy" to stir his conscious.

Mr. Lemp was asked if he knew who "Pal" was, and said he did not. "Might it not have been a woman friend to whom Mrs. Lemp wrote in a moment of discouragement?" Mr. Lemp said he thought not.

"Then you think it was a man?"

"Yes."

Mr. Lemp said "Vella" referred to in the note was his wife's sister, and that "Ham and Ella" were her brother, A. H. Handlan, Jr. and his wife.

"Did you ever speak to Mrs. Lemp about finding the letter?" asked Judge Dillon, Lillian's co-counsel. When Lemp replied in the negative, the Judge said, "That's remarkable!" to which Lemp's attorney replied, "Not at all."

Lillian stated that the "decoy" was also a way to check and see if he was reading her correspondence.

Mr. Lehmann, William's attorney attacked the letter by saying, "It was written either to gladden the heart of another, or to crush the heart of her husband. Either of these theories is replete with room for thought. I am not sure that it is not worse for a woman to have written this letter, intending that her husband should see it, than to have written it for another."

By this time, both Lillian and William were showing the strain of the trial. What had begun as a way to gain custody of their small son, by proving the other parent was unworthy and unfit, had turned into a media sideshow with headlines lashing out at both parents. It was becoming obvious, by their body language and haggard appearances, that they regretted using such a public forum to air their dirty laundry, and lambast a person they had once loved. Like a storm put into motion, there was no reining it in now. There would be no winner in this tragedy that played as morose and dark as any penning of Shakespeare's. But the final blow was still to be delivered and Billy was the target.

What had begun as Billy's glib dismissal of alleged parties in his home when his wife was away, soon turned into an avalanche of testimony from several witnesses that the wealthy brewery owner was unfaithful to his wife, not once, but often.

Questioned about the visits of women to his home, testified to by some of Mrs. Lemp's witnesses, Lemp said such a visit took place but once, and that the guests were Mrs. A. H. Handlan, Jr., wife of his brother-in-law, and Mrs. Burt Evill, a widow.

He and his brother, Edwin Lemp, were the hosts, Billy testified. The party met at Cherokee Garden, and going to the Lemp home, stayed there an hour. He mixed wine and Apollinaire for the party. This was in the summer of 1906, while Mrs. Lemp was away from home.

"I upset a table, a little dinky affair," he added.

The women then left the house, he said, and he accompanied them to the gate. He admitted that he didn't tell his wife of the visit upon her return from the east.

"Mrs. Evill was often at the house when the Madame was at home," he said, "and by her invitation."

Lemp denied he had ever taken Mrs. Evill to a garden or theater.

"Did you think it was right to ask a lady to your home when your wife was away?" he was asked.

"When she was my sister-in-law?" he asked.

Lehmann objected to the question, it was sustained.

Billy may have skipped past that accusation, but it was about to get worse.

"THE QUEEN OF TENDERLOIN"

Asked whether he had visited houses conducted by certain women, four of whom were named, he said he knew them all, but had not been at their houses since he was married. He admitted paying the funeral expenses of Lulu Morrison, saying he did so at the solicitation of his brother, Louis, and as an act of charity. But the accusations only got worse from there.

St. Louis, February 11: "Sensational evidence full of scandal, concerning William J. Lemp, Jr., with women of unsavory reputation, even with the "Queen of Tenderloin" herself, was brought out by Mrs. Sue E. Langley, a face specialist, in her testimony bearing on the divorce suit of that young millionaire.

"Expecting some unusual developments, the court room was crowded to the doors, and 2,000 curious spectators were turned away from the stuffy little room. Those who gained admission were not disappointed.

"For the first time, the bravado attitude of Lemp was shaken when Mrs. Langley testified that she had twice treated Mrs. Lulu Morrison, known as the "Queen of Tenderloin," in the belief she was Mrs. Lemp. Lemp was identified as the man who entered the Morrison house as the face specialist left on her second visit.

"On my first visit," declared the witness, "I heard servants address the patient as Mrs. Lemp, but I later learned that she was the notorious "Queen of Tenderloin." After that I refused to treat her further."

"Another witness was Jacob Rosenstein of Chicago, who was formerly in the lady's tailoring business in St. Louis. He said a girl, by the name of Dolly Housel, who recently moved to Dallas, Texas, contracted a bill for lace handkerchiefs and lace curtains. When she returned to St. Louis, the Dallas firm sent the bill to Rosenstein, who presented it to Miss Housel. With the woman at the time was Lemp, and he promptly drew a $50 bill from his pocket and handed it over, with the remark that it might be applied to the account. Mr. Rosenstein said he had spotted the brewer in the homes of other "women of bad character" after his marriage to Lillian.

"A deposition was read from Pearl Ritchie of Chicago. This was taken last Saturday at the Mullanphy Hospital where the witness is an invalid. The Ritchie woman tells of visits to questionable "resorts" made by Lemp after his marriage. One such woman was Molly Edwards, known as "Molly Polly, a woman of questionable character."

Finally, Mr. Robert L. Johnson, William's chauffeur, told of driving Mr. Lemp on many evenings while he was accompanied by women who were drinking. He said the women often ended up at Lemp's home, and sometimes he went to theirs.

In a glib moment, Lemp would regret, he had spoken with his father-in-law, A. H. Handlan, at the Mercantile Club in 1905. Mr. Handlan told William that he had treated his daughter so badly that she had every ground for divorce "in the law dictionary" except that of infidelity. He said William responded by saying, if necessary, he could give her that ground also.

St. Louis, and any city that carried newspapers, now knew William's most hidden, and shameful secrets. The proud brewery owner, father, and dutiful son, had been laid low in the public's opinion, and in his own. He must have felt some relief that his mother had not been alive to see this. His family had been dragged through the mud and impaled on every reporter's pen.

There was nothing left but the summations by the attorneys. They were eloquent and designed to pluck at the heartstrings of their audience. Indeed, by the time they finished, sobs could be heard coming from the gallery. Lillian dropped her veil to cover her face, but her chin could be seen quivering. William turned away with tears in his eyes.

THE VERDICT

There was almost a sense of loss for the citizens of St. Louis as the trial entered its final day. The gossip, scandal, and high emotion that had dominated every breakfast table, tea party, business office, and department store was coming to an end. The loss of excitement would leave a void in the minds of those who had fed off the picked over carcasses of William and Lillian Lemp for over a week.

On February 18, 1909, Judge Hitchcock rapped his gavel for silence and handed down his verdict. He granted Lillian an absolute decree of divorce. "The divorce was granted on the ground of desertion alone," he stated. He said Lemp had managed to refute every charge leveled at him but one…he had moved out of the house, stopped providing income, paying the bills, or caring for his family. "The plaintiff is not entitled to a decree on any other ground charged and in all other issues brought forth, the court finds in favor of the defendant."

Lillian was awarded $6,000 a year in alimony, payable in quarterly installments of $1,500, due on the first day of March, June, September, and December. A $30,000 bond from Billy was to be submitted to the court as a way to guarantee the payments.

The meager awarding of only weekend visits with his son was awarded to William. He could have little Billy from 9 a.m. Saturday morning until 8:00 p.m. Sunday evening, beginning February 20, 1909. William would be allowed to have the boy for two consecutive weeks to compensate him for Lillian's usual trip with little Billy (who was now 8) to a summer resort.

Before court was adjourned, on the most-sensationalized divorce trial in St. Louis history, Mr. Leahy had one more bone to pick. He was appalled at the amount awarded his client, and that she did not retain sole custody of the child. With the settlement as it stood, he argued "she would be tied down" to one place in order to comply with William's visitation rights. He said the alimony awarded "practically creates a license for a rich man to get as many divorces as he wished."

Lillian was determined to get her share of William's money. When the state denied her request for a second trial, she took it to the Missouri Supreme Court. Her attorney, Mr. Leahy was once more by her side. He argued that Mr. Lemp might dispose of his fortune, or lose it in the future, and a one lump payment of $250,000 made more sense. It would allow the child a proper education and upbringing.

The court finally awarded Lillian Handlan Lemp a lump sum of $100,000, the largest settlement at that time in a divorce case.

With the banging of the gavel, the Lemp divorce saga came to an end. Newspaper headlines were relegated to back page filler as some publications, reluctant to let go of the sensationalism that had filled the publisher's coffers for most of 1909, rehashed and embellished the sad details of a family's demise. Large ads for the day's fashions and automobiles took precedence over the fading story.

Ads that ran on the same pages of the Lemp divorce trial recap of 1909.

Aftermath

According to the 1910 census, Billy was back in the house at 3343 South Thirteenth Street. Four servants are listed as living with him, including a gardener to tend the vast acreage that had been little Billy's playground. He was now indeed "master of the house," but one, no doubt left with a great deal of pain.

Lillian and her son lived with her parents on Lindell Boulevard in the fashionable Central West End of St. Louis. By 1915, she was residing at the Manhattan Hotel in New York City and Billy III, who was then 14 years old, was living with her.

Billy continued to run the brewery that was literally steps from his front door, rode his horses, and added more buildings to the ever-expanding complex.

In 1909, the year of the divorce, he gave the okay for a new Boiler House and Smoke Stack to be built. The stack could be seen for miles around and still stands today. He also included a Repair Shop. One year later in 1910, more offices and shops were added as Lemp Beer and its sidekicks continued to sell well. And in 1911, the final building was added under Billy's tutelage: Stock House #3.

Billy was lambasted later when he sold the brewery during the Prohibition era, but the author believes he got the short end of the stick in the media coverage of his lack of interest in saving the brewery. During Billy's reign, he continued to build, land new contracts, invent new beer products, and employ a remarkable marketing campaign that covered everything from print ads to chargers, corkscrews to automobile signage, labels, packaging and more. This was during a time when his private life was in tatters, he lost his wife and son (and a good chunk of his reputation), and was staggering from the loss of his mother.

His siblings were scattering to the wind, and there seemed to be a rift between himself and Louis. The prostitution scandal that came out during the trial may have been the reason the attorneys kept asking Billy about Louis and their estrangement. The deposition where Billy stated he only knew of Lulu Morrison because his brother Louis had asked him to help with her funeral costs, literally put Louis' name out there as associating with a well-known prostitute, during the time Louis himself was married. It may have precipitated Louis selling out his stocks in the company and moving to New York in 1906. Odds are, his wife was not happy about the whole thing, and perhaps blamed Billy. None of the society pages ever showed Agnes Walsh as attending functions with the Lemp family, whether it was her husband's horse races, concerts or other events. As mentioned earlier in the book, Louis and Agnes were not listed in attendance for Elsa's wedding in 1910.

The William J. Lemp Brewing Company had launched some of the most-famous beers in the world: Standard Lager, Gulmbacher, Extra Pale, Extra Export, and the one people still speak of today, Falstaff.

William Lemp Jr. chose the jolly character of Falstaff for Lemp Beer as an embodiment of the good times. The jovial, indulgent and raucous fellow is a character in Shakespeare's **Henry IV**, and the **Merry Wives of Windsor.**

He is a prominent figure in the Lemp chargers (plates) that Billy began producing in 1910, and quickly became collector's items.

THE TALE OF TWO HOUSES

Two Lemp mansions sat catty-corner from each other on South Thirteenth. The street itself had undergone changes during the Lemp's time there. The city changed the streets with French-bearing names around 1890, and 2nd Carondolet became Thirteenth Street. It was changed again to DeMenil Place when the 55-freeway sliced through its north end, taking the carriage house of William Lemp, Sr.'s mansion with it.

Whether Charles had mentioned he was moving to the Racquet Club, leaving the Lemp Mansion empty, or it was for more pragmatic reasons to facilitate the growing need for more office space, Billy turned Lemp Mansion into its first commercial metamorphoses, in 1911.

As for his home at 3343, he lived there until 1914. In 1910, he built his escape from the prying eyes of St. Louis society, a home where he could be alone…that is until he met a fellow German from another beer brewing legacy…Ellie Limberg.

Chapter Thirteen

BILLY, ELLIE & ALSWEL

William and Ellie Lemp at Alswel --1915 Graphic
Design by Rebecca F. Pittman

ALSWEL

At 12696 Alswel Lane in Sunset Hills, Kirkwood,
Missouri, sits an imposing estate in a motif seldom seen in the
rustic hills surrounding it. The Tyrolean chalet is a large
cypress-clad house set at the top of a bluff two-hundred feet
above the Meramec River. The house has two full stories and a
third level in the lea of the all-embracing gable roof. From the
entrance side, the embankment nearly hides the ground floor,

which is concrete construction. The upper stories are surfaced in cypress planks, applied shiplap-style on the second story, vertically on the third. The same material forms brackets, balustrades and friezes. The interior is unusually arranged, with most of the public rooms on the level below the entry, a large reception hall and four bedrooms at entry level, and four more bedrooms on the third floor. Interior detailing reflects the Craftsman movement.

The main staircase opens into the ground floor living room by way of a landing which has three steps down at both ends. This irregularly shaped room has a large alcove extending under the overhanging balcony toward the river. The fireplace combines bricks of an unusual aggregate composition with a micaceous limestone. The wainscoting is said to be sugi, or Japanese cypress; bookcases with leaded-glass doors are fitted into this paneling next to the fireplace and next to the stair.

On the north side of the house is an entry area walled in red brick, with a powder room to one side. This entry leads to the northeast room, called the billiard room. One of the most carefully detailed rooms in the house, it has a tile floor, beamed ceiling, and walls surfaced to wainscot level with gray-brown brick laid with recessed gray joints. The brick fireplace is trimmed with rock-faced stones and flanked by cabinets with glass doors. The windows in this room as well as the windows in its door have muntins in a pattern of nine circles with diamond-shaped interstices.

The service rooms on the ground floor include a kitchen lined with white-enameled brick, a butler's pantry, a scullery, and a boiler room, which extends under the entrance porch and drops about ten feet below the level of the other ground-floor rooms.

Four more bedrooms and two baths are located on the third floor, which centers on a large hall. Occupying most of this room is the art glass window, lighting the living hall below. It is surrounded by a white-painted balustrade. Above it opens a rectangular lantern or cupola.

Steps descend on both sides of the house from the entrance drive to the backyard, which extends in a gentle grade about 120 feet to a stone retaining wall. At the north end of the wall is an octagonal pavilion with a cupola, while a little beyond the south end is a circular stone tower with a flat wooden roof arranged as a viewing platform. Beyond the line of the wall, the ground drops steeply about 150 feet down a wooded hillside to the flood plain of the Meramec River. Since the ground on the other side of the river is much lower, the view from the house is almost panoramic. –Description courtesy of the National Register of Historic Places.

The remote wilderness Billy had chosen to build his 200-acre sanctuary, affording him a chance to indulge his love of hunting and fishing, was not a well-kept secret. In the next few years, the family friend, brewer "Papa Joe" Griesedieck, and the stove maker Louis Stockstrom, acquired adjacent properties about a mile and a half south of Meramec Highlands, where they built private estates as retreats from the city. Later, houses for year-round occupancy were built. Billy's younger brother Edwin built *Cragwold* on a hill overlooking the river in 1911, the same year brewer August Busch built the palatial mansion at *Grant's Farm* on Gravois Road closer to the city. The next year Anheuser Busch converted a nearby restaurant into the Sunset Hills Country Club, and in 1913, Busch's son Adolphus Busch III built *Grandview* adjacent to it.

This area may have been attractive to so many brewers in part because it was easily accessible via Gravois Road to the southern part of the city, where most of the breweries were located. *Cragwold* has a half-timbered exterior, *Grant's Farm* is a French Chateau of the late sixteenth century, and *Grandview* is Colonial Revival. Alswel stands out for its iconic style. Besides the main house, the grounds were home to several smaller structures all emulating the Swiss-chalet design. These were guest houses and home to Billy's servants.

In 1914, Billy made the move that would end an era of the Lemp brewery presidents making their home on Thirteenth Street. He relocated full-time to his beloved *Alswel*. Lemp Mansion was now the brewery office headquarters, and the home Billy, Lillian and Billy III had shared, sat empty. It was finally razed to make way for the expansion of the brewery and a future owner, the International Shoe Company. From Adam Lemp's inception of Lemp Beer—when he lived above the small saloon—to William J. Lemp, Sr.'s building of two homes on Thirteenth Street, within walking distance of the new brewery, the head of the lager beer dynasty had always made his home nearby. Billy changed that dynamic when he left for the hills and created Alswel, a name that perhaps he chose as a talisman against future sadness.

Ellie Koehler Limberg

St. Louis Post-Dispatch May 19, 1915.

St. Louis Post-Dispatch: May 19, 1915. The marriage of Mrs. Ellie Koehler Limberg, daughter of Mrs. Caspar Koehler of 4651 Lindell Boulevard, and William J. Lemp, which took place yesterday afternoon, is the outcome of almost a lifelong friendship and a six years' courtship.

Since the summer of 1909 or 1910, when Mr. Lemp traveled to Europe with Mrs. Koehler's party, which included her daughters, Mrs. Ottilie Krausnick, Mrs. Limberg and her son, Edward A. Limberg, rumor has set the date of the marriage many times. So constantly have they been seen together that the engagement was generally understood.

The ceremony was performed at 5 o'clock at the home of the bride's son, who married Miss Virginia Foster last autumn. The Rev. John W. Day of the Church of the Messiah officiated and only the nearest relatives were present.

The bride is the widow of Rudolph Limberg, who was associated with the Columbia Brewing Company, of which the late Caspar Koehler was president. The latter died while traveling in Europe for his health, about ten years ago. Mrs. Lemp is considered very attractive, and is so youthful in appearance and manner that she looks more like her son's sister than his mother. She is one of a group of fashionable women who have interested themselves in the St. Louis Maternity Hospital, and it is said that much of the credit for the success of the recent fashion show was due to her untiring efforts.

Mr. Lemp recently completed a large home on the Gravois Road, St. Louis County, where he and his bride will reside when they return from their wedding trip.

Mr. Lemp is the president of the Lemp Brewing Company, and the brother of Charles A. and Edwin A. Lemp, and Mrs. Thomas Wright, who was Miss Elsa Lemp. He married Lillian Handlan, daughter of A. H. Handlan, in 1899, and in 1909, she obtained a divorce, after several years of separation. There was one child, William J. Lemp III, who was awarded to his mother, with the provision that he was to spend certain proportions of time with his father.

And yet another newspaper, reported the couple had gone to White Sulphur Springs, Virginia, for their honeymoon. Friends of the couple professed surprise when told that Lemp and Mrs. Limberg had taken out a marriage license earlier in the day and said they not been told of the plans of the couple. The ceremony, which was performed on May 18, 1915, had been kept quiet and only a select company of relatives was invited. Servants had been instructed to tell any visitors that the family was "out" and no marriage had taken place there.

It happened that Lillian was in St. Louis that day, and when told of her former husband's marriage, expressed surprise but refused to comment. On her last visit to St. Louis, during the holidays, an attempt was made to serve papers on her in a suit for attorney fees brought as a result of her divorce litigation. Mrs. Lemp escaped from the Planter's Hotel in a taxicab.

Ellie was four years William's senior. Lillian had been ten years his junior. Perhaps he hoped this marriage would bring stability to his life with a more mature, less theatrical, union.

Ellie's brother owned land adjacent to Alswel, and although business rivals, the two families had been friends for many years. Following their marriage, the couple settled down at the wilderness retreat. The following years were the heyday of Alswel. Here they entertained friends and family and watched sunsets reflecting in the Meramec River. The playboy who had at one time complained there were not enough places to spend his money, seemed to have settled down and found peace at last.

Ellie Koehler Limberg Lemp.
Photo courtesy of Lemp Mansion

Chapter Fourteen

THE FINAL DAYS OF LEMP BREWERY

St. Louis, Missouri: 1915

Billy struggled on after 1915, trying to hang on to the family brewery. Anheuser-Busch was ramping up and the William J. Lemp Brewery dropped to the second largest brewer in St. Louis. He continued to manage his ice houses and other interests in hopes of making it through the changing times. William Marion Reedy wrote of him in 1912, "Verily he do cut some ice."

He remodeled Lemp Mansion, his old family home, into brewery offices in 1911. The porte cochere came down and in its place, was a more commercial-looking overhang, making the residence appear more like an Italianate-style office complex. He had the interior renovated to include wall partitions for offices for architects, bookkeepers, secretaries, department heads, and a waiting area. The biggest addition was a large room that sat atop the atrium. When electricity was wired up to homes and businesses in 1914, it replaced the gasoliers throughout the building. Some people during the introduction of electricity feared it gave off deadly vapors and were hesitant to adopt it. But the Lemps had always been on the forefront of new technology, and for Billy, his new offices would reflect the modern new world.

THE FIRST BEER DELIVERED BY AIR

Donald Roussin of *BeerHistory.com* shares this fascinating story of one of Lemp Beer's most-astounding achievements:

The William J. Lemp Brewing Company issued over 130 different postcards in the years preceding Prohibition. These postcards, some humorous, others featuring real photos, are avidly sought after by many collectors. One of the rarer of the Lemp photo postcards, shows a crowd of people standing in the brewery loading yard, off Cherokee Street, grouped around an early "glider" type aircraft, not much advanced from the Wright brothers' machine that had made its maiden flight at Kitty Hawk less than a decade prior. A wooden beer bottle case marked 'Brewed in the Brewery of Lemp' can be seen being loaded onto the airplane. The postcard carries the caption, 'Falstaff is the first Bottled Beer to be delivered by aeroplane.'

Photos courtesy of Donald Roussin of *BeerHistory.com*

Loading Lemp Beer aboard its historic flight.

Another seldom seen Lemp photo postcard shows the same airplane, now airborne, flying above the Lemp brewery engine house. The postcard carries that same caption and in addition is marked 'Circling the Lemp Smoke Stack.' (see photo on page 288)

Neither of these two postcards carries a date; no "from" or "to" information, or other details of the flight.

However, there is a story behind the 'The First Beer to be Delivered by Air' Lemp postcards. William J. Lemp, Jr., was an early supporter of aviation, and used its novelty value for advertisements, as well as for promotions of flying events he sponsored. These postcards were issued to celebrate the first delivery of beer via an airplane (at least as far as can be ascertained), which occurred in 1912. The following is an excerpt from a letter dated September 22, 1967, addressed to the 'Advertising Manager, Falstaff Brewing Corporation,' from a John G. Shea, which tells, as they say, "the rest of the story:" 'Your advertising of Falstaff beer in the New York newspapers rings an ancient bell, which, I thought had long since been silenced by the years. Several years ago, as a professional writer on aviation history, I had an opportunity to chronicle the start of scheduled airplane transportation -- which originated between St. Petersburg and Tampa, Florida, in 1914. Visiting St. Pete, I had the pleasure of meeting with Jay Dee Smith -- an 'early bird' airplane pilot, and mechanic to the Benoist aircraft used in the world's first scheduled airline operations.

Tony Jannus flying the Benoist airplane.
Photo courtesy of St. Petersburg Museum of History.

A chap by the name of Tony Jannus was the pilot of the first airline operation. Jannus was the Lindbergh of that era. He had established several altitude and long distance flying records prior to 'settling down' to pilot the first Benoist 'airliners.' Now among his records was a flight in 1912, in a Benoist-type aircraft from St. Louis to New Orleans. And who sponsored this flight? The Lemp Brewery!

Here's the rest of the story that you should be told before it gets lost in the labyrinths of time: Smith, who serviced the Benoist aircraft, followed Jannus down the rivers by land. The epic flight started at St. Louis with the Mayor, and various officers of the Lemp Brewery, strapping a case of Falstaff bottled beer to the wing, behind the pilot's perch. Jannus was instructed to deliver the case of Falstaff to the Mayor of New Orleans. The flight was to be made in short, daily hops. First day out, Smith -- upon meeting up with Jannus at a predesignated spot along the river -- noticed the pilot was feeling no pain. Further observation revealed the case of beer had been broached -- and Jannus was joyously engaged with the twelfth bottle.

"How about the Mayor of New Orleans?" Smith inquired. "No Problem," Jannus chortled. –"Case flies much better empty!"

Photo of the "first bottled beer" being delivered by "aeroplane" circling the
Lemp Smoke Stack.
Photo courtesy of Donald Roussin, *BeerHistory.com*

Teddy Roosevelt in a Lemp ad promoting the Lemp Brewery brands. – Courtesy of Donald Roussin, **BeerHistory.com**.

William J. Lemp, Jr. put together another first for the Lemp Brewing Company. His advertising genius put Lemp Beer in the history books. The brewery had been the first to introduce lager beer to America, first to add refrigeration, first to build a pipeline from the brewing facility directly into the bottling plant, first to own their own railroad in the brewing industry, and now first to deliver beer by air. And this latter victory belonged to Billy.

Billy was also one of the first to utilize the new trucks rolling off the assembly line.

Packard trucks are popular with the Elk Liquor company. Fourteen horses were put out of work when Charles Reilley, local distributor for the Lemp Brewing company, purchased two two-ton Packard trucks to handle the Elk Liquor company's service in distributing the Lemp products.

According to Mr. Reilley, the truck service is fully 100 per cent more satisfactory than the horse delivery. "The trucks are cheaper to maintain," said Mr. Reilley yesterday. "Besides they are efficient at all times, carry heavier loads and give much faster service."

The brewery continued to thrive, although William Lemp, Jr. was aware the competition was always closing in on him.

1912, marked another occasion of Lemp Beer landing in the headlines, but on a more tragic note:

Titanic sinking on April 12, 1912. Photo courtesy History.com

LEMP BEER GOES DOWN ON THE TITANIC

St. Louis, Mo.—April 16, 1912. Twenty thousand bottles of beer and ale, including several cases of Lemp Lager Beer imported from St. Louis, went down to the bottom of the Atlantic with the *RMS Titanic*. Brewery heiress Elsa Lemp had planned to book passage on the *Titanic*, but lost interest when she discovered that no first-class tickets were still available. The price of a first-class ticket was $4,700*.

Lillian Handlan Lemp, the former wife of Lemp Brewing Company president William Lemp, Jr., and her son William Lemp III, were in Southampton when the Titanic shoved off, and they watched her sail out to sea. *$4,700 is the equivalent of $69,600 today.

These days were hectic ones for the owner of the Lemp brewery, but Billy had also started a new life. He was married to Ellie Limberg, and the headlines touting his feats in the brewing industry were finally eclipsing the crippling details of his divorce. He had a beautiful home in the country, and friends and family who loved him. For William Lemp, Jr., "the reluctant king," this was at least a respite from the earlier pain—until the headlines announcing the death knoll for brewers sounded on January 16, 1920. Prohibition was Billy's *coup de' grace.*

The United States Senate proposed the Eighteenth Amendment on December 18, 1917. Upon being approved by a 36th state on January 16, 1919, the amendment was ratified as a part of the Constitution. By the terms of the amendment, the country went dry one year later, on Jan. 17, 1920. Coincidentally, 1920 went down in history as the most-corrupt year in the history of St. Louis for police officers on the take. Bootleggers were profiting while breweries and saloons were hanging on by their teeth.

On November 18, 1918, prior to ratification of the Eighteenth Amendment, the U.S. Congress passed the temporary Wartime Prohibition Act which banned the sale of alcoholic beverages having an alcohol content of greater than 2.75 percent. (This act, which was intended to save grain for the war effort, was passed after the armistice ending World War I was signed on November 11, 1918.)

The Wartime Prohibition Act took effect June 30, 1919, with July 1, 1919, becoming known as the "Thirsty-First." On October 28, 1919 Congress passed the Volstead Act, the popular name for the National Prohibition Act, over President Woodrow Wilson's veto. The act established the legal definition of intoxicating liquors as well as penalties for producing them. Although the Volstead Act prohibited the sale of alcohol, the federal government lacked resources to enforce it. By 1925, in New York City alone, there were anywhere from 30,000 to 100,000 "speakeasy" clubs.

While Prohibition was successful in reducing the amount of liquor consumed, it stimulated the proliferation of rampant underground, organized and widespread criminal activity. Many were astonished and disenchanted with the rise of spectacular gangland crimes (such as Chicago's Saint Valentine's Day Massacre), when prohibition was supposed to reduce crime. Prohibition lost its advocates one by one, while the wet opposition talked of personal liberty, new tax revenues from legal beer and liquor, and the scourge of organized crime.

Brewery owners struggled through these frantic years, creating "near-beers" and adding soda beverages to their product lines, but many did not fare well.

While the other breweries were updating equipment, adding new product lines, and doggedly refusing to close their doors under the new mandate, Billy was losing hope. Cerva, his answer to Busch's "near beer" Bevo, was not making enough revenue to pay for the massive overhead costs of the brewery. He was not alone.

Donald Roussin of *Beer History.com* has a very comprehensive website dedicated to the history of beer. He is an avid collector of beer memorabilia and touts an accumulation of merchandise most beer connoisseurs would envy. He had this to say about the sad fallout of prohibition, and the lives it took:

THE "DUTCH (DEUTSCH) ACT"

Suicides by prominent St. Louis German-Americans, which included a number of brewers, became so notorious that their affliction became known as the "Dutch Act." The phrase was coined by the St. Louis Police Department who had to investigate all the untimely deaths. Four members of the Lemp family took their own lives. William Lemp Sr. was the first. He was 67-years-old.

William Lemp, Jr. was soon to follow. Doubting that Prohibition would ever end, he sold his company's famous Falstaff trademark to aspiring beverage producer "Papa Joe" Griesedieck. Then, after receiving only eight cents on the dollar for his auctioned brewery, Lemp became increasingly morose and depressed. Months later, on December 29, 1922, the 55-year-old Lemp shot himself in the heart in his mansion office. Charles Lemp was the family's final suicide. William Jr.'s brother had worked at the brewery in his younger days before going on to a successful career in banking and politics. But the old bachelor grew ever more reclusive with age, and in 1949, aged 77, and bothered by arthritis, Charles shot himself in his bed at the Lemp mansion.

Other suicides notable in St. Louis brewing history include P. H. Nolan, Otto Stifel, and August Busch.

Patrick Henry Nolan was vice-president and general manager of the Mutual Brewing Company of St. Louis, which erected a brewery at 236 S. Boyle in 1912. Largely owned by area saloon operators, the brewery was hit by financial problems late in 1914, and Nolan committed suicide at the brewery office the night before a scheduled appearance in bankruptcy court.

Otto Stifel of the Union Brewery was the next brewer to take his own life. Angry over the passage of Prohibition, saddled with large gambling and other debts, and facing a loss of his lifestyle, after losing much of his inheritance, Stifel shot himself in the mouth at his beloved Valley Park farm in August, 1920. He left several rambling suicide notes, blaming Prohibition and money problems caused by allegedly unscrupulous family and business associates for his mental state.

Anheuser-Busch brewer August A. Busch was yet another suicide victim. The son of Adolphus Busch, August A. had scrambled during the years of Prohibition to keep the family business going. With the repeal in 1933, the future seemed promising for the company. But ill health began to overtake Busch, and after complaining of recurring chest pains, the morning of February 13, 1934, he decided to end it all, using a revolver kept in the nightstand at his *Grant's Farm* bedroom. The 68-year old brewer left an unsigned note reading "Goodbye precious mama and adorable children."

It is interesting to note that both William J. Lemp, Sr., and the son of his good friend Adolphus Busch, August A. Busch, shot themselves on February 13th. Adolphus Busch was a pallbearer at William, Sr.'s funeral in 1904, and August was a close friend of Billy's.

Chapter Fifteen

"HAVEN'T I HAD ENOUGH?"

"Haven't I had enough?" Those were the last words William J. Lemp Jr. said to his secretary on the morning of December 29, 1922.

William J. Lemp, Jr. was a complex man. He was admired for his directness and business acumen. During testimony given at his divorce trial, he admitted to behavior that many would have dodged. You can see the mentality that caused others to say that where Billy was concerned "his word was as good as a bond." He openly admitted to Lillian's father that he had been unfaithful to the man's daughter. For Billy, there was a complicated moral code by which he lived: a playboy adulterer with a conscience set for telling the truth. A man who would easily shoot down a neighbor's cat for disturbing his sleep, yet a father devoted to his son. A friend who could slam down drinks as easily as a bawdy Elizabethan...knocking down men with slight provocation, yet a collector of the finest art known anywhere. His collection of Oriental furs and ivories, bronzes, and bric-a-brac, was unrivaled in most cities. His home was a pantheon of exquisite taste and refinement, and he was incredibly close to his mother.

In 1912, William Reedy in an article said of Billy: "discerning people will see the fundamental quality of Billy Lemp in the fact that it was he who called the most popular brand of his brewery product, "Falstaff." There's a fine business, fine sense of humor, noble literary association and historic perspective in the name."

For all he accomplished in his lifetime for his father's brewery, this author does not believe Billy sat easy beneath the crown. Charles was 2nd Vice President and Treasurer in 1910, but his heart was in politics and other ventures; Louis left in 1906 when their mother died; Edwin was the quiet force in the background (and eventually left as well to his secluded *Cragwold*), leaving Billy to steer the wheel of a sinking ship. The divorce headlines had left his reputation in tatters, his son was split between two states, and wherever he looked on Thirteenth Street were the ghosts of loss.

GERMANS GO HOME!

The world was changing in more places than Thirteenth Street, in St. Louis. The people, who had embraced German beer, were now looking at any name with an umlaut as a possible spy or enemy.

On June 28, 1914, the Archduke and heir to the Austria Hungary throne, Franz Ferdinand, and his wife Sofia, were gunned down and killed as they rode in an open-top automobile during an impromptu parade in Sarajevo, by Yugoslav nationalist Gavrilo Princip. This set off a diplomatic crisis when Austria-Hungary delivered an ultimatum to the Kingdom of Serbia. Entangled international alliances that had formed over the previous decades were invoked. Within weeks, the major powers were at war and conflict soon spread around the world. The United States joined the Allies in 1917, and we were at war with Germany.

The Tolerance Movement jumped on American's new distrust of German immigrants and used it to fuel their fight against alcohol. Most of the breweries were flying under German leadership, if not German names. Lemp, Griesedieck, Busch, Stumpf...the list went on and on. Sales dropped and

Prohibition grew ever closer to the gates of the giant brewing corporations.

Billy felt the hot breath of change upon his neck as he bent over the ledgers of the William J. Lemp Brewing Company. Other brewers were already turning out "near beers" in an effort to beat Prohibition to the punch, if and when, it did knock at their doors. Billy joined the movement and created Cerva, his answer to "near beer." With only a 2.75% alcohol content, it was basically a fermented cereal product and the sales of it floundered. It was soon apparent it would never sustain the monster brewing plant. Cerva was dropped in June, of 1919.

When Anheuser-Busch announced they had built the largest bottling plant in the world for their "near bear" Bevo, Billy felt his time was up. He had let the equipment slide in an effort to cut costs and Busch had steamrolled ahead. Like a morose game of dominoes, the brewery fell in swift stages.

William Zimmerman, an employee at the brewery said, "Lemp didn't have any farewell ceremonies. We just came to work one morning and found the place locked up. It never opened again," he said.

William J. Lemp, Jr. saw no hope for the future of brewing beer. To have an amendment repealed was almost impossible in his mind. He had plenty of money, and other investments upon which to retire. But the decision to liquidate the giant corporation his grandfather and father had poured their life into was not an easy one. For months, he wrestled with the repercussions selling off the brewery would bring to the Lemp name. He made this statement at the time:

"We have done nothing since Prohibition," he said. "I am tired of seeing all the weeds in the courtyard and the dust upon the windows. I am out of the brewery business for good. I am 54-years-old, and it is time to quit."

But others felt at some point Americans would pressure Congress to overturn the ruling. It had brought nothing but anarchy, poverty, and crime to the cities. The underworld had used Prohibition as a stepping stone for gangs and mobsters to run a corrupt government.

One of the brewers who believed beer would make a comeback, was Joseph "Papa Joe" Griesedieck. He was struggling with a floundering brewery business and needed a lifeline.

On October 22, 1920, the creditors of Griesedieck Beverage Company (GBC) filed an involuntary petition in bankruptcy, for approximately $450,000 owed ($4.9 million in 2010). The creditors agreed to let Griesedieck serve as receiver, under a bond of $50,000 ($544,000 in 2010). The GBC was certainly not the only brewery to fall victim to Prohibition. Brewers across the country were shutting their doors in the face of financial losses and uncertainty over the duration of the dry period. At the time, no one knew how long Prohibition would last: would brewers see Repeal in a year, a decade, or ever? They had to decide whether to muddle through by selling "near beer" and soft drinks or to dissolve their companies.

After Prohibition had been in effect for a few years, more and more St. Louis brewers started opting for the latter. In 1917, the city directory listed twenty-seven breweries. By 1918, the year in which the Eighteenth Amendment was ratified, that number had already dropped to twenty. In 1922, only nine breweries were listed in the city directory. The breweries of Griesedieck's former corporation, the Independent Breweries Company, were among those that had closed. By December 1919, when Billy Lemp announced his plans to sell the brewery, the company had become the second largest beer producer in St. Louis, after Anheuser-Busch. Their Falstaff label, brewed since June 1899, was nationally known. Billy had chosen the character of Falstaff as he wanted his beer to be associated with the character's "eat drink and be merry" mantra. By December 1919, the company had been out of the brewing business for a few months, having produced its last batch of real beer in October 1918, and its last batch of near beer, Cerva, in June

1919. William J. Lemp, Jr., later confided to his Vice-President that he believed Prohibition would be long. Moreover, he did not foresee beer ever regaining the commercial prominence it once held.

Out of this family's downfall, the Griesedieck's saw a way to save the Griesedieck Beverage Company while carrying on a piece of the Lemp tradition. Joseph and Alvin Griesedieck approached William J. Lemp, Jr., with whom Joseph was close friends, about purchasing the Falstaff trademark and shield, which they would use as the centerpiece of a new company.

Billy's first reaction to the offer was to decline it...emphatically. He would not see his family's label flying under any other flagship. It was the last vestige of pride he had after making the heart rending decision to shut down the plant.

But the Griesedieck's reasoned with him. In this way, the Lemp brand would live on. Alvin Griesedieck, in his book *The Falstaff Story,* recalls their meeting with Billy at his office in Lemp Mansion:

"I can remember the meeting at the Lemp office on South Thirteenth Street, across the street from the Lemp plant. Father wanted me to go with him, which I did.

"We were ushered into Mr. Lemp's office by Mr. Vahlkamp, secretary of the William J. Lemp Brewing Company. Mr. Vahlkamp, with his long white beard, was a very picturesque old gentleman, then I think somewhere in his seventies.

"Mr. Lemp knew all about our financial difficulties, and I believe in spite of his reputation for hardness and coldness in his business dealings, he consented to negotiate terms purely out of sympathy and a kindly feeling for my dad. Naturally, this was a matter to be approved by all the directors of the William J. Lemp Brewing Company, but Mr. Lemp was able to secure this in a relatively short time."

Once "Papa Joe" convinced Billy that he was only interested in the Falstaff trade mark, and would not be using the name Lemp itself, Billy relented and made him a remarkable deal. For only $25,000, the Griesedieck's purchased the Falstaff name and logo staff. The payments were made in increments: $5,000 in cash, and the balance due in three months. Billy later extended the time for the final payment to nine months, and used Griesedieck's First Mortgage Bonds for $20,000 as collateral.

Alvin Griesedieck –St. Louis Library

There was only one thing left to do regarding the large brick edifices that Billy saw every day of his life. The decision must have been the hardest of all. He may have spent countless hours trying to figure a way to change the brewery buildings into some other income-producing plant, but in the end, he put it up for auction.

PUBLIC AUCTION SALE

of the

GREAT LEMP BREWING PLANT

Wednesday, June 28th, 1922

18 Buildings. Heavy Construction. Power Plant Rare Shipping Facilities. Railroad Sidings. Vacant Property . Adjoining Buildings. Build to Suit

With that announcement, made by Joseph P. Day Auctioneer, Inc., Billy had moved his final pawn. The building which was valued at $7 million in 1919, was now only worth about $3.5. Billy had hoped to coupe at least $1,050,000 from the sale.

On June 28, 1922, the auction gavel sounded and the bidding began. Ultimately, five companies bought off the birth child of William J. Lemp, Sr. in pieces. The International Shoe Company took the lion's share of the buildings. When the dust had settled, the final tally was made on the sale.

The magnificent brewery that had set so many records in beer brewing history, ranking first in St. Louis and 9th in the nation, covering 11 city blocks, with flagship branches in numerous other cities, went for the disappointing sum of $585,000. The final gavel came crashing down upon the final tenuous tethers of Billy's faltering conscious.

The day after the sale, Billy was still reeling from the shock. "How would anybody feel to get eight cents on the dollar for a great plant like that?" he asked angrily. "They told us when Prohibition came that we could make something out of our plants, but look what happened. We obeyed the law, too."

Billy made the announcement that he would proceed to liquidate the corporation, selling off saloon corner sites and other land the company owned, and that he would thereafter "take it easy" on his farm.

However, Billy put *Alswel* up for sale shortly after that announcement. The 192-acres of farm and timber land, fronting the Meramec River was priced to sell at $175,000 (about $2.5 million in 2014). He told those around him he planned to take Ellie and travel the world for two years, and then decide what the future held for him. Nearing his mid-fifties, Billy Lemp was ready to lay aside the mantel of responsibility he had shouldered since his early 20's and enjoy life.

Yet the months following the auction of the brewery, found him more and more restless, distracted and ill. He sought out doctors and was hospitalized for myriad ailments. He complained constantly of aches and pains, nervousness and chills. Co-workers at the Lemp Mansion offices said he would repeatedly move from radiator to radiator in his office, where he would stand to keep warm. His lethargy concerning day-to-day business on the remaining investments he oversaw was remarked upon. The staff still arrived at the offices each morning. There were still loose-ends and transactions to wrap up concerning the sale of the brewery, and other investments. It had only been five months since the auction.

Radiators in Billy's "office" are beneath the two windows. He died approximately where the 4th chair is sitting at the top, on the right side.

Lemp Mansion's room that Billy used for his office. According to report measurements, Billy's desk would have been centered in front of the fireplace. The room is now used for dining. The fireplace is original. – Photo by Rebecca F. Pittman

Billy sat at his massive desk in the room northwest of the front door of his childhood home. It was surreal to come here and do business from a room that had once been the formal lady's parlor of the house in which he grew up. Christmas decorations still adorned the marble mantelpiece that stood behind his desk chair. He thought back a few days to the scene at his room at the Chase Hotel. He had tried to put on a brave and happy face for Ellie as they opened festively-wrapped Christmas presents and made plans for their world tour. He saw the hope in her eyes that this would be the start of a new life for them both; one in which the brewery's shadow no longer hovered overhead.

His heart began pounding and he felt the onset of the familiar chest pains he had been having. Within moments his palms were sweating, and he felt light-headed. The panic attack grew as he heard co-workers begin to enter through the front door to begin the few days of business since the Christmas break.

According to several newspaper, coroner and police reports, the following transpired on the morning of Friday, December 29, 1922:

Billy Lemp was in his office at 9 a.m. when Henry Vahlkamp, vice-president of the brewery company, and Lemp's personal secretary, Miss Olivia Borsches, arrived. Vahlkamp said that Lemp's face was flushed, and he had been extremely nervous for two months. Recently Lemp had complained of nervous chills, and "when in his office, he would stand frequently for several minutes before the heating radiators."

Vahlkamp said he greeted Lemp: "Well, how do you feel today?"

"Oh, I am feeling worse," Lemp replied.

According to Vahlkamp, he was resting his elbow upon his desk and held his forehead in his hand.

"You look better," Vahlkamp said, hoping to cheer him.

"I may look better, but I'm feeling worse," Lemp repeated. Vahlkamp then left and went to his office on the second floor of the mansion.

About this time, Miss Berchek telephoned Ellie Lemp at the Chase Hotel, where the Lemps had been living since the sale of *Alswel,* to discuss some correspondence matters with her. While talking to Mrs. Lemp, and relaying questions posed by her to Mr. Lemp, Billy took the phone and spoke to his wife himself. Miss Berchek said his voice was very low and quiet and she did not overhear what words were said between the two. It would be the last time Ellie Lemp would hear her husband's voice.

During the coroner's inquest, which was the following day, Miss Berchek was asked to relay what happened that morning. She said after he hung up the phone from his wife, she asked him a question about some blueprints that needed to be copied.

"At first, he said it was alright, what I had, and then he said, 'On second thought, you had better go downstairs and ask Mr. Norton (the brewery's architect).' While I was on my way downstairs, I heard this noise. It didn't sound like a shot to me, because they had been doing some work in the basement…and I thought the men had dropped something. It sounded like a piece of iron falling, to me. I went to talk to Mr. Norton, and when I came up a porter had Mr. Lemp lying on a pillow. The porter had heard the noise from down in the basement and came upstairs; he was the only one who realized it was a shot. When he came in the office he didn't see anything in there and had to walk up to Mr. Lemp's desk and he saw his feet lying under the table. He started around back of his desk and got to Mr. Lemp just as he was giving three gasps. He called for help and the men from the other side of the office came over and laid him on this pillow, and he was on the pillow when I came in the room."

Lemp was lying on his back in the northwest corner of his office, a .38 caliber revolver near his right hand. Officer John H. Schamm told a reporter from the *St. Louis Star* that Lemp had apparently dragged a large chair from it accustomed place around to the wrong side of his desk in a space of about four feet between the desk and the west wall of his office. Lemp was evidently sitting in this chair when he opened his vest and fired through his shirt into his chest. The initial report said two shots were heard, and two shots fired, leaving two wounds half an inch apart near his heart. There were two discharged shells from the gun, and the first thought was that during a spasm from the first shot, the gun fired again. However, during the inquest, it was established that only one of the two shells had been recently fired, leaving one chamber empty, perhaps as a safety precaution. The fact that one person reported hearing two shots was not gone into, nor the two marks first reported on Lemp's chest.

Dr. F. W. Abeken lived just around the corner from the Lemp offices at 914 Utah Street. He and police officers arrived to find William dead. Before his body could be removed to a private undertaking establishment, Billy III was made known of the accident and came bursting into the office. He was 21-years-old and staying in St. Louis. Kneeling beside his dead father, he cried, "You knew I knew it. I was afraid this was coming."

No note was found on or around Billy, though Captain William Doyle of the Wyoming Street Police Station searched.

News reached Ellie at the Chase Hotel that her husband was dead, only minutes after she had spoken to him by phone. She was reported to be prostate with grief and refused visitors at the hotel. She could not bring herself to come to the office.

Billy's ironic words he had spoken, when he viewed his sister Elsa, only two years earlier, as she lay in her bed, dead from a supposed self-inflicted gunshot wound, now hung over the small office where the dead man lay: "This is the Lemp family for you."

Billy was reportedly depressed and visibly low-spirited as he sat during the inquest over Elsa's body. Just as the family had been that day in 1920, they were now staggered from the sudden and violent loss of the third president of the William J. Lemp Brewing Company. The Lemp tradition would continue as the coffin of Billy Lemp rested in the twin parlors of Lemp Mansion, just as his father's had done before him. On December 31, 1922, at 2:00 in the afternoon, flowers again perfumed the air of the family home, condolences came in from far and wide, and once again, a young man named Billy Lemp sat near his father's casket, and cried.

Photos taken by local newspapers show the curious bystanders at the house the day of the suicide. Young boys in cloth caps and knickers lean against the trees of the front yard and watch, needing to be a witness to this historic unfolding of events. Men in bowler hats prowl the sloping lawn, while others loiter on the sidewalk.

The day of Billy's death. Lemp Mansion.
Photo courtesy of the *St. Louis Post-Dispatch.*

Where horse and buggies had parked before Lemp Mansion during William Lemp, Sr.'s funeral, the scene was now one of cars sporting the latest technology from the 1920's. The hitching post sat uselessly embedded in the cement sidewalk, recalling simpler times.

Shockwaves spread through the St. Louis social sector. How could one family lose three wealthy members to suicide? Surely there was a strain of madness in the Lemps. Could perhaps a stealthy hit man be knocking off the affluent members one by one? The gossip ran rampant, unsympathetic to the lives that were left behind after the flowers wilted and the hours and days ahead had to be faced alone. The socialite playboy who had thrown the lively parties at club settings, found himself in the love of horses, and whose messy divorce made history in St. Louis annals, was now incongruously still. It was almost too much to take in.

The funeral of Billy Lemp on December 31, 1922
Photo courtesy of the *St. Louis Dispatch*

The newspapers' headlines encapsulated the dead man's life in succinct, unemotional caps:

LEMP KILLS HIMSELF IN BREWERY OFFICE

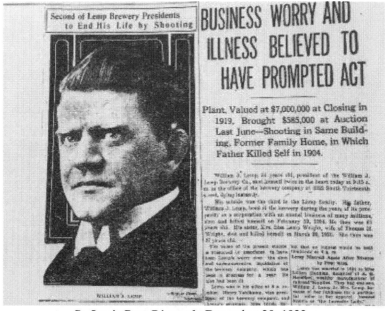

Second of Lemp Brewery Presidents to End His Life by Shooting

BUSINESS WORRY AND ILLNESS BELIEVED TO HAVE PROMPTED ACT

Plant, Valued at $7,000,000 at Closing in 1919, Brought $585,000 at Auction Last June—Shooting in Same Building, Former Family Home, in Which Father Killed Self in 1904.

St. Louis Post-Dispatch: December 29, 1922.

At the funeral, Henry Vahlkamp, who had been with the Lemp family and their brewery for 54 years, recalled that Billy had confided in him that he did not think beer would ever make a comeback to its prior importance. He said Billy had grown increasingly nervous two to three weeks prior to his death.

Miss Berchek mirrored Vahlkamp's assessment that Billy was not well. "Well, he had been feeling decidedly ill for the past three or four weeks. He was suffering with chills; I would call it a nervous chill, and was very morose...he was always very particular about things, and very precise. But for the last three or four weeks he didn't seem to care. He didn't fight back at anything. He just let everything go, contrary to his former attitude towards things; and Thursday afternoon, he said to me, 'I have had enough doctors, haven't I?' Later he said, 'Don't you think I have had enough trouble? I have had about enough.'"

Miss Berchek said Billy had been in the hospital three times recently for short periods.

While Billy's son and co-workers saw the man's slow and steady deterioration of mind, others were more surprised to hear of his death.

August A. Busch, who had been a close friend of the Lemp family for years, said he had just seen Billy a week before. "At that time, he seemed cheerful and there was no indication that he was worrying either about the business situation or anything else. He was a hard worker and personally looked after the operation of his farm. He was a fine fellow, and it is hard to believe he has taken his own life." Yet, August would follow suit shortly after.

William Lemp, Jr.'s will left primarily everything to his wife, Ellie, and his son Billy III. Billy's son would obtain half of his inheritance now, and the other half upon turning 30. Charles Lemp was named his executor. Billy's jewelry was given to his son, with the exception of some pieces left to Ellie. The boy was also bequeathed Billy's fishing gear and hunting equipment. Most of Billy's estate came from a series of bonds, investments, and stocks, namely: $40,000 in Phillips Petroleum; $34,000 in the Kinloch Long Distance Telephone Company; $60,000 in Consolidated Coal Company, and $50,000 in a Mexican railroad investment. *Alswel's* revenue was not reported, nor was stock from the Lemp brewery. The will was filed on January 4, 1923, five days after his death. His net value came out to $878,431, the least of all the Lemp's reported assets.

Ellie Kohler Lemp passed away on February 21, 1941, at the age of 77, from a second cerebral hemorrhage. She died at home at #2 Lenox Place, in St. Louis, and is buried there in the Bellefontaine Cemetery.

One last irony...

Human beings plague themselves with "What if's?" The 20/20 hindsight that makes us suddenly wise comes always a little too late. For Billy Lemp, the headlines that would have saved his brewery and his life were posthumously delivered:

On March 22, 1933, President Franklin Roosevelt signed into law the Cullen-Harrison Act, legalizing beer with an alcohol content of 3.2 percent (by weight) and wine of similarly low alcohol content. On December 5, 1933, ratification of the Twenty-First Amendment repealed the Eighteenth Amendment. However, United States federal law still prohibited the manufacture of distilled spirits without meeting numerous licensing requirements that made it impractical to produce spirits for personal beverage use.

For those tenacious souls who hung on to their breweries, selling "near beers", sodas, glucose, sugar, corn syrup, ice cream, candy and anything else they could think of to survive, the announcement was nothing less than miraculous. Little- by-little the regulations fell away, and left rising from the ashes was none other than the man who had sat in Billy's office that day in 1920, and made a deal to purchase the trademark and logo for Falstaff beer: Joseph "Papa Joe" Griesedieck.

"It was a big moment in the progress of Falstaff when Louis Becker, Internal Revenue officer, gave Federal Permit Number 1, covering relegalized beer, to Falstaff Founder Joseph Griesedieck in 1933."

While the caption beneath the photo credits Griesedieck with the founding of Falstaff beer, he actually founded the Falstaff Brewing Company, not the original beer, after buying the rights from Billy. You could not take that honor away from William J. Lemp, Jr.

Falstaff logos: With Lemp's name, and without.
–Lemp Mansion

Chapter Sixteen

William J. Lemp III

IN HIS FATHER'S IMAGE

William J. Lemp III was born on September 24, 1900, in St. Louis, Missouri. As a young boy, he watched his parents, William J. Lemp, Jr. and Lillian Handlan Lemp embroiled in a bitter divorce. If some of his mother's allegations were true, then the boy had witnessed live chickens being fed to the monkeys in the stable behind his home when he was only 4 or 5 years old. His father had an affinity for firearms and the boy often ate dinner while staring at a revolver laid next to his father's plate. He was living across the street in 1904, when his grandfather shot himself in the temple and died. Even at four years of age, he could not have missed the media circus and

314

strangers thronging the street outside his home. He may have been spared the funeral, but he would have been told his grandfather was gone.

When William III and his mother were ousted from their home in May of 1908, he was 8 years of age. They went to live with his grandparents, and in later years, to an apartment in New York City. His visitation rights with his father may have been regularly observed, but there is no record of the amount of time Billy Jr. spent with his son. The sense of security and a safety net beneath the boy's feet was probably never in place.

WILLIAM J. LEMP III SANTA CLAUS FOR POOR CHILDREN

St. Louis-Post Dispatch: December 13, 1908.

"King of St. Louis fairies, tiny Oberon of the joyous Christmastide is William J. Lemp III, whose father, the millionaire brewer, and whose mother, "the Lavender Lady" are fighting in court for him.

He is the one boy in St. Louis who not only need have no fear that Santa Claus will forget him, but who has, as well, the privilege of buying hundreds of dollars' worth of toys, candies and dolls to make other children happy.

He has but to wave the magic wand and anything that he sees in the big downtown stores is his...and will be added to the presents which will gladden hearts of other little boys and girls on the great feast day.

Following the custom of his father, grandfather and great-grandfather before him, he yesterday spent $350 in buying Christmas presents for the children of the levee district, who are pupils of the Old Cathedral School on Walnut street.

Hundreds of these children are orphans or children of parents who are too poor to make them happy on Christmas, and it has been the practice of the Lemp family for years to send candy and toys to the school each year for those unfortunate ones.

In the company of his father for first time in ten weeks, the boy made the rounds of the various shops in an automobile and bought enough toys and candy to send many thrills of real Christmas glee to the hearts of the poor...The little fellow picked out all the gifts himself, and personally supervised all the lavish buying...handling each toy to check that it worked properly.

Dozens and dozens of tin horns, toy guns, dolls, building blocks, steam engines, horses, sheep, elephants, Teddy bears and other things were laid aside...Mr. Lemp paid the bill at once, and gave instructions for their delivery.

The father stood by and approved the boy's purchases, and in so doing was reminded of his own boyhood. Adam Lemp established the custom of remembering the poor children of Old Cathedral School at Christmas time, and William J. Lemp, Jr. used to accompany his father, William J. Lemp, Sr. and pick out the toys and candy much as did his own son yesterday morning. Not once since the custom began have the children of Old Cathedral been forgotten at Christmas by the Lemp family.

By the ruling of Judge Kinsey in the Circuit Court Friday, the Saturday visits of William J. Lemp III to his father have been restored. Early in the morning, a big automobile drove up to the mother's home, and Mr. Lemp got William J. III.

By the custom established by Adam Lemp, the toys and candy will be delivered by the firms from which they were purchased to the Old Cathedral School Thursday, the day before Christmas, and William J. Lemp Jr. will be there to attend the distribution, just as were his father and grandfather in his lifetime. Last year the father wanted William J. III to be there, but his mother would not allow it.

It is doubtful if he can be there Thursday, though he is very anxious. The Court authorized his father to have the child only on Saturdays, but Mrs. Lemp will be appealed to by her husband to allow the child to go to the school Thursday and see his bounty distributed to the poor.

The rivalry between Mr. and Mrs. Lemp for the affections of their son will be the means of giving William J. III a double Christmas. Friday is Christmas day and on that day Mrs. Lemp will give her boy all the presents she thinks good for him, to make him happy. It is said the mother has already purchased lavish gifts of every description for him. The day following Christmas will be Saturday, the father's day, and William J. Lemp Jr. has bought stacks and stacks of toys and candy for the boy. Mechanical toys of every description and wagon loads of other things...have been bought by the father."

In 1921, William Lemp III, the lost little boy, was now a grown man. Yet he was dealt another blow by none other than his maternal grandfather. On June 1, 1921, Alexander H. Handlan, Lillian's father, died. His will was duly filed and its contents made headlines. It contained a discrimination clause against his grandson, William J. Lemp III. Handlan's will, which was published after the 77-year-old President of Buck Manufacturing Company died in his summer home in Oconomowoc, Wisconsin, was actually made out on April 27, 1920. It stipulated that "William III (now 20 years old) would only receive $5,000 of his mother's inheritance when she died." Lillian was awarded 13% of her father's estate. The amount of Mr. Handlan's estate was not disclosed. Nothing was given to the boy at the time; only upon the death of his mother, who, as it turns out, outlived him.

"The reason for this discrimination," the will states, "is the fear he might come under the influence of his father. It pains me to make such discrimination, but if he is to be dominated and influenced by his father, and deprived of his mother's training, I believe it would be unwise to give him any considerable sum of money. I want my grandson to realize this discrimination is wholly on account of his father's treatment of my daughter, his mother."

Lillian Handlan Lemp died March 29, 1960, at the ripe old age of 84, outliving both her ex-husband and son. According to her obituary, she died of infirmities at Jewish Hospital. Funeral services were held at 2 p.m. at the Donnelly undertaking establishment, 3840 Lindell Boulevard, followed by entombment at Bellefontaine Cemetery. She never remarried after her divorce from Billy, and asked to be buried in the Lemp Mausoleum in Bellefontaine Cemetery, in St. Louis, with the other Lemps. Edwin Lemp gave his permission and she is interred there.

In 1928, William Lemp III married a beautiful young socialite, Agnes. This author could find no information on the ceremony. There were no children from the marriage.

The 1930 census shows Billy III and Agnes living in Manhattan on East 48th street, renting an apartment. He was 30, as was she. His occupation is listed as "Investor: Various." Shortly after that year, they moved into his late-father's *Alswel*, in St. Louis county. The Board of Finance held the mortgage to the property after it was auctioned off by Billy Jr.'s executors in 1925, three years after his suicide.

Agnes P. Lemp on her wedding day, 1928
Photo courtesy of Lemp Mansion

In 1934, one year after Prohibition was repealed, Billy III and his wife Agnes began suffering serious setbacks. When Billy could not keep up *Alswel's* mortgage payments, the Church sued the Lemps for interest and principal in 1934. Finally, the property was foreclosed on. It was valued at that time at $200,000.

In 1937, Agnes threw in the towel. She petitioned for a divorce, stating Billy had abandoned her on March 14, 1936, without notice, and without any provocation on her part. She said their financial situation was so bleak that she was forced to pawn a $2,000 bracelet and other jewelry just to survive. At a time when women of her means wouldn't dream of holding down a job, she was forced to seek employment at a department store one Christmas season.

At some point after the divorce, Billy III moved back into *Alswel* and rented it from the current owners. The 1940 census shows him living there with two servants: Gustan Rudolph, age 60, a "Yardman," and Gustan's wife, Emma Rudolf, age 56, a "Maid." He is 40 years old and living on Gravois Road. His occupation is listed as "Brewery Proprietor."

Billy III's title as owner of a brewery was due to his efforts to resurrect Lemp Beer. In 1939, he put his finger to the post Prohibition era winds and decided it was time to pull the Phoenix from the ashes. He entered into a contract with Central Breweries, Incorporated, of East St. Louis, on August 25, 1939. The agreement was for the licensing of the Lemp name for their beer manufacturing. Billy would be paid royalties for all beer sold using the name 'Lemp.'

The resurrection of the William J. Lemp Brewing Company in October, 1939, was heralded with a huge marketing campaign. Through full-page ads in newspapers and other print media, Adam Lemp's child was reborn. On November 1, 1939, Lemp Beer was once again rolling off the assembly line.

William J. Lemp III must have felt immense pride in his accomplishment to bring back the business his family had fought to grow throughout their lifetimes. His grandfather, William J. Lemp, Sr. had come to this country at the age of 12 to embark on his life-long endeavor to carry on his own father's brewing heritage. Surely Lemp Beer would once again dominate the industry.

It looked like all systems were go. Lemp Beer was again being printed on labels, beer cartons, bottle caps and merchandise.

An example of the large ads running in newspapers announcing
the return of Lemp Beer. – St. Louis Library

The response to the re-release of Lemp Beer was
overwhelming. The public welcomed the long-lost lager with
open arms. It looked as though, finally, the company was back.

But what would a Lemp success story be without its tragic
ending? By September of 1940, serious financial troubles began
assaulting the fledgling company. Whether the person in charge
of finance had little training in the art of bookkeeping, or the

company overextended itself in its excitement to be back on the charts, outstanding liabilities came tumbling in at an alarming rate. These included:

- $8,300 owed in back taxes
- $120,000 in outstanding accounts
- $34,000 in advancements from the officers and other investors to the corporation
- $108,000 in interest on the second mortgage came due

The assets on the books at the time showed only $150,000. This included 13,000 barrels of beer in the inventory.

One month later, on December 19, 1940, any trading in the Lemp Beer company stock was suspended on the St. Louis Stock Exchange. The stockholder's interest was lost and the company was declared insolvent. Total bankruptcy followed only a few months later, in 1941.

The final assault came on March 1, 1945, when Ems Brewing Company, who had taken over the brewery in December of 1939, canceled the contract with William J. Lemp III and discontinued using the Lemp name.

After over 100 years of Lemp Beer being brewed in St. Louis, the only remaining sign of its glory days was the brick brewery on the corner of Cherokee and Thirteenth Streets; its proud tower still emblazoned with the name LEMP. Incongruously, its interior was home to shoe manufacturing. The expansion of the International Shoe Company buildings had rolled over the home of Billy and Lillian Lemp. Where little Billy III's playground had been, was now a row of metal buildings and a parking lot.

Only three years later, at the age of 43, William J. Lemp III was crossing a street in downtown when he suddenly dropped dead of a heart attack—just as his Uncle Frederick had died of heart complications decades earlier. If the Kennedy's were cursed, the Lemp family must have been born under the same alignment of planets.

You can still see the faded International Shoe Co. logo on the side of Lemp Brewery, as it faces DeMenil Place. Photo courtesy of Ron Bueker.

Chapter Seventeen

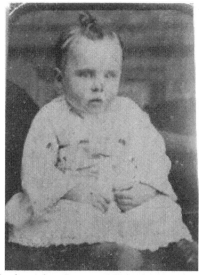

Charles Adam Lemp, 1872, one year old.
Photo Courtesy of Lemp Mansion

CHARLES LEMP
The Prodigal Son

Charles Adam Lemp was born on December 30, 1871, the third son of William and Julia Lemp. He was one year younger than Louis, two years older than Frederick, and nine years Edwin's senior. Billy was four years older and was looked upon as the "big brother" by his siblings.

Like his brothers before him, Charles attended the St. Louis schools. He was dedicated, focused, and already looking at politics as a possible avocation.

Charles Lemp in 1889, at the age of 18
Photo courtesy of Lemp Mansion

The 1895, the census shows him living at Lemp Mansion and "at school" at the age of 24. One year later, he was encouraged to run for a political office in St. Louis, which shows the reach the young man already had in the community.

LEMP WILL RUN

St. Louis Post-Dispatch: October 22, 1896.

Charles Lemp, the Democratic nominee for Congress in the Tenth District, who has declined to accept the nomination tendered him by the State Committee, was visited Thursday by Chairman Cook of the State Committee and Chairman Harvey W. Salmade of the Executive Committee.

They urged him to make the race, and made the statement that, as his name was already on the ticket, he could not very well get it off. It is probable that Mr. Lemp will make the race.

Charles was living at a boarding house at 3401 S. 13th Street, in 1901. He was 30 years old and listed as Treasurer of the William J. Lemp Brewing Company. While fulfilling that position he continued his interest in the political arena, and ventured out into other investments. He helped his father recruit other states for the World's Fair, as William sat on the Board of Directors. One such feat was published on November 16, 1901. It shows a fun side of Charles Lemp:

SOUTHERNERS HAVE SHOWN GREAT HOSPITALITY TO THEIR GUESTS

Mississippi Exhibit Assured

St. Louis Republic: November 16, 1901. Holly Spring, Miss.

What has been the most enjoyable, as well as the most successful, day spent by the excursion party of St. Louis merchants and manufacturers in the South, has just been closed with a reception at Holly Springs, Mississippi.

It is now assured that the State of Mississippi will exhibit richly at the Louisiana Purchase Exhibition (the 1904 World's Fair). All local business leagues have exerted themselves to excel one another in hospitality while the member's wives and daughters have showered roses and chrysanthemums upon their guests.

Today has been a frolic upon cotton plantations and groves hung with Spanish grey moss. Charles Lemp has run a special engine at 60 miles per hour, while a number of business men have stood on the roofs of the cars to throw World's Fair souvenir buttons to people lining the parade route.

The article went on to say that Governor Langino of Mississippi assured the group from St. Louis that they would be exhibiting at the World's Fair. Charles and the other members were shown around Jackson, the capitol of Mississippi, and then entertained at the Columbia Club.

Charles rose quickly in power in St. Louis politics. His list of friends included Circuit Court Judges, members of the St. Louis police force, bank presidents and many others. He was a notary public, and seemed to be called upon often to bail dignitaries out of jail.

"SNAKE" KINNEY IS INDITED

St. Louis Republic: April 18, 1902. Thomas E. Kinney, member of the House of Delegates from the Fifth Ward, appeared at Four Courts yesterday to give bond in the sum of $800 to answer the charge of assault to kill proffered in an indictment by the last Grand Jury. Kinney is charged with assaulting Daniel Shea at the Union Market early on the morning of March 5. Kinney gave bond signed by Charles Lemp, son of the brewer.

Charles popped up on the other side of law on more than one occasion. He was subpoenaed, along with Tony Stuever, and Phillip Stock, all St. Louis brewers. It was learned that the

Grand Jury was investigating a report that an attempt was made to secure money from brewers to effect the passage of the beer compromise bill by which brewers were released from paying fines for violation of the beer inspection law on the condition that they pay a stipulated sum into the State treasury and obey the law in the future. The former Lieutenant Governor of Missouri, John A. Lee, was on the stand, and broke down into tears when he was accused of being connected to the "boodling" charge. [Boodling is a bribe, or other illicit payment.]

The case got uglier when Lee said he was approached by "a well-dressed stranger, whom he did not know," in the corridor of a hotel in Kansas City, directly after making his confession to "boodling" in Jefferson City, Missouri. The stranger offered Lee $1,000 a month for a year if he would leave the country for that length of time. He said the money would be paid for his absence from Missouri. Lee turned down the bribe, and went to Chicago for a week before returning to St. Louis.

"A subpoena was issued for William J. Lemp, President of the Lemp Brewing Company, but was not served, the Sheriff stating that he could not be located at home. Another was issued for Charles Lemp, who will be asked to tell what he knows about money which was raised to pass the beer compromise bill." –*St. Louis Republic*, January 22, 1904.

The fact that William J. Lemp committed suicide, only three weeks after this case was under investigation, gives one pause. He was also being sued for stocks he sold out of turn in an amount totally over $400,000. When his best friend, Captain Pabst, passed away from cancer only a month before this all went down, William may have felt the floor disappearing from beneath him. It's possible Charles knew much more about the strain his father was under than did the rest of the family. According to the previous newspaper report, Charles and

William, Sr. are the only Lemp names associated with the investigation of the brewery's connection to the "boodling" charge. Charles' involvement may have been due to the fact he was the brewery Treasurer, or he had helped set up the bribe. Billy's, Louis', and Edwin's names do not appear in the article.

Billy was asked during his divorce trial if he had spied on his wife's telegrams. Under oath, Billy said there had been a misunderstanding—it was the other "Mrs. Lemp" whose telegrams he had asked for. Why would Billy be interested in his mother's telegrams? Perhaps William had Julia sending telegrams in his stead to correspond with the people involved during the time Lee was approached by "a stranger" offering him a bribe in Kansas City. Spies may not have been looking for telegrams from Julia Lemp, but they would have been very interested in any sent by William. If William had any part with bribing a witness, it would mean prison time.

Politics and Dodging Taxes

Charles made the papers again when he was interviewed on June 29, 1904 about his political affiliations:

"According to Charles Lemp, who departed last night for the Joplin convention, A. C. Stuever and George J. Taney will be the district delegates to the Democratic National Convention from the Tenth District.

"I understand this has been agreed upon," he said. "I expect to be a State Committeeman from the district with James McCaffery. I do not believe there will be any opposition to this settlement of the Tenth District situation." –*St. Louis Republic:* June, 29, 1904.

But, alas, Charles was once more before the Grand Jury on September 29, 1905, this time for dodging his taxes:

TAX DODGERS

The Holt County Sentinel (Oregon, Mo.): "In bunches of five, the thirty millionaires of the city of St. Louis, are being called before the Grand Jury of that city to explain away the incongruity between their petty personal property tax and their style of living. The inquiry is based on the significant fact that the tax receipts credit the millionaires summoned, with possessing only about $850,000, while the deposits in the St. Louis banks aggregate more than $200,000,000.

Among the plutocrats, who are being called upon when they are reached by the Sheriff's men with a subpoena, and the tax valuations of their personal property, are:

Festus J. Wade, banker.......... $3,200
Geo. F. Tower, manufacturer...   700
Otto F. Stifel, brewer.....   2,000
A.C. Stuever, brewer.....   1,300
Charles Lemp, brewer....   300
Henry Ziegenheim, banker....   1,200
Henry Nicholaus, brewer.....   1,560

The St. Louis Grand Jury is doubtless skeptical as to the poverty of a number of these men, as shown on the tax books.

Others were named, but it is interesting that Charles sited the least amount of property. Ziegenheim, who cited only $1,200, was a neighbor of the Lemps on Thirteenth Street.

While Charles continued to rise in the ranks of his father's brewery, his name appeared more often in the national newspapers for things other than brewing suds. The image of the mild-mannered, stern, and boring gentleman many associate with Charles A. Lemp, is not the man who simply could not outrun the ubiquitous eye of the newspaper reporters.

The Chanute Times (Chanute, Kansas) reported this on September 22, 1905:

St. Louis: Judge Foster overruled the motion in arrest of judgement made some time ago on behalf of Zach Mulhall, convicted last January of shooting Ernest Morgan on the Pike at the World's Fair.

Charles Lemp, bondsman for Mulhall, was ordered to bring him in to be sentenced.

And on May 29, 1913, Charles just barely missed being brought in himself when he was spotted by a snooping reporter, gambling at an illegal cock fight.

MILLIONAIRES SCARED BY NEWSPAPER MAN

Honolulu Star-Bulletin: May 29, 1913:

St. Louis: A cocking main, a novel weekend entertainment provided for a small party of men by Robert A. D. Walsh, vice-president of the Mississippi Glass Company, on the country estate of his brother, Julius F. Walsh, Jr., of New York and St. Louis, near Ferguson, was suddenly terminated by the unexpected appearance of a reporter.

Among the wealthy guests present was Charles A. Lemp, the millionaire brewer. The betting was heavy.

The reporter was discovered by one of the guests after the first go and Walsh immediately called the rest of the main off, despite the protests of his guests.

Charles had a lighter side. His antics made the headlines along with the scandals.

DRINK UP ME HEARTIES!

Mexico Missouri Message-- A delegation from the notorious Jefferson Club was very much in evidence at the capitol Monday night. It is needless to say that the delegation got drunk. Drunk is a mild word to apply to their hilarity. They were cultivating a jag of monstrous proportions.

Charles Lemp, the brewer, who, by the way, looks more like a professor of Greek in a theological school than a politician, was ubiquitous and saw that no man went to bed thirsty. One refrain echoed all over Jefferson City:

"Beer, beer, we want more beer,
Beer beer, we want Falstaff beer."

Those two lines of drunken doggerel were sung to the tune of "My Country Tis of Thee." Try it yourself, and in singing hold the first syllable of Falstaff and you will see how easily the noble air can be adapted to trash. Political criticism has it that this is the last kick of the Jefferson Club. One thing is certain, one seldom has an opportunity to see such a gang of depraved rowdies and plug-uglies as the Jefferson Club brought to Jefferson City.

An interesting accounting of the Jefferson Club, to which Charles was nominated to Board of Directors, is that it boasted over 8,000 members, held a bank account totaling over $12,000 (that's $314,000 in 2014) with no attachments, and listed Richard Hanlon who sat on the Board of Police Commissioners, as its Vice-President. It was a club whose member's directory was filled with the names of some of biggest power-hitters in Missouri.

Racquet Club, St. Louis, where Charles made his home for 19 years.
Photo courtesy St. Louis Public Library

333

By 1910, Charles had risen at the brewery to 2nd Vice-President and Treasurer. He had moved into the Racquet Club in downtown St. Louis, after staying for a short period in his home at Lemp Mansion, after his mother's death. It was at this time that Billy began renovations to the family home to turn it into the company offices. Whether Charles was going to move, and Billy saw it as a way to utilize the empty home for the brewery's growing needs, or he asked Charles to move out of the needed space, citing the brewery owned the estate, we don't know. Either way, Charles moved out.

He remained at the Racquet Club for 19 years. Yearly travels to exotic places around the world became his passion. He never married, but instead set out to acquire an impressive collection of art. Charles frequented galleries wherever he went and became known for his "eye" for a worthy investment. His acquisitory nature sent gallery owners rushing to assist him when he crossed their doorway. Money was literally no object.

In 1917, Charles left the William J. Lemp Brewing Company and became Vice-President of the German Savings Institution, in downtown St. Louis, at Broadway and Pine. His investment portfolio grew, as did his banking undertakings. In 1921, he signed on at Liberty Central Trust. When automobiles began dominating the transportation industry, he became president of the Indemnity Company of America, as an automobile casualty insurance dealer.

During Charles reign at Indemnity Company of America, he hired Billy's son, William J. Lemp III, who became a Treasurer and Vice President.

Charles was the primary owner of the East St. Louis, Columbia, and Waterloo electric line until it closed its door in 1932. He owned real estate in various cities, and managed his income well. At his death, his estimated assets totaled over $3.2 million. (That's $29.7 million in 2014's dollars.)

In 1922, *The Evening World* newspaper from New York City published a cute article Charles posted for his amusement. It shows a lighthearted side to the often-stuffy man.

IT'S A GIFT

"From my window, I watched a crew of men at work in an excavation, my attention being drawn to one man in particular. After watching this gentleman's antics for ten minutes, I am convinced that I have discovered the World's Champion Staller. While I studied his really scientific loafing, I observed the approach of two of his bosses. Now, said I to myself, the poor fellow will have to do a little real work. Did he? The minute they were opposite him he took off one shoe and shook an imaginary pebble out of it. Then he put the shoe on. Then he walked to the other end of the job and "drank" water out of an absolutely empty bottle, not forgetting to wipe his mouth. Suddenly he grabbed a spade and set off to another part of the job, the first speed he had shown. He's a genius."—Charles Lemp.

Charles sought relaxation through travel. He had friends all over the country and would often stay at their estates for weeks at a time. As usual, the reporters found him out and dutifully reported his whereabouts:

1914: "Charles A. Lemp, son of a prominent St. Louis brewer, is a member of a party of several wealthy tourists who arrived at Honolulu in the Matson Navigation steamer *Wilhelmina* and will remain in this city until the sailing of the Toyo Kisen Kaisha line *Hong Kong Maru* for Japan and China. Mr. Lemp is on a leisurely tour of the world." – *Honolulu Star-Bulletin,* 1918.

"Charles Lemp of St. Louis To Pass Spring Season Here:

Charles Lemp of St. Louis will be a guest at the Peter Edes Bradshaw country place for an indefinite period this spring. Mr. Lemp and his host are week-ending in Prescott." –*Arizona Republican*

Charles' passports bore stamps from Puerto Rico, Southampton, France, Germany, Japan and other ports of call. His art collection grew, as did his need for a more secure and spacious place to put it all. The Racquet Club was hardly conducive to showcasing and storing his rare finds, one of which was a Picasso.

Charles knew where he could find three large fireproof vaults that had kept his parent's art collections safe for years. They measured 15' wide by 13' high by 25' deep and sat at the end of the hallways where he used to play. In 1928, Charles restored Lemp Mansion to the way he remembered it, removed the temporary walls that had housed brewery cubicles, took out the old elevator and replaced the main staircase …and in 1929, he went home.

****

Charles Adam Lemp stood in the foyer of his childhood home and looked up the main staircase, newly carpeted in a red runner. It was as if his mother might come down from the second floor at any moment and walk toward him, her long bengaline gown sweeping the carpet in soft tones—like someone whispering. If he closed his eyes and listened real hard, he might hear the sound of his father showering in the marble tub down the hall, or the squeals of his sisters as Billy and Louis chased them through the hallways.

He sniffed the air as the smell of dinner cooking wafted up the back stairs from the kitchen where Mrs. Lena Bittner was preparing his evening meal---not Mathilda Bressler, the cook with whom he grew up, but a woman who had been with him for some time. She, and her husband Albert, were now his constant companions.

Lemp Mansion main staircase. Photo by Rebecca F. Pittman

Charles looked about him and his eyes came to rest on the room across from him, nearest the front door. He looked to the left of the parlor's fireplace without moving from his spot. The room had been Billy's office when the house was used for business purposes.

"That's where he shot himself," his mind murmured. "There...by the west window." He shuddered, hearing the sharp report of the gun in his mind. Billy had given up. Just

like their father, Billy had used a gun as a way out of the burdens that bent him and tortured his mind.

Albert Bittner, Lena's husband, and the only other servant, entered through the front door, and Charles jumped. The man doffed his fabric cap, and scraped his shoes against a door mat before entering. An excited red dog bounded in behind Albert and ran toward his master's dangling hand. Charles' rubbed the Doberman Pincher's coarse hair, appreciating the momentary feel of life. Albert smiled at his employer and walked down the hallway toward the back stairs to the basement, Cerva racing after him. It was dinner time for the dog and the backstairs meant the kitchen, and food.

A piece of caked mud fell from Albert's heel and Charles stiffened. Removing a handkerchief from his front pocket he stepped to the repugnant intruder, carefully enfolded it into the linen without touching it, and carried it out the front door, where he tossed it away from him. Upon entering the house, he threw the tarnished handkerchief into a waste bin. There would be new rules about shoes in the house, he decided. They must be left outside. He walked to the bathroom down the hallway and scrubbed his hands beneath the hot water from the sink faucet until his flesh was red.

*As the years passed, Charles retreated from the hectic world of politics. He ran his business ventures from a home office. Prohibition had taken his family's legacy, leaving only the brick shell he could see from every west-facing window of the house. The name **LEMP**, staring down at him at night from the tall tower, that glowered over the houses across the street from him, seemed to taunt him to remember...remember it all. But so many of his family were gone now. Billy, Elsa, Frederick, Father and Mother. Everything had changed.*

Before Charles shut away the world, during his later years, he continued to scour art galleries, and made some unusual friends; people who appreciated art as much as he did. They were connoisseurs who knew their Manet's from their Monet's. One such person was Vincent Price, the famous actor of horror films, who was born and raised in St. Louis. His father had run a prosperous candy empire and was well-known throughout the Gateway City. Vincent was closer to the younger Lemp's ages, and was friends with them. Before Hollywood claimed Vincent's time, he and Charles would prowl art galleries and discuss politics. The two had much in common and Mr. Price was a frequent guest at Lemp Mansion; no doubt ogling Charles' impressive collection of paintings, bronzes, sculptures, bric-a-brac, rugs…and a very large display of guns.

Vincent Price. Photo courtesy of Screen World

THE LEMP MANSION WAS ONE OF VINCENT PRICE'S HAUNTS

By Ron Elz of *The Saint Louis Globe Democrat*
(With gratitude to Tom Stockman)

St. Louis Globe Democrat: "By 1983, the Lemp Mansion in South St. Louis had become Vincent Price's idea of the perfect place for dinner: a haunted house that served Beef

Wellington and Lobster Louisville. As the star of "House on Haunted Hill," "The Haunted Palace," and a gourmet cook book author, he would have been right at home.

"It turns out that Price had already been told to make himself at home at the mansion years earlier by beer baron Charles Lemp.

"As fellow industrialists, candy maker Vincent Price Sr., the actor's pop, moved in the same circles as the Lemp boys. The Prices were wealthy but the Lemps of Lemp Beer symbolized mega-money and everybody in the country knew it. Whether you were in Deadwood, South Dakota, New York, New York, London, Berlin, Rome, Paris, Hong Kong, or Calcutta, you could find Lemp beer. It was on ice at Failoni's in Dogtown, Pozza's 7 Steps on the Hill, the Dry Dock in Lemay, and Delmonico's in Manhattan. They were comparable to today's Waltons of Walmart, Bill Gates of Microsoft, the automotive Fords and, of course, the Anheuser-Busch Busch's. Lemp was a national shipping brewery when Coors was a quirky little beer maker wedged in between the Rocky Mountains.

"And it wasn't just beer money. Charles Lemp was a founding director of Phillips Petroleum, and an oil portrait of him still hangs in the oil giant's corporate headquarters in 2011.

"Charles was also a lover of art, and this common passion caused him and the much younger Price to become fast friends. Price had to wipe drool from his lips as he watched Lemp write massive checks for rare works of art without blinking an eye. Lemp traveled extensively, buying treasures as he went. Jaunts to Germany, Italy, England, Spain, India and West Africa, usually resulted in large crates of art arriving at Lemp Mansion. He was an avid collector of European Art Deco (not surprising since Germany, the land of his ancestors, was at the center of the art style). His collection included paintings by Picasso, Salvador Dali and Georgia O'Keefe.

"Price frequently stayed at Lemp Mansion as a guest of Charles, who maintained it as his principle residence after

Prohibition shuttered the Lemp Brewery. Vincent didn't need makeup to turn green with envy as he admired Lemp's rare and wonderful collection. Price was also friends with Charles' favorite nephew, Billy Lemp III, who was more his age.

"Once Price had gone off to Hollywood, Charles Lemp began to drift toward dementia that seemed to haunt a family that was both blessed and cursed.

"Lemp had always been a little quirky. Price knew firsthand, for example, that if he came to stay at Lemp Mansion, there was a mandatory wake-up call at 5 a.m.

"But as time passed, Lemp got closer and closer to going off the deep end. Just like billionaire Howard Hughes, Lemp became terrified of germs and illness. Visitors were required to remove their shoes before stepping through the front door and he refused to shake hands with anyone. He frequently showered five or six times a day, and anything that he touched from outside the mansion, including money, had to be washed before he would handle it.

"His eccentricities increased as he got older. Lemp became more and more reclusive, another form of behavior he shared with Hughes, and closer to home, Springfield, Missouri mogul John Q. Hammons.

"Eventually Lemp stopped receiving visitors altogether, including old friends and family-members. He was also suffering from arthritis; a painfully dangerous malady for a member of a family known to be manic-depressive.

Vincent Price, Sr., was known as the "candy mogul." He created a candy manufacturing business in St. Louis, that rose to be the largest in the world, by 1922. The International Candy Company made the Price's a wealthy family, although Vincent Price, Jr. preferred to call them "well to do." The 9-story building still stands at 4230 Gravois Avenue in St. Louis, though it is no longer operating.

As an interesting collateral affiliation with the Lemps, Vincent Price, Sr. posted an article shortly after Prohibition came raining down on the beer barons of St. Louis. It seems the removal of alcohol was impacting candy as well:

DRY LAWS' EFFECTS ON CANDY EXPLAINED
By Vincent Price, Sr.

The Ogden Standard Examiner (Ogden, Utah)

Chicago, May 24, 1922. Prohibition's effect upon the candy industry was explained at Tuesday's session of the Associated Retail Confectioner's, one of the four branches of the industry holding simultaneous gatherings here, by Vincent L. Price of St. Louis.

"There are there kinds of drinking men," he said, "the one who drank because he had to have it, the other drank to quench his thirst, and the third who imbibed for sociability. The two latter lasses are the one who have been the greatest benefit to the candy business. This is especially true in smaller towns, where the candy store is a sort of social center. The whole family partakes of drinks, and more candy is sold.

"The savings bank was the greatest gainer by the closer of saloons, the soft drinks next, ice cream third, movies and theaters fourth and our industry fifth."

Mr. Price told the retailers that the consumption of confectionary last year was 14 pounds per capita, compared to 10 pounds in the pre-war period.

Charles spent his days primarily in his second-floor bedroom at Lemp Mansion, which is today named for him. The round office atop the atrium Billy had built, when he converted the home into offices, was now Charles private office. It had an adjoining door into his bedroom, and another that lead out onto the 2nd floor landing. As he began to experience discomfort from the onset of arthritis, he may have regretted having the elevator removed.

As time passed, the pain became too much to navigate the stairs. A new bedroom was created for him on the first floor, where he recreated the set-up he had enjoyed upstairs. He moved the dining room furniture to another room on the main floor, and the old dining room became his bedroom. The area beneath the upstairs office, the first-floor atrium, was his new place to handle business as needed, and house the books that had become his vehicle for escaping the endless hours. It also put him close to his father's private bathroom that housed not only a free-standing shower for his frequent ablutions, but also a foot bath.

In the 19th century, people believed that by bathing the feet in cold water you could ward off colds and all manner of illness. This was probably installed during William Lemp, Sr.'s lifetime, but Charles, with his fear of germs, and his need for constant bathing, may have used the small porcelain tub frequently.

The Bitner's had been with Charles before he returned to Lemp Mansion. They were with him at the Racquet Club until he moved back into the mansion, in 1929. They were devoted to him and knew him probably better than anyone alive. It appears they were living out back in the two-story brick building that had been the elaborate two-story Lemp carriage house. The upper floor had been an apartment for the stable man, and it's possible Charles remodeled it for the Bitner's to give them a private home of their own. Old illustrations of the mansion show the Carriage House with chimneys. They would have been mere steps from the basement door to the mansion. It is also probably why they didn't hear the gun shot. Lena Bittner gave her address to the police as "rear" of the mansion, such as a guest house would be.

We do know they were at Lemp Mansion the morning Charles decided to take his life. He would be the fourth, and last, of the Lemp family to choose a gun as his way out of a life that now brought him only anxiety and pain.

****

Charles Lemp pulled the velvet curtain aside and looked out toward the carriage house where he could see the light burning through the upstairs' window. Albert Bittner had locked the basement door a few minutes before, after telling him goodnight around 8 p.m., and walked the few steps through the back courtyard to his home in the old Lemp building. Fog was rolling in from the Mississippi, causing the outside world to shimmer in swirls of distorted shapes. The Bittner's light became hazy, sinking into the white miasma, pushing them farther away.

Thunder suddenly shook the old mansion. Charles watched for lightening forks but the fog made it hard to see. He dropped the curtain and turned to face his room. The house settled in around him; its creaking rafters shuddering beneath each onslaught of thunder. Cerva, his dog, perked up his ears and moaned pitifully as the loud rumblings rattled along the dark hallways and shivered the ancient glass windows of the house.

The 77-year-old-man ran a hand over his wrinkled face and trembled. The pain in his joints was unbearable and he sank into a large chair near the radiator. He felt bone-tired. The dog ambled over to him on stiff legs, and the two aging companions sat near each other as the storm thundered on. Charles ran his fingers along his pet's head, looked into its rheumy eyes, and made his decision.

As the thunder exploded outside the windows of Lemp Mansion on that "dark and stormy night," two other explosions blended into the cacophony of noise.

According to the Coroner's report, and that of the responding officers, this is what happened on the morning of May 10, 1949, at 3322 South Thirteen Street. As you will see, there is some confusion over which floor they are referring to in the Lemp home. For Albert Bittner, the Lemp mansion's basement was the "first floor" of the house. For the officer, the first floor was the floor off the main entrance.

Col. Jeremiah O'Connell, Chief of Police. Complaint #89,650:

had been found dead. Sergeant Frank Zengerling and Patrolman Clarence Junior of this District, in charge of Scout Car #33, report that at 8:40 o'clock this a.m., while they were cruising north on 13th Street in the 3300 block of South 13th Street, they were summoned by Richard Hawes Jr., residing at #15 Picardy Lane, Clayton, Missouri, who informed them that he had received a telephone call at his home, from one Lena Bittner, residing at 3322 rear South 13th Street, who is employed as a housekeeper for Charles Lemp, of 3322 South 13th Street, who stated that her employer

At this time, the above officers were joined by Patrolman Stanley Cunningham of this District, and were directed by Lena Bittner to a first floor rear bedroom at the above address, where they found one, Charles Adam Lemp, 77—Missouri—single— retired, residing at 3322 South 13th Street, lying in bed, clad in a white broadcloth short sleeve shirt, resting on his back, with his head to the west and feet to the east, his left arm lying at his left side and his right arm and hand resting on his right chest, his right hand lightly clasping a revolver. The body was covered to the chest with a sheet and blanket. The officers report that Charles Lemp was apparently dead, a bullet apparently having entered his head just above the right ear and emerged from the left side of the head, about 2 ½ inches above the ear.

The officers report that the bed light was burning and the bottom drawer of a bedside table was partly open and contained an empty leather revolver holster. A .38 caliber spent bullet was found embedded in some feathers, which were forced out of the left side of the pillow on which Charles Lemp was resting, at the left side of his head.

Dr. Joseph Falk, with offices in the Humbolt Building, Grand and Washington Avenue, arrived at the home of Charles Lemp and pronounced him dead at about 9:10 o'clock this a.m.

The afore mentioned revolver, which the deceased man had in his right hand, is a .38 caliber Army Colt Special, serial #485071 and the cylinder contained 5 loaded cartridges and one empty cartridge, the empty shell being under the hammer.

A note written in pencil on manila paper was found leaning against drawers of a roll top desk, in an office located to the south of the deceased man's bedroom, and is quoted herewith:

St. Louis, Mo
May 9th 1949
In case I am found dead blame it on no one but me.

(signed) Ch. A. Lemp

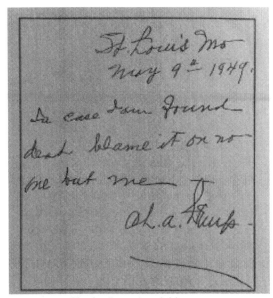

Charles Lemp's suicide note
Courtesy of the St. Louis Medical Examiner's Office

The aforementioned note was found by Richard Hawes, Jr. and turned over to the officers.

Detective Corporal William Ferie and Detective Francis McGovern of the Homicide Squad arrived at the scene and assisted in the investigation.

The body of the deceased man was conveyed in an ambulance of the City Undertaker, accompanied by officer Cunningham, to the City Morgue, where it was found to bear no marks of violence, other than the above gunshot wounds. There was no personal property on the body.

The Officers report that they interviewed Lena Bittner and she stated that she last saw the deceased man alive about 6:00 o'clock last p.m. and was not aware of his death until about 8:00 this a.m. when she was informed of same by her husband at that time.

Albert Bittner, husband of Lena Bittner, was interviewed by the officers and he stated that he had been employed as a servant by the deceased man for the past 32 years and that he last saw him alive at about 8:00 o'clock last p.m., at which time Charles Lemp complained of being "very nervous." Bittner further stated that about 6:30 o'clock this a.m., he left his quarters and went to the kitchen on the first floor of the Lemp home and prepared breakfast for his employer and placed same on a tray on the desk in the afore mentioned office, adjoining the deceased man's bedroom, as has been his practice for years. He stated that at that time, the door leading to the bedroom was closed as usual and that he did not look into the bedroom. He stated that he then went to other parts of the house and about 8:00 o'clock this a.m. he returned to the office for the purpose of removing the tray and dishes, and when he found that the food had not been eaten, he opened the bedroom door to see if his employer had awakened, and at this time, he found him as afore described. He stated he then returned to his quarters and informed his wife of the above and she called Richard Hawes, Jr. who is a friend of the family. Both Lena and Albert Bittner stated that they heard no unusual noise during the night. They added that Charles Lemp resided by himself.

The officers report that when they arrived at the home of Charles Lemp, all the windows were closed.

Edwin Lemp, residing at *Cragwold Farm*, Kirkwood, Missouri, brother of Charles Lemp, later came to the home and took charge of same.

The aforementioned revolver, spent bullet and suicide note, are being held at this station as evidence and will be forwarded to the Coroner's Office in the usual manner.

The here-in mentioned persons constitute the witnesses in the above case and they have been notified to be in the Coroner's Office at 9:00 o'clock a.m. on May 11, 1949.

> Respectfully,
> John A. Buck
> Captain Commanding

Charles Adam Lemp in later years
Photo courtesy of St. Louis Public Library

THE INQUEST

The Coroner's inquest was held the next morning in the Coroner's Court, City of St. Louis, State of Missouri. This differs vastly from the hurried inquest done over Elsa's body in 1920. Joseph A. Quinn, Deputy Coroner, and a jury presided over the questioning before ruling on their verdict. In this case, the jury was allowed to hear the evidence, unlike Elsa's case, where they signed a blank document and were not present at the questioning of the witnesses.

Here are some of the pertinent questions asked regarding Charles Lemp and his death:

Coroner Quinn is questioning Officer Frank Zengerling (3rd District): Q. You found him where? A. In the rear bedroom of the Lemp home at 3322 So. 13th street.

Q. When you arrived there was the room where you found the man in order? A. Yes.

Q. Any evidence of a struggle? A. No.

Q. Any evidence of any windows or doors being forced by any outsider? A. No.

Q. Did you find any note? A. One.

Q. You found this note? A. Yes.

Q. Did you talk to anyone concerning the note as to whether it was his signature or not? A. The signature was identified by his brother Edwin Lemp.

Q. All indications from your investigation pointed to suicide? A. Yes.

Q. Is there anything further you can add to your report at this time?

A. Only the statement of the servants.

Q. Are they here this morning? A. Yes.

Lena Bittner testifies:

Q. Your address? A. 3322 So. 13th Street.

Q. Are you related to Charles Lemp? A. No, I just worked for him. Q. How long have you worked for him? A. About twenty-eight or twenty-nine years.

Q. At any time did Mr. Lemp ever indicate to you in any manner that he desired to take his life? A. No, he never said a word.

Q. Has he been under the care of a doctor lately? A. Yes.

Q. Do you know what he was being treated for? A. He had arthritis.

Q. Do you know the last time the doctor treated him? A. It was about two or three weeks before he went to Arizona.

Q. Were you present when this accident happened? A. Yes.

Q. There have been no strangers in the home? A. No.

Q. As far as you know he had no enemies of any kind? A. No. Q. Other than this sickness do you know of any reason why he should want to take his life? A. No, he never mentioned anything to us.

Albert Bittner testifies:

Q. You worked for Mr. Lemp? A. Yes, since 1916. Q. Did you find his body? A. Yes. Q. Did he ever indicate to you that he desired to take his life? A. No. Q. You knew that he was under the care of a doctor? A. Yes, I took him to the doctor. Q. Did you see the note after the body was found by you? A. No.

Coroner's Inquest, May 11, 1949, verdict read as follows: Hemorrhage due to Gunshot wound in head, self-inflicted in the bedroom of his home 3322 So. 13th Street, on May 10th, 1949, 9:10 o'clock a.m.

SUICIDE

The signatures of the six jurors are found at the bottom of the page, along with the signature of Deputy Coroner, Joseph A. Quinn.

Charles was cremated in the Missouri Crematory and the remains were taken afterwards to the John L. Ziegenhein Funeral Home, 7027 Gravois Road. The ashes were collected by Edwin Lemp.

There were unusual requests made to the funeral home by Charles in a letter received at Ziegenhein Funeral Home dated April, 1941. In the letter, Charles states that immediately upon his death his body should be conveyed by ambulance to the Missouri Crematory. The ashes were to be placed in a wicker box and buried on his farm.

He ordered that his body not to be washed, changed or clothed. He further instructed there were to be no services performed, nor any notice of death or obituary published. He instructed these orders be carried out regardless of any wishes made by his family and that he had already paid the funeral home in full and notified them of these last requests.

Charles Lemp was a man used to being obeyed, and he was in death, as he was in life. Everything was done as he requested, and Edwin dutifully picked up his brother's remains on May 11, 1949, one day after Charles was found dead at Lemp Mansion. The question of "the farm" mentioned has puzzled people for a long time. Searches have not revealed a farm owned by Charles. Richard Lay of the Bellefontaine Cemetery in St. Louis, confided to the author, he believed "the farm" was Edwin's farm, *Cragwold*, a place Charles had visited frequently. Richard said the Lemp's considered *Cragwold* the family farm. It does make sense that Charles would want his ashes buried somewhere where someone who loved him would watch over them.

The papers pounced on the fourth suicide of the Lemp family. Two such headlines were:

CHARLES LEMP ESTATE VALUED AT $3,455,000

CHARLES A. LEMP, EX-BREWER, KILLS SELF AS DID THREE OTHERS IN FAMILY

The St. Louis Dispatch, later on the day Charles died, reported that "the bedroom, in which the body was found shortly after 8:00 o'clock this morning, adjoins the library room, in which, in 1922, his brother, William J. Lemp, Jr. shot and killed himself." It stated again farther down the page "Charles Lemp, a bachelor, was accustomed to eat breakfast in his bedroom, the food being left on a tray in the large library room adjoining. This morning, Mrs. Lena Bittner, the cook, placed the tray as usual and later noticed it had not been touched. She called her husband, who entered the bedroom, and found the body."

There is some confusion here as to the room in which Charles died. The police report stated twice that Mrs. Bittner escorted the officers to a bedroom at "the rear of the house on the first floor." The report also says "a note written in pencil on manila paper was found leaning against drawers of a roll top desk in an office located to the south of deceased man's bedroom." It also states the room "adjoins" the bedroom.

The room in which William Lemp, Jr. shot himself is directly to the left of the main front door. The room next to it, which is today used as the restaurant bar at Lemp Mansion, is also very near the front door, and was originally the Lemp's library. It does not have an adjoining door into the room where Billy died, and that room is to the west of the bar/library room, not to the south. It can hardly be described as a room "at the rear of the house."

The confusion may come from the fact that Charles's office probably doubled as his "library." Someone may have said, "He died in the room next to where William died," and it was assumed they meant literally right next to it, rather than the room a few steps down the hallway.

(Another error lists Mrs. Bittner as bringing Charles' tray and alerting her husband, when it was Mr. Bittner who brought the tray, and checked on Charles later when he found the breakfast uneaten.) In the 1900s, a big paper put out two publications a day: the morning and late afternoon. The afternoon paper would often say FINAL in the header to indicate which paper it was. To "out-scoop" the competition was the name of the game and stories were hastily published, especially ones guaranteed to sensationalize.

Charles Lemp bedroom, Lemp Mansion, today. This is the first room Charles occupied until arthritis made it too painful to climb the stairs. You can see the door to the upper atrium office at the top left. The large door straight ahead leads out to the hallway. He later took the dining room as his bedroom which is directly beneath this room. Photo courtesy of Ron Bueker

Dining Room Charles later used as a bedroom, where he died. You can see the door to the atrium office to the right.

The two atrium offices Charles used, one below and one above.
Photo courtesy Ron Bueker

There is only one room in Lemp Mansion that has "adjoining" doors leading to a room that could be used as an office on the *south* side, and that is the dining room, to the "rear" of the house. It is the last room on that floor, at the "rear." The room Mr. Bittner used to leave his employer's breakfast each morning was the atrium. I believe Charles kept the two large double doors leading to the dining room from the main hallway closed and locked, and had his headboard against them. The police report said his head was to the west and his feet to the east, and that is the only place a bed could be placed to satisfy those coordinates. The small door at the northeast corner of the room, to the right of the fireplace, led out to the side hall, and was close to his father's private bathroom, and the servant's stairs to the kitchen. It made it convenient to the cloistered lifestyle he was now living.

Mr. Bittner would have entered the atrium from the main hall door to leave the breakfast tray. When he returned later and found the food untouched, he opened the door that "adjoins" the dining room to the atrium and found his employer dead.

355

One wonders if Mr. Bittner wishes he had looked around the office as he sat down the tray and seen the note himself leaning there against the roll top desk. Instead, Richard Hawes, Jr. found it when he arrived at the home. Richard is the husband of Marion Lemp, Frederick Lemp's daughter, and is thus, Charles' nephew-in-law. His direct descendent, Christy Hawes Bond, who authored the impressive *Gateway Families* history book of her family, told me she remembered being told Charles died on the first floor.

It was to this same Marion Lemp Hawes that Charles left most of his estate. After the probate was taken, state inheritance taxes removal of $301,572, federal estate tax of $1,172,301, and executor's commission of $170,361, the remainder of Charles' estate is as follows:

$855,158 to a niece, Mrs. Marion Lemp Hawes, wife of Richard S. Hawes, Jr., 15 Picardy Lane, Ladue; $438,725 to each of two grandnieces, Mrs. Anne Marie Brewer and Mrs. Phyllis Olivieri, both of Hempstead, Long Island, N.Y., and $47,335 to a brother, Edwin A. Lemp.

Mrs. Brewer and Mrs. Olivieri are children of Charles Lemp's late nephew Geoffrey Konta, Annie Lemp's son. Edwin Lemp and St. Louis Union Trust Company were executors of the estate. Charles's assets were listed as: Corporation stocks $3,011,210; bonds, $118,920; cash, $236,745; real estate, $47,250; chattels, goods and miscellaneous, $40,352.

An interesting note: On May 10, 1949, sunrise was at 5:26 a.m. Charles' suicide note was dated May 9, 1949. The police record says "the bed light was burning" when they arrived after he was found shot, at 8:00 a.m. It is possible he shot himself during the night, or even before midnight, when he dated his note May 9th. The almanac states the night of May 9th had "fog, thunder and lightning."

Lemp Mansion in the 1940s

There were probate inventory records from Lemp Mansion that were written up shortly after Charles's death. By then, most of the expensive art had probably been removed by Edwin, and possibly Richard Hawes, Jr. Or, it may have been locked away in the vaults to be picked up by Edwin at a later date, but it is more probable it was immediately taken away for safe keeping. The paintings alone would have been worth millions.

The probate records list items found "on the unused 2nd and 3rd floors" of the mansion, underscoring that Charles or the servants were not living upstairs. Some of the "chattels" (property other than real estate) listed on the probate records are as follows:

Main residence:

Lot of firearms consisting of 2 double-barreled shotguns, 1 American Flint-Lock rifle, 1 Moorish Flint-Lock rifle, 4 sabers and swords, 4 fencing foils, 2 percussion rifles, 1 old American rifle.

1   Balance of unimportant chattels in unused 2nd and 3rd floors, comprising walnut cabinet, mirrored wardrobe, 6 Vienna bentwood chairs, brass bed, marble washstand, oak table and oak cabinet, 1 grass rug, 2 old pottery figures, oak rocker, old couch, 3 fire extinguishers, 30 old picnic chairs, lot of iron bed parts, lot of discarded picture frames, etc.

2   Lot of personal clothing and apparel, including no special items of valuable importance,

3   Lot of table linens, bed linens, blankets, comforters and kindred soft goods throughout the house.

----

4   1 old crotch mahogany covered box containing 2 braided hair and gold bracelets, 1 gentleman's Elgin pocket watch, 1 gentleman's signet ring initialed CAL, 1 elk's tooth watch fob, 5 pieces of metal. (These may have been in Charles' old room)

----

1 Mahogany chiffonier

1 oak and leather dining room suite comprising extension table and 9 chairs

1 Bohemian rose crystal decanter

1 Post-Victorian mahogany cabinet

1 four-paneled embroidered Oriental screen (depleted condition)

1 lot of taxidermy specimens, animals and fish

1 Chinese Oriental room rug, size 9' x 12'

A three-piece American Gorham sterling silver tea set comprising tea pot, cream jug and sugar bowl, and two Continental plated

silver candlesticks, and an American silver demi-tasse pot.

    Nine dining room chairs, where nine members of the Lemp family had once sat. It seems the dining room furnishings were all kept together in one room as if Charles still saw them all seated there, like a scene from Dickens' novel *Great Expectations*. The character of Miss Havisham in the story also has a father who is a brewer. She was given great wealth and never married, remaining alone in her decaying mansion. The dining table lay set with dishes and crystal, as it had been for her wedding day that was never realized; the food now moldy and cob-web infested.

The rest of Charles Lemp's inventory included fishing poles, gaffing hooks, tennis rackets, deep sea reel, more guns, boots and hunting clothes—remnants of the active outdoors life he had once known.

The basement contained a dazzling array of crystal ware:

Limoges, Coal port cups and saucers, 5 Bohemian liqueur glasses, 13 Bohemian wine hocks, 12 Continental wine goblets (air twist stems), 11 large Bohemian cut crystal beer glasses, 8 gold-encrusted champagne glasses, 4 Bohemian goblets.

The kitchen contained sterling silver pitchers; julep cups; Spode and Copeland porcelain dinner services; pottery and crystal tableware; pots, pans, and kitchen utensils; spices, coffee, oil and other sundries. Pages depicting the furnishings in the rest of the house were missing. But from this, it appears Charles wanted the first floor to resemble the opulent home he had known. The upper floors had rooms filled with left-overs from his family and his own past life.

The end of Charles Adam Lemp's life can be summed up in the words of Miss Havisham from *Great Expectations*:

"I have been shut up in these rooms a long time (I don't know how long; you know what time the clocks keep here)..."

Chapter Eighteen

Edwin Alvin Lemp 1881 at 1 year old
Photo courtesy of Lemp Mansion Museum

EDWIN ALVIN LEMP
My Brother's Keeper

Edwin Alvin Lemp was the last of the Lemp male children born to William and Julia, but the first child to enter the world at Lemp Mansion. Born on August 28, 1880, Edwin's cries echoed through the second-floor hallways. His six brothers and sisters were anywhere from five to thirteen years older than he. Billy, the oldest, was already a teenager when little Edwin was being rocked to sleep at night by his mother or a nanny. His little sister Elsa was born three years later. It was she he was closest to in age, and thus began a life-long bond between the two.

Edwin at three years old in 1883
Photo courtesy of Lemp Mansion

Following in his brother's footsteps, Edwin went through the school system, and upon graduation, entered into the brewery business. As an older brother departed, he took over their role and moved up in the ranks. He was steadfast and easy-going—the constant anchor during times of chaos.

When William Lemp died in 1904, Edwin was only 24-years-old. It was he and Billy who came running on the day they were told their father had just shot himself in their home across the street from the brewery. Within moments, they were at the locked door of his bedroom and kicked and shouldered the door open. For a young man, who had a more sensitive side than the other Lemp boys, it must have been traumatic and heartbreaking to see his father lying there with a wound in his head and still breathing. For an hour, the boys stayed by their father's side, praying for a miracle, even though the doctors said nothing could be done for him. He finally passed away without acknowledging or recognizing his loved ones around him.

It was Edwin who walked with somber steps to the brewery offices to make the announcement that William J. Lemp Sr. was dead of a self-inflicted gunshot wound. He knew it would be the St. Louis paper's headlines by evening. He asked that the American flag atop the building be lowered to half-mast. Then he, along with Henry Vahlkamp, began calling the other branches and companies owned by the William J. Lemp Brewing Company and delivered the dreadful news to all who were incorporated with them. The flags were lowered at each company.

The next few days after his father's death were a blur. There were funeral arrangements, out-of-town friends, and the care of their mother, who was totally grief-stricken. Myriad business details had to be attended to, not the least of which was their part in the World's Fair, which was starting in two months. Edwin did his part to honor the Lemp's involvement in the World's Fair beer exhibit, which was created in the Tyrolean Alps motif:

The St. Louis Republic: *June 12, 1904.*
Friday evening Edwin Lemp gave a dinner at the Tyrolean Alps in honor of Miss Ehret, daughter of multimillionaire Ehret of New York. Among the guests were Miss Elsa Lemp, Miss Stella Schnaider, Edgar C. Lackland, Jr., and Joseph Buse.

—

Hosting dinners became Edwin's claim to fame. His love of cooking was matched only by his enjoyment in creating entertainments for his friends and family. He hooked up a grill next to his office at the brewery and often cooked steaks for the workers and friends.

One of Edwin's many events made the Entertainment page of *The Saint Louis Republic* on May 7, 1905.

Edwin Lemp Gives Unique Supper for Apollo Club in South Side Rathskeller

"The Apollo Club had one of their novel evenings with Edwin Lemp last week, after the closing season concert. Nobody in St. Louis entertains in quite the original manner that Mr. Lemp has done for some time, probably for the very good and sufficient reason that nobody else has quite the same facilities.

"A year or two ago Mr. Lemp, who is naturally hospitable, and whose facility for giving his friends a rare good time amount to positive genius, fitted up a corner of one of the big rathskellers, down on South Thirteenth Street, and has converted it into a "growlery"* that those privileged persons who are invited into it find unusually interesting. The walls bid fair to become famous, for every time an artist friend—and many from both this city and others—gets inside, he whips out his pencils or his bit of crayon and proceeds to immortalize himself by an original decoration. This may be a bit of sketchy scenery, a cartoon of Mr. Lemp or somebody who is also a guest at the particular luncheon or supper party, or a funny portrait of the artist himself. The smooth white pine of the partitions are fast becoming covered with genuine works of art, all dedicated to Mr. Lemp.

"A spread in the "growlery" is well worth one's while. A big oaken table ornaments the center of the room, surrounded by oak chairs, all put together in the ingenious Continental fashion without nails. A side table and huge gas burner forms the only other furniture, and at this latter the host, who is also the chef, presides. That is the great charm of these suppers—having the dishes made and acquiring a prodigious appetite, while odors of broiling beefsteaks, or English chops float up to the high rafters.

"Mr. Lemp is a cook of exceedingly modest speech where his own abilities along this line are concerned, but the Apollo and those favored few of his women friends who have been invited to the "growlery" wax enthusiastic when they tell of his proficiency. He appears to have natural aptitude for the task, and knows to a "T" when the steaks and broiled mushrooms or onions are at their ripest perfection.

"With all this "toothsomeness" in the way of a repast, and with a host whose entertaining powers along conversational channels are pronounced, a luncheon or a supper at the "growlery" have become much coveted affairs. The Apollos are bidden to come down usually several times each year, and when the hearty supper is over, a piano is brought in, and for several hours their best and most rollicking songs roll out right merrily. Mr. Lemp's evenings have become a regular institution with the Apollo Club.

*A growlery is defined as "a retreat for ill-humor." The description of the "rathskellers" Edwin used sounds like the empty lagering cellars, reached by elevator from the original Brew House.

In later years, when Edwin moved to his country retreat at *Cragwold*, his dinners became legendary. There was a *joy de vivre* about Edwin that set him apart from his brothers. He enjoyed life for the sake of it and reveled in its finest elements of taste and style. To make others happy and include them in his dinners was one of his greatest joys. He traveled extensively, collecting exquisite art pieces that were placed carefully about his home in just the right setting. It was known throughout St. Louis, that Edwin Lemp had a sense of humor, and didn't care a fig what others thought of it.

MISS OVERSTOLZ QUEEN OF THE UNION CLUB BALL

St. Louis Republic: February 15, 1901:
"Miss Marie Overstolz was unanimously chosen queen at the Union Club masque ball last night, and Edwin Lemp, son of William J. Lemp, who was gowned as Cleopatra, was also unanimously chosen first maid of honor, but the contretemps that would have resulted from the mistake was prevented by a member of the Entertainment Committee, who was aware that "Cleopatra" was a man, and forcibly dragged him from his escorts. Last year Mr. Lemp fooled the judges with his "Zaza"

costume. The Judges then chose Miss Natalie Geisel as first maid of honor and Miss Stella Rassieur second maid of honor.

Edwin was also escorted from another formal function, for underdressing this time. He was a member of the fashionable Liederkranz Club, as was his father before him, and Billy. It was an all-German-American club who had some very fastidious rules of dress when it came to their social functions. On one particular occasion, Edwin showed up at the swanky New Year's Eve event dressed only in work clothes, and walked out onto the ballroom floor at 4 a.m. with a member's female relative. What followed, in Edwin's own words, once again, made the papers:

St. Louis Post-Dispatch: *December 31, 1911.* New Year's Eve.

"I arrived at the club early New Year's morning with five other fellows. I knew of the rule requiring full dress, but I did not think it would be in effect at that late hour.

"I met a lady whom I have long known and asked her to dance with me. We were dancing when Moritz Elyssel, president of the club, stopped me, and ordered me from the floor. I didn't argue with him, but stopped dancing at once and walked out of the ballroom.

"The next day I was told by friends that Elyssel had said I took women of questionable character to the club on New Year's morning. As there were no women with me when I went to the club, this made me angry, and I wrote my resignation and sent it to the club."

Edwin A. Lemp   Ancestry.com photo

While Edwin never married, he was often sighted out in society for different gatherings, entertainments, and sporting events with a female companion. He made the society pages on a regular basis, sometimes with his sister Elsa in tow, and at other times with various well-to-do socialites. Some were mere blurbs under small gossip columns, such as:

St. Louis Republic: *August 16, 1903*: Miss Lillian Wahl and Edwin Lemp of St. Louis are visiting in Milwaukee.

St. Louis Republic: February 25, 1902:   Edwin Lemp attended the performance last evening with a man friend.

St. Louis Republic *November 7, 1902*: At the horse competition was Edwin A. Lemp with Miss Tinker, and her parents Mr. and Mrs. Tinker.

The lists continued: "Edwin Lemp escorted Elsa Lemp"; "Edwin Lemp was in attendance with Mrs. Gustav Pabst, and Miss Elsa Lemp at the Olympic last evening"; "Edwin Lemp and his sister, Miss Elsa Lemp in the Lemp Box at the Apollo Club"; Lemp box seats with Billy at various horse competitions; and an announcement in the *Seattle Post-Intelligencer* on July 5, 1896 that "Miss Elsa Lemp and Mr. Edwin Lemp are staying at the Tacoma Hotel."

One did get the impression that Edwin took a more laid-back approach to life than did his high-powered brothers. For Billy, Louis, and Charles, winning was everything—for Edwin, he was just out for the scenery and the fun.

During a large fox hunting party, that was widely covered by the Missouri papers, Edwin seems to pale in comparison to the other riders who were "in it to win it." The women in town rode "like Amazons" according to one newspaper article, but alas, Edwin was more like Ferdinand the Bull sniffing the flowers:

St. Louis Republic *November 3, 1901.* "Yet who ever heard of anybody riding to hounds? Last fall it was, I believe, that Gussie Busch, Edwin Lemp, and one or two others started out right merrily, with a pack and some good riding horses, but they tarried on the way, and their enthusiasm never forced them beyond the first good stiff fence."

Edwin Lemp school days
Photo courtesy of Lemp Mansion Museum

From a young age, Edwin displayed a sensitive side and it showed in his quiet, delicate face, framed with wavy blond hair. He resembled a young Greek thespian whose features differed vastly from the prominent brooding brows of his male family members. According to his April 18, 1900, passport, he was 19-years-old, a "student," and stood "5' 5 ½ tall," with blond hair and blue-gray eyes. The interesting thing about the passport, is

Henry Vahlkamp, the brewery secretary, signs as witness to Edwin's citizenship and that he has known the boy during his lifetime. The Lemp family's other passports usually had family members' signatures bearing witness. Why Henry was chosen, is unclear. He may have simply been convenient that day.

Edwin is still living at Lemp Mansion in 1900, and is the only child remaining in the house other than Elsa. When Julia Lemp passed away in 1906, Edwin bought a suite in the toney St. Regis Apartments at 4954 Lindell Boulevard, in St. Louis. He invited Elsa to share the rooms and she moved in with him. They had two servants in the spacious apartment: Margaret Moore (39), and Barbara Vehu (17). The death of both their parents drove the two siblings even closer together. Elsa was 23 and Edwin was 26. Elsa was now the richest single woman in St. Louis; a position that brought with it fears that no doubt caused her to rely on her older brother for support and comfort.

Edwin Lemp, the easy-going, affable man who enjoyed life, nature, and entertaining those closest to him, was not someone without backbone. His consistency in his integrity, steadfastness and love of his family seems to have put him front and center whenever something needed to be done, no matter how onerous.

It was Edwin who helped kick down his father's bedroom door on the day of his suicide; Edwin (along with his siblings) who was at his mother's bedside when she died of cancer; Edwin who testified at Billy's divorce trial to help his brother's defense against Lillian's allegations of impropriety; Edwin who took care of his little sister Elsa when their parents died; Edwin who was Best Man for his sister Hilda's wedding (even though Gustav had two brothers); Edwin who gave Elsa away at her wedding to Thomas Wright in place of their father; Edwin who came running when news reached him that his sister was shot (and even though Billy was there as well, it is Edwin's name on Elsa's death certificate as the "informant"); Edwin who was asked to handle his dead brother Charles' estate and bury his ashes according to his wishes; Edwin whose name appears on countless documents on his family's behalf, and is awarded the position of curator of his niece Marion Lemp, after his brother Frederick dies. He is even sued because of it:

Allowance for Marion Lemp

St. Louis Republic: *September 29, 1904*: Probate Judge Crews yesterday made an order against Edwin A. Lemp, curator of Marion Lemp, a minor, for $700 for her support in the past, and $100 a month for her support in the future. The order was made on the application of Mrs. Irene V. Lemp, mother of Marion Lemp.

There were bad feelings after Julia Lemp's will was read where Marion Lemp's inheritance was concerned. Frederick, Marion's father, was deceased, and upon his death, William J. Lemp, Sr. had left it to his wife Julia to handle the bequests to their children and grandchildren. Julia must have given Irene and Marion what would have been Frederick's share, if he was still alive. Frederick's widow must have felt they were entitled to more, including the value the brewery had accumulated since her husband's death, not the value at the time.

So, Edwin was sued, and Marion was granted additional money for her support.

Thus, in Julia's will it stated, "To Mrs. Irene Lemp, widow of her son, Frederick W. Lemp, and her granddaughter, Marion, she leaves nothing, stating that she has purchased from them the part of the estate which would go to the deceased son's heirs."

As mentioned earlier, Edwin was also sued, along with his brothers Billy, Charles, and Louis for a stock issue concerning his father from 1902. When William died, the aggrieved party,

Mr. Richard A. Jackson, a Chicago lawyer, came after the brothers, as William's executors, for $403,000.

In an odd twist of fate, Edwin was involved in not one, but two, automobile accidents where a pedestrian was struck, in one case, fatally.

1906 proved to be the year that a dark cloud settled over the Lemp family and stayed there. It was the year Julia Lemp passed away from cancer, Billy's divorce was heating up, the brothers were involved in a major law suit culminating from a faulty transaction of their father's from four years earlier, and Louis Lemp quit the business and moved to New York.

It was also the year that Edwin Lemp was involved in a vehicular homicide while accompanying a wealthy widow in her car.

CHAUFFEUR IS HELD, MRS. NOLKER AND MR. LEMP NOT BLAMED

St. Louis-Post Dispatch: *July 11, 1906.* August Schmitt, chauffeur for Mrs. F. W. Nolker, of 4440 Lindell Boulevard, whose big automobile struck and killed Ernest Shank of 5362 Goodfellow Avenue as he was leaving a street car at Easton and Arlington avenues, Monday night, was found guilty of criminal carelessness by the Coroner's jury Wednesday and was ordered held by the police. The verdict was returned after Mrs. Nolker, Edwin Lemp, son of the millionaire brewer, who was her companion in the auto, the chauffeur and others who saw the accident had described it.

Edward A. Lemp, the young brewer who accompanied Mrs. Nolker on the fatal jaunt, told practically the same story as that related by Mrs. Nolker. He was faultlessly attired in a morning suit, wearing gloves and carrying a soft straw hat. He spoke frankly, leaning forward in his chair, but holding himself in a rather military pose.

"I noticed that two passengers were about to get off the car in front of us," he said, "and when the car started to slow down the chauffeur ran the machine close to the curb.

"The man stepped from the car, paused for an instant and then seemed to run forward a little. His hat blew off and he hesitated, and then took a step back, and we struck him. The auto was only about a foot from the curb and was going about twelve miles an hour. I think not more than 15."

When asked if the chauffeur had tooted the horn or made any other signal of warning, Mr. Lemp said he had sounded the horn.

Other witnesses testified they heard no horn and that the car was moving faster than indicated.

The verdict read as follows:

"We, the jury, find that August Schmitt did not exercise proper precaution in approaching the car from which passengers were about to alight and was running his automobile at an excessive rate of speed; in violation of the city ordinances. Verdict, criminal carelessness."

Mr. Lemp, Mrs. Nolker, and most of the rest of the room left after the verdict was read.

In 1920, Edwin was once again a passenger when his friend's automobile struck a woman crossing a street as they rushed to 13 Hortense Place, home of Elsa Lemp Wright, after being told she had committed suicide. In both cases Edwin was not driving.

With wealth always come contentions, and with the Lemp family, there were many privileges, yet many burdens. For Edwin, the stress of the brewery business, the constant drama of estranged family relationships, and his need to retreat from it all, drove him to the wilderness outside St. Louis, where he created a sanctuary. He named it *Cragwold.*

"Twenty years ago, Edwin A. Lemp, not long out of college, took a tent and went out and pitched camp on a high cliff overlooking the Meramec River, not far from Windsor Springs. Every weekend for three summers he went there, roamed there, occasionally entertained his friends camp style. It is on the site first chosen for his camp that Lemp now gives what are probably the most famous dinner parties in St. Louis. In the years that have elapsed he has dedicated himself to the arts of the host."

This passage, from an old magazine article housed at the St. Louis Library, encapsulates Edwin's first encounter, and love of, the land that became the foundation for his beautiful wilderness retreat: *Cragwold.*

Cragwold in Kirkwood, Missouri
Photo courtesy National Landmarks Association

Edwin began construction on *Cragwold* in 1911, the time his brother Billy began conducting the brewery's business from Lemp Mansion. During the time his dream home was being created, he remained with the brewery while living at St. Regis Apartments. Elsa was now married to Thomas Wright and Edwin felt she was looked after. In 1913, disillusioned with the fast-paced world of St. Louis, business dealings and the pursuit of money, he quit the brewery and moved to his escape that entailed everything he loved: nature, art, fine food and entertaining. With architects Clymer and Drischler, the 3000 feet of land running parallel to the Meramec River, became an amazing fortress of stone and timber. Its observation tower can be seen from the river. Here Edwin could forget the world and find peace and happiness. He was 33-years-old. He had found the land that became his sanctuary only 4 years earlier in 1909, and now he would walk its grounds, inhabit it with friends, and an eccentric collection of birds and animals from around the world. Here he created the world as he saw it...without tragedy and loss.

Edwin had always loved to travel, but after moving to *Cragwold*, he preferred to spend his days creating the elements that made the acreage truly remarkable: a stone bridge here, a pool there, an aviary, cottages. He found his need to leave becoming less and less vital.

"Entering the private road to *Cragwold*, one drives for half a mile through rough, wooded country, left in its natural state. The road winds sharply up and down hill. Then, abruptly, there is a commanding gateway and just beyond, the road runs through the farmyard. Here, too, there has been no attempt at formal landscaping. The farm buildings have been left as they originally were—weathered wood and field stone, tall picket fences, bordered by hollyhocks. Another transition and one comes out into a bluegrass park. The drive winds broadly, edged at its highest point by a group of silver and blue spruce and low cedars. The house itself is set so perfectly in its natural environment that it almost escapes notice.

Cragwold
Photo courtesy National Landmarks Association

"It is one story, made of rough plaster, timbered, set on a high retaining wall of field stone, and almost covered with ivy. The planting around it, which was done under Lemp's direction, is extremely skillful. There are poplars, an occasional larch, spruces and cedars, all so arranged as to give the effect of alleys and courts, each one opening onto a new vista.

"Around three sides of the house are a broad, flagged terrace, or porch, and it is here that Lemp spends much of his time from early spring until late in the fall. He has a view that extends 50 or 60 miles out across the Meramec Valley, including almost the entire circle of the horizon. It never grows monotonous, he says."—Magazine excerpt housed at the St. Louis Library.

Cragwold terrace.

The 11,000-square foot, single story home, is a sprawling estate centered around a large glass-enclosed atrium. The plan mirrors that of Roman architecture where the rooms were clustered around a central open area. It is this area where Edwin lavished his time and money. It began as a kind of conservatory with a few plants and a parrot or two. It evolved, under Edwin's careful design, into a tropical setting for one of the most valuable collections of tropical and semi-tropical birds in the country. Hundreds of birds of every variety fly within the confines of the glass atrium. He made headlines on June 20, 1910, which read: "Edwin A. Lemp of St. Louis set an American record purchase price, by paying $1250 for six white Orpingtons, a male bird and five young hens. The check was exhibited in Kansas City as marking an epoch in poultry deals."

The Romanesque layout of *Cragwold* around a central element.
Here the atrium has been replaced with a fountain.

Around the walls and about the center pool of the atrium were placed special glass aquariums, filled with tropical fish. Each stood upon a carved marble and bronze base. As in Roman-style homes, branching off the main atrium are three or four guest rooms, Edwin's own room, a study, kitchen and service pantries, a living room (that extends the breadth of the house), and the dining room.

LET ME ENTERTAIN YOU

Edwin's haven—the dining room at *Cragwold*.
Photo courtesy of the National Landmarks Association

With Edwin's love of food and entertaining, it is no wonder the dining room of *Cragwold* became his favorite area of the house.

The small grill he created in the adjoining offices at the Lemp Brewery, where he would cook steaks over charcoal and serve them to friends, workers and family, was just the start of Edwin's life-long love affair with culinary events. His reputation for his dinner parties had spread from St. Louis to throughout the country and an invitation to one of his fetes was coveted.

Edwin's dining events were never impromptu. The greatest care went into every detail, from the planning of the menu, to the dishes and linens, and of course, the food selection itself. Customarily, he would invite guests from 10 days to two weeks in advance, and once he decided the guest list, no changes or additions were allowed. His German cook, who was lauded for her culinary skills, would go over every menu selection with Edwin. He then chose the floral arrangements and made sure all was to his exact specifications.

One of Edwin's friends had this to say about the dining experience at *Cragwold*: "I have traveled a good deal all over the world," he says, "and I have nowhere encountered such dinners. They are perfect in every detail. And formal, very formal. They are not necessarily elaborate dinners; usually a soup, an entrée, the meat course, a salad and dessert.

"The soup for example may be a very simple soup but it is perfectly prepared. Of course, Mr. Lemp is very fortunate in his cook. She prepares a great many foreign dishes, even the names of which are unknown in the country. She has no specialties in the ordinary sense, for everything she prepares is excellent."

Edwin was also famous for his Sunday night suppers where dozens of different hors d'oeuvres and several salads were offered. His "kitchen dinners" were another of the invitations close friends awaited. Three or four intimate friends were invited into the kitchen at *Cragwold* where Edwin donned a white apron and cap, and began to prepare a first-rate dinner.

The servants were given a holiday as Edwin set about, with his usual eye for detail, to arrange the linens, silver and china in the humbler kitchen setting. Edwin's specialties for these dinners were scrambled eggs, steak and a special kind of baked potato. At his more formal dinners, the menu might offer veal or venison marinated in sherry for weeks and prepared by a process that required days of effort.

The basement pantry was a veritable storehouse of delicacies. Rows of imported caviars, foie gras, anchovies, pickled mushrooms, brandied peaches, canned goods of every kind. Condiments, such as mustard and pepper were ground by the cook from seed. A New York farm shipped out certain kinds of sauces, and a special kind of pickle came from Milwaukee.

Edwin entertained the greats, and near-greats who came to St. Louis. One such party was for Frieda Innescort and other principals of the Theater Guild Company. Henri Deering, the pianist was a frequent guest, and Edwin kept the baby grand piano in the living room in perfect playing condition.

When asked to recall an evening that stood out in his mind, Edwin recalled the occasion of a dinner to Michel Guiskoff, who was then concert master of the St. Louis Symphony Orchestra. It was a night of perfect moonlight and after dinner Guiskoff took his violin and played beside the pool in the garden, to the distant accompaniment of the piano in the living room.

Edwin's days were spent in relaxed refinement. He would often walk his wooded estate after breakfast. After, he would read or play the piano. Three or four days a week, he drove into the city to his office on Seventh, not far from Olive, to transact his personal affairs, and hook up with old friends. During summer months, he spent a good deal of time in his swimming pool. Flanked on either side by lily ponds and edged with low cedars and tall silver papyrus grasses, it was fitted into the most formal spot in the garden. Due to his hours of basking in the sun, he became almost a mahogany color.

Cragwold driveway (above), and pool –
courtesy National Landmarks Association

When asked if he missed his old life, Edwin answered, "No, it was simply that I saw no need to make more money. It seems to me that this is the curse of America. Everyone is always making more money. I was confident that I could organize my life in the way I wanted to. Of course, I was very fortunate in having an income."

By the 1920s, the estate grounds became home to hoofed mammals from many continents, including South America and Africa. Lemp used his estate as an exotic animal farm and a licensed Federal Game Farm. He bought, sold, and traded animals with many zoos around the country, especially with the St. Louis Zoo. He was consulted on creating several environments for them, including the decorations for the bird house, and the construction efforts for the antelope house, which was completed in 1935.

No flesh-eating animals were kept on Edwin's estate. The 140 acres of *Cragwold* housed such exotic species as buffalo, sacred cattle from India, Siberian Yaks, llamas and Barbary sheep. The fowl population was prodigious, with species from around the world. Twelve varieties of pheasants and two pea fowl strutted about the grounds. Edwin was a member of the Zoological Board of Control, which governed the St. Louis Zoo. His contributions of time, money and animals was well-known throughout the community.

Edwin's love of animals was matched only by his love for refinement and the arts. He had traveled the world and acquired an impressive collection of paintings, bronzes, rare prints and other acquisitions. His attire was always impeccable and his clothes filled several closets of his home. A lover of books, Edwin's library was filled with rarities and every title that interested him. He would often read throughout the night.

As the years went by, he became more reclusive. He belonged to no clubs. The trips to town became less frequent, and his famous invitations for parties and small gatherings tapered off, until finally he was left with his books, his two German shepherds—Mike and Edith—that usually slept with him. His household staff consisted of two butlers, a cook, a maid, and a gentleman whose job was to care for the birds. Each night at 6 p.m., unless guests were expected, the gates of *Cragwold* were closed and locked. He wandered his cherished grounds and watched the animals with interest, stopping to run an aging hand along their feathered or coarse skin.

Edwin kept a companion at *Cragwold*, as his withdrawal from the public became more pronounced. One such gentleman was Tom Dooley (his son was the famous Doctor Tom Dooley), and George Vierheller, the former director of the St. Louis Zoo. He had a fear of being left totally alone. It may have been due to his family's history that now included four suicides. Or perhaps, the ghosts of a haunted history of family tragedy walked the recesses of his mind when the night closed in around him.

John Bopp was the caretaker of *Cragwold* for over 30 years. He was a loyal and constant employee and friend to Edwin. He kept Edwin's secrets, refusing to divulge anything that Mr. Lemp may have confided to him in private. It was perhaps this integrity that led Edwin to bequeath to John Bopp his final wish.

Edwin walked along his flagstone terrace and looked out over the sweeping vistas below him. A watery reflection of the moon hanging above the Meramec River shimmered in the distance. An owl hooted, various cackling and cawing sounds came from the nocturnal birds that roamed his grounds.

He stopped at the stone retaining wall and looked down at the veined, tanned hands he had placed there. He was 90-years-old. He was still surprised at the passing of time...its relentless trek across his world and his memories. His family had spent many happy days here with him at Cragwold. His darling Elsa had been a constant visitor here. He could still hear her laughter and see her shadow slip amongst the trees. The only peace he ever saw ease the wrinkles of his brother Charles's face was when he sat here on this terrace and looked out at the great expanse of Missouri wilderness. His father and mother had not lived to see its creation, but he felt them here with him all the time. Some of their art they collected in their lifetime hung from his walls, and he had cherished pieces of his father's jewelry and clothing. Billy spent much of his time at Alswel, his own retreat nearby, ...at least until...

The memories came flooding back in the moonlight. The dispute over his father and mother's wills by various family members, wanting more than was offered them. So much of the art and family memorabilia was now in his hands---trickled down over the years, as each one of his brothers and sisters died before him. He didn't want what he knew was coming when he died. He was the last of the Lemps. The family name on his father's side would end with him. He would finalize the legacy.

Edwin Alvin Lemp died at the age of 90, on November 30, 1970. He died with his pets and a few treasured friends near his side. To John Bopp, he left his final wishes. And then, the last remaining heir to William J. Lemp's empire, died.

On an isolated plot of the *Cragwold* farm, John Bopp carried out Edwin Lemp's final request. Before him sat the pile he had accumulated from the sprawling house, the gilt frames glinting in the moonlight. Painted masterpieces passed down through the Lemp bequests looked back at him in disbelief as he held the un-lit match in his trembling hand. Ledgers of family history, diaries, and documents, detailing a lifetime of Lemp heritage, waited beneath the gasoline-soaked bindings. It was all here...the lives of William, Julia, Billy, Charles, Frederick, Louis, Hilda, Annie, Edwin and Elsa. The drawings and ideas that created a beer brewing empire and introduced the world to lager beer in 1838, lay bound in weathered ledgers.

With a deep sigh, John Bopp looked down at the pyre—
and lit the match.

Cragwold was added to the National Register of Historic
Places in November, 2009. Today, the estate is privately
owned.

Chapter Nineteen

Myths, Mysteries and Musings

Lemp Mansion's history is as layered as the underground caves that sit beneath it. So many rumors and distortions have been added to her legacy that it is hard to sort the truth from the sensationalized.

For the sake of integrity, this author tried to research, double-check, and validate every piece of information she included within these pages. While she took liberties with the blocks of text in italics, where a story is told about each person, they are based on the trends of the day, tradition and facts known about the person. It is her way of trying to bring the Lemp family to life.

But there are a few stories that persist about the Mansion. The author will address a few of them here, in her own words:

Zeke, the Monkey-Faced Boy

After speaking with Betsy Burnett-Belanger, the tour guide at Lemp Mansion about Zeke, during my initial interview with her, I checked on the dates and information she gave me. The full story is listed in the Hauntings section of the book under her name. I will say here, that I found it probable a boy of his age could have lived in the mansion. There are other reasons, as well, that people may have reported seeing faces at the attic windows of a child with distorted features.

That there were, at one time, eight children of varying ages living at Lemp Mansion is a fact, even though Annie was a teenager by the time Elsa and Edwin were born. Grandchildren also played along the shadowed halls of the attic where rumors of a child with deformities was said to live. According to the stories, people crossing on the sidewalk below said they saw a boy with an odd "monkey-like" face peering down at them from the third-floor window.

After looking out from the windows on the attic floor that are accessible to the Mansion's guests, there seemed to be only one that could be easily seen from the sidewalk below, and that is the dormer window in the Louis Lemp Suite, which looks south toward the DeMenil Mansion. The adjoining room, the Frederick Lemp Suite, has a matching dormer window facing north, but it would have looked down on the park-like grounds of the mansion. The windows in the Elsa Lemp Room also face north. To the east was the Michael Keber house which backed up to the mansion in the 1800s and 1900s.

There is a crawl space that wraps three sides of the attic floor, with small windows spaced every few feet apart. During the time the small Lemp children lived there, it may have been a fun place to play hide-and-seek. It would not be hard to picture Billy, Frederick, Louis, Charles or Edwin, at a young age, pressing their faces to the window glass, distorting their features as they stuck their tongues out at the people below. Today, the doors to the crawl space are locked.

I did come across an entry on Ancestry.com about Zeke. It said he lived in the Mansion until 1940. There are rumors posted over the years of a boy living at the mansion with Charles after William and Julia died. When I contacted the person on Ancestry who had posted the entry, he didn't respond. Betsy Burnett-Belanger said Zeke died at 16 years of age and I traced that to be 1910 when he died.

Another entry said there was another son named Albert Lemp, born after Billy. When I contacted the person, who posted that entry, he admitted it was an error.

The rumor that Zeke was a child of one of the maids is unlikely. All of them I found in the census reports were unmarried, and I doubt Julia would have condoned an illegitimate child under her roof. As we will see, in the next section of the book dealing with the hauntings of Lemp Mansion, there are numerous reports, and EVP's of a young child playing on the attic floor…the irony is, it's often a little girl! Please see that section for more information about Zeke.

Charles Lemp Shot His Dog and Then Himself

This story has long been reported. I asked Paul Pointer, co-owner of Lemp Mansion, during an interview in 2012, if he knew anything about the persisting rumors that Charles Lemp shot his dog and then himself, as he did not want to leave his treasured pet alone.

Paul told me the Bittner's, Charles trusted servants who had been with him for over 28 years, talked to him in later years. They were quite elderly by then, but wanted to visit the home once more. They told Paul that Charles left two notes that morning when he prepared to die. One was addressed just to them. In the note, among other last requests, he told them he shot his dog. He may have asked them to bury it for him.

Nothing was said to Paul about where the dog was shot, or where it was buried. But it seems this mystery has some validity to it. As the police found only one spent chamber in Charles' gun, it may be he reloaded after shooting his dog, or used a different gun entirely. The probate records show the house was filled with guns.

Musing:
Henry Vahlkamp

Throughout the saga of the Lemp family, one name runs through their stories like a fine thread.

Henry Vahlkamp, Lemp Brewery secretary, was listed in almost every Lemp newspaper report, Lemp wedding, divorce, probate court filings, and trial witness summons. His signature is even offered on some of their passports to verify their citizenry. It was his office phone that received the heart-stopping notice from Martha Wetzel, the maid at Lemp Mansion, that she heard a gunshot in William Sr.'s room, and Mr. Lemp was not answering his locked door. It was he who had to inform William's sons that something very wrong was going on at home with their father.

Henry was in his 70's on the day he ushered the Griesedieck's into Billy's office at Lemp Mansion to discuss the sale of the Falstaff logo and trademark. Billy died only two years after that, and it was Vahlkamp that was one of the last three people to speak to him alive.

From the celebrations that echoed throughout the Lemp Brewery offices on the day it became incorporated as the William J. Lemp Brewing Company, to the toasts made for the first railway purchase for a brewery, and the first beer delivered by air, Henry was there. He witnessed the signatures of countless documents, and kept the Lemp's secrets. He attended their funerals and remained loyal until there was nothing left of the Lemp brewing dynasty. He was never mentioned as a beneficiary in any of their wills, but I have no doubt the stock he owned in the company made him a very wealthy man.

He was the unsung hero who had their backs, and was as much a family member as an employee could be.

Paul Pointer, co-owner of Lemp Mansion, shared a rare document with me concerning Henry. It is a short biography written by Mr. Vahlkamp called "Notes on My Life" by Henry Vahlkamp. In it he gives a short synopsis of his life, stating he was born on June 26, 1845 in Lippstadt, Wesphaliar, Germany, the son of an accountant. He attended technical schools and served in the Prussian Army.

"Thanks to my knowledge of languages I soon found work in the New York office of a Lennap textile company. I then went to San Francisco by way of the Isthmus of Panama. The trip from New York to San Francisco took 22 days.

"On the coast of the Pacific Ocean I managed my existence at times through hard, strenuous but honest work as well I could.

"In 1868 the two overland railroads, the Union Pacific and Central Pacific were finished...I spent time in Salt Lake City, Denver, and Cheyenne, all places which were in a state of flux and where, as in the entire region from Nevada to Nebraska, one could see typical scenes of the Wild West. Indians, cowboys, professional gamblers, miners of the worst sort, and highwaymen played major roles in the area.

"I reached St. Louis, my actual destination, in late 1869. In the winter of 1869-70, I was employed in the lumber business of Richard Schulenberg. In June 1870, I had the bad luck to suffer nearly fatal sunstroke in Schulenberg's lumberyard. This incident put an end to my outdoor activity for a long time. Wm. J. Lemp offered me a job in his company; in five minutes we had come to terms and I began my new duties, by Mr. Lemp's wish, the same day that we had come to terms on the job, the salary, etc. I won't go into all the details but the duties assigned to me were not easy.

"The first 12 to 24 months, I had to get up at 4 a.m. I worked until 6 a.m., then had breakfast, rested two hours and was on duty from 9 a.m. for 12 to 13 hours straight except for the midday and evening meal breaks. I worked as a stamp sticker—commonly called "Papsackel" in the brewery lingo—and was in charge of city deliveries, shipping, served as a cashier, did account books and correspondence, at that time 2/3 in German and 1/3 in English, I played a major role in the visits of foreigners, in short, I was a jack-of-all-trades, and nevertheless satisfied with my modest 65 dollars a month.

"The relationship between the employer, Wm. J. Lemp, and this employee lasted 35 years, that is until the death of Mr. Lemp in 1904, remained friendly, yes became more than friendly. In the course of time, Mr. Lemp trusted me with the absolute commercial direction of his company and he didn't omit to add me to the conferences about the technical operation of the brewery business. When the Wm. J. Lemp Brewing Co. was incorporated in the year 1892, he made me secretary of the new company, also I was a member of the board of directors. Later, I held the office of Vice President and remained in that position until the company broke up in 1925. My relationship with Mr. Lemp and the successors at the Wm. J. Lemp Brewing Company lasted exactly 56 years. Since that time, I have withdrawn into private life."

Henry Vahlkamp married twice in his lifetime, once to Helene Hay, and after her death, to her sister Caroline Hay. He fathered 14 children—12 of whom survived. Henry died in St. Louis in 1931.

Passport photo of Henry Vahlkamp from 1920,
two years before he found Billy shot. Ancestry.com

John Lemp The Other Lemp Brewer

The Lemps dominated the beer industry in more areas than just St. Louis. John Lemp, second-cousin to William J. Lemp, Sr., left his mark on Boise, Idaho, in the mid-1800s as well.

Nicknamed "The Beer Baron of Boise," John Lemp had a huge impact on the early development of Boise. He was involved in mining, banking, land development, hotels and eventually became mayor of Boise. In 1852, Lemp came to America from Germany, like so many immigrants after the failure of the 1848 revolution. He made his way to Louisville, Kentucky. Gold brought him to Colorado and later to the Boise Basin. In 1863, Lemp arrived in the Boise Valley, yet the prospects of gold were minimal and he soon found himself buying a brewery on Main Street in downtown Boise City. The story goes that he traded a teacup filled with gold dust for the Idaho Brewing Company on 6th and Main. He later owned several saloons and built some substantial warehouses and business houses, including the Lemp Block on Main Street. He was also a major stockholder in the First National Bank of Idaho and the Boise Rapid Transit Company, and served as president of the bank from 1882 to 1889. Lemp was city councilman for about twenty years and served as mayor of Boise from 1874 to 1876. He was a millionaire several times over. He and his wife, Catherine, had 13 children and lived in a 10-bedroom house on Grove Street.

Karl Lemp, Jr. is a St. Louis resident, and direct descendent of John Lemp. I had the pleasure of having lunch with him at Lemp Mansion, along with his good friend, Tom Stockman, Paul Pointer, Patty Pointer-Brinker, and my partner, Ron Bueker, in December of 2014. Karl is rightly proud of his Lemp heritage and is collecting family memorabilia and stories.

Left to right: Tom Stockman, Karl Lemp, Jr., Rebecca F. Pittman, Paul Pointer, Patty Pointer-Brinker, in the Lemp Mansion atrium. December 6, 2014.

Chapter Twenty
BELLEFONTAINE CEMETERY

At the top of Prospect Road, #30 on the Bellefontaine Cemetery map, sits the Lemp Mausoleum. It overlooks Broadway Avenue, far from the main gate of Bellefontaine on West Florissant Avenue. The winding drive that takes you to this solemn tomb is beautiful and peaceful; the tombstones lining its pathway marked with the names that made St. Louis great.

Lemp Mausoleum – photo Rebecca F. Pittman

Nominated to the National Register of Historic Places, Bellefontaine Cemetery was built in 1849. It is open to all religions, and is a perpetual care cemetery. The architecture of the buildings, mausoleums, and larger monuments display influences from Classical, Romanesque, Gothic, Egyptian, and modern architecture. Noted architects include George Ingham Barnett, Eames and Young, and Henry Bacon.

Bellefontaine is a Level II arboretum, with over 5,000 trees and woody shrubs from over 200 species. They plant 350 to 500 new trees and shrubs each year.

Some of the names chiseled into stone here encompass the span of St. Louis history. Here are a few of the notables:

• William Clark – Co-captain of Lewis and Clark Expedition

• Captain James Buchannan Eads –Eads Bridge builder

• Sterling Price – Missouri Governor & Confederate General

• James S. McDonnell, Jr.—Founder of McDonnell Douglas

• Sara Teasdale—1st Pulitzer Prize winning poet

• Adolphus Busch—Founder of Anheuser-Busch Brewery

• Henry M. Shreve—Designed 1st river-going steamship. Shreveport, Louisiana is named for him.

The list goes on and on, like a Who's Who of St. Louis royalty.

Adolphus Busch tomb, Bellefontaine Cemetery

Richard Lay of Bellefontaine Cemetery was kind enough to give my partner Ron Bueker and I a tour of the Lemp Mausoleum. It was incredibly surreal to stand inside the white marble room and look at the chiseled names of a family I had been learning about for over two years. There is a feeling of finality to it—they were real, they lived, and they died.

Interior of Lemp Mausoleum. Photo by Rebecca F. Pittman

Elsa Lemp Wright tomb   William J. Lemp, Sr.
Photos by Rebecca F. Pittman

Inside the Lemp Mausoleum.

Stained Glass Window in Lemp Mausoleum
Photo by Rebecca F. Pittman

Richard Lay informed us the Lemp Mausoleum is the largest in Bellefontaine Cemetery. The stain-glassed windows (German inspired) send a soft effusion of ochre-toned light throughout the marble room. The window's pale purple lilies against an olive and leaf-green background, with golden yellow medallions is stunning.

The Lemp tomb is also the only mausoleum in the cemetery wired for electricity. Richard Lay related a rather amusing story concerning this resting place and Edwin Lemp, who acted as the caretaker for the tomb, as his family members each passed away before him.

It seems that someone visiting the tomb, possibly a person working on repairs or cleaning, left an electric heater, plugged into the electricity there, running for over a month. They had obviously departed without shutting it off, bolting the door behind them. The first Edwin learned of it was when he received the electric bill for the mausoleum for an astronomical amount. He marched over to the tomb, and not only turned off the heater, he cut the wires to the entire electrical system.

The button for electricity can be seen here on the marble column inside the tomb. Photo by Rebecca F. Pittman

The names of the Lemp family interred in the Lemp
Mausoleum in Bellefontaine Cemetery are:
William J. Lemp, Sr.
Julia Feickert Lemp
Jacob and Elizabeth Feickert
William J. Lemp, Jr.
William J. Lemp, Jr. III
Lillian Handlan Lemp
Elsa Lemp Wright
Patricia Lemp Wright (Elsa's stillborn daughter)
Edwin A. Lemp
Louis Lemp
Agnes Walsh Lemp
Edwin L. Pabst
Louise Lemp Pabst (daughter of Louis and Agnes, married her
cousin Edwin L. Pabst, son of Hilda and Gustav Pabst) There
are 17 empty vaults in the mausoleum.

As mentioned earlier, Lillian asked to be interred in the
Lemp tomb. Edwin said "Yes." Charles Lemp was cremated
and his remains buried elsewhere.

Richard Lay told me that William Lemp, Sr.'s vault
placement was not an accident. He lies next to his beloved
Frederick "where his heart would be closet to his son's."

Photo by Rebecca F. Pittman

There is a suspicion that the unnamed crypt sitting in the
upper left-hand corner of the tomb, just above Elsa's still-born

baby, may have been for Zeke. It is odd that it is surrounded by crypts with chiseled names.

If you are in St. Louis, don't miss the chance to see this beautiful cemetery. The winding roads through hills, statuesque trees, and marbled head stones is truly a time-altering experience. It is still an operating cemetery.

My deepest appreciation to Richard Lay for taking his time to talk to us and show us this beautiful tribute to an amazing family.

Chapter Twenty-One

THE CAVES

The labyrinth of cave tunnels running beneath the streets of Cherokee and DeMenil were more than just a place to store beer as it lagered, or as a unique novelty for parties and recreation—it was a place of history in the rugged outback of St. Louis.

When Adam Lemp peered into a rough opening in the rock in 1845, and discovered a cave system that could maintain a temperature cold enough to store his beer, the beginnings of the Lemp/Cherokee Cave was born. The area was wilderness, sitting just outside the city limits of St. Louis proper. The Mississippi River wrapped around it in a soft curve that was later called Chatillion's Bend in honor of the large house sitting atop the small hill near the cave entrance.

Adam brought in workmen who expanded the cave, eventually cutting a large hole in its top to facilitate dropping ice from the Mississippi into the cavern to reduce the constant temperature of 50° to around 35-40° year-round. Only 20% of the vast underground cavern was excavated, leaving the rest unaltered.

In 1850, Adam was joined in the "neighborhood" by a fur trader named Henry Chatillon. He built a simple farmhouse on Arsenal Hill close to Adam's cellar house that Lemp built atop his new cave storage area. In 1856, Dr. Nicholas DeMenil purchased the land and began renovating it. He took Chatillon's small farmhouse and added several rooms and a portico. To the east, he developed a beautiful garden that overlooked the Mississippi just as it wound its way around toward the west.

DeMenil Mansion in 2014. —Photo Ron Bueker

The caves attracted other brewers who saw the built-in refrigeration they provided. In 1865, DeMenil was approached by the owners of the small Minnehaha Brewery, Charles Fritschle and Louis Zepp, who leased the southwest corner of the property and built a small, two-story wood frame brewing house. DeMenil had been using the cave beneath his house as storage for perishable items. Here was a way to make a tidy income leasing the cave to the brewery. Where Adam's was merely a rudimentary structure designed to facilitate a place to store beer, the Minnehaha operation was brewing its beer *at* the site.

Lemp Brewery delivery wagons haul down Cherokee Street at Broadway, along the north side of the plant. On the hill near the center of the photograph is the DeMenil Mansion.
Photo courtesy of the DeMenil Mansion

Unfortunately, the Minnehaha Brewery went out of business two years later. During the two years it had operated, it was using another part of the same cave Adam Lemp was using. A wall was erected to separate the two entities. Later, when William J. Lemp, Adam's son, decided to build a brewery over the cave instead of hauling beer from his father's store on 2nd Street, he struck a deal with DeMenil. If he would allow William to run pipelines from the new brewery to the mansion Lemp was renovating a few feet to the north of him, William would share the hot and cold running water he was piping in.

Another labyrinth of pipes carried beer to Lemp Mansion, giving the family beer on tap whenever they wanted it.

Dr. Nicholas DeMenil (left) was part of St. Louis' French-Catholic aristocracy. He regarded his neighbor, William Lemp (right) as a "beer-swilling, sausage-eater." Lemp, a German-Lutheran who was far wealthier than DeMenil, had little regard for the "snooty" side of St. Louis and Frenchmen in general. The best that could be said of their relationship was that they generally ignored each other. The fact that DeMenil operated the Minnehaha Brewery directly across the street from Lemp's brewing plant merely served to make an already frosty situation downright icy. However, pragmatism won out, and the pipelines for the water and beer were installed through DeMenil's half of the caves.

When artificial refrigeration was installed in the late 1870s, the cave was no longer needed to house the beer barrels. The Lemps, always on the innovative edge, decided to turn the cool underground caverns into a play area. Just below Cherokee Street, down a metal spiral staircase, they built a theater, complete with floodlights and seating. Fake walls resembling the rough cave stone were made to store scenery and act as "wings" from which actors made their entrances and exits.

Stairs leading to theater area in Lemp Cave. Photo courtesy of Jordan Woerndle of www.trickykegstands.com

Two hundred feet east of this entertainment was a large cement reservoir that had been used for the beer. It now became a heated swimming pool, using the hot water from the brewery. A ballroom was made from the more cavernous, finished areas. No one in St. Louis could boast such an underground playground built by the Lemps. Some of Edwin's famous "growlery" dinners were staged here. Many of the paranormal reality shows have shot footage from the cave tunnels, showing remnants from the Lemp's party days still standing; shadowed and decomposing, but refusing to fade completely into the past. The only remaining entrance into this area is locked; the others sealed, or long gone.

Lemp Cave swimming pool. Photos courtesy of Jordan Woerndle of
www.trickykegstands.com

Lemp Cave Ballroom & location of Edwin's "growleries."

While the public entered the cave system, upon invitation, down the winding stairs, the Lemps traveled from their mansions via a quarried tunnel linking the house to the cave system and the lagering cellars of the brewery. This passageway was also used by the Lemps to travel to work during inclement weather, or, as a means to avoid the prying eyes of the public. Both Billy and William's homes had a spiral staircase linking their properties to the cave labyrinth.

Prohibition saw the end of the Lemp's use of the cave. The spiral staircases, in some places, were broken apart, their metal rungs demolished for safety reasons. Most entrances were sealed shut. But the side of the cave beneath the DeMenil Mansion was not yet finished.

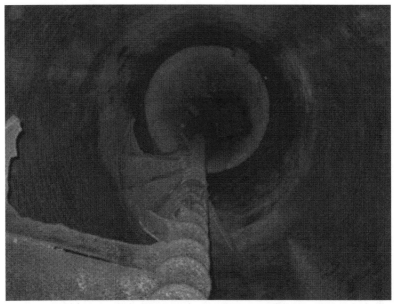

Broken steps to the spiral staircases. Photo courtesy of Jordan Woerndle of www.trickykegstands.com

Sometime earlier a fire broke out in the cave. Though one was reported in the Bottling Storage House in 1902, it is doubtful the firehoses, still seen today in a blackened area of the cave, remained from that fire. If it did, then the fire broke out in the wood-paneled room near the swimming pool and spread up through a shaft leading into the Storage House, or vice versa. There are remnants of old fire hoses still lying about the cave floor, and blackened walls can be seen around a door leading possibly to the refrigeration area of the cave.

(See photo on following page. Photo courtesy of Jordan Woerndle of www.trickykegstands.com)

In November of 1946, a pharmaceutical manufacturer named Lee Hess saw the cave's potential as an entertainment venue of a different sort. He would construct a "show cave" and charge the public to come and see its wonders. He bought the old DeMenil house and the rights to the cave belonging to the defunct Minnehaha Brewery.

Photo courtesy St. Louis Public Library

Calling his new attraction "Cherokee Cave," Hess built a parking lot and museum on the grounds. The cost to convert the cave and make it a navigable playground nearly cost Hess his fortune. He and his wife moved into two rooms of the DeMenil Mansion, and his partner, Albert Hoffman, who managed the cave, moved into the other. The rest of the mansion was unlived in.

Photo courtesy of DeMenil Mansion

Finally, in April of 1950, the exact time Lemp Mansion opened its doors as a boarding house, "Cherokee Cave" was opened for business. The tour was impressive. The public could view underground wonders that Hess had given colorful names: Petrified Falls, Wishing Well Lake, and the Spaghetti Room where slender stalactites hung from the ceiling like tendrils of pasta.

The cave ran for ten years. In 1960 the Missouri Highway Department purchased the cave and land around it. There was a new highway going in, and the DeMenil property, house and cave were in the way. And so was the house at 3322 South Thirteenth Street called Lemp Mansion.

The cave was lost, but Hess refused to stand by and watch the historic mansion fall beneath a wrecking ball. He, along with a handful of other determined citizens battled to keep the historic home intact. They finally succeeded, and in an uncommon act for a government-run agency, the enormous highway cut a swath around the two mansions. The Landmarks Association played a big part, purchasing DeMenil for $40,000. Later, in 1975, Richard L. Pointer and his family rescued Lemp Mansion again, oddly enough, for the same price.

In 1964, the highway department demolished the cave entrance and museum. It was assumed the cave had been filled in. In the mid-1960s, curious spelunkers found a way into the underground cave and found large portions of it intact. They reported seeing the rooms created by the Lemps, long passageways, rotted beer casks, and rooms finished with brick and stone. The old pool was still there, filled with mud. A metal railing leading down to the old theater still remained and the room that once echoed with the sounds of laughter and theatrical orations could still be seen, the fake scenery walls lying in rubble.

The cave had one last gasp of glory when, during Hess's excavation of the area for his wondrous show attraction, he came across a number of prehistoric bones, including those of a Pleistocene peccary, a predecessor of today's wild boar. The museum of National History in New York sent out a team of paleontologists to help with the digging. A few of the bones were given to Hess to showcase in his museum.

Entrance to Lemp Mansion property from cave being sealed in 1980.
Photo courtesy of St. Louis Library

Today, the cave entrance leading from the Lemp Mansion property is sealed. The underground lagering cellars can be reached via elevator from the brewery, but only a chosen few are allowed to view them, for safety reasons. In years past, the area was used for a Haunted House venue, and people reported they saw and heard things not on the original attraction's menu. It seems the Lemp's may still be walking their cherished labyrinth of stone passages, 36 feet below the surface.

Chapter Twenty-Two

LEMP MANSION

The story of Lemp Mansion begins with its creation in 1868. It was one of two homes built on the 5-acre tract of land Adam Lemp purchased to build his cave storage system. The other mansion was created for William Lemp's stepmother, Louise Bauer Lemp, Adam's third, and last, wife. William and Julia lived in the home with their young family while Julia's parents, the Feickerts, lived in what is today Lemp Mansion. The houses were cata-corner across the street from each other, the Bauer house at 3335 Carondolet, and Lemp Mansion at 3322. Billy and Lillian later used the Bauer house as their residence after their marriage, in 1899. (Carondolet was changed to Thirteenth Street, and later, to DeMenil Place, and 3335 was changed to 3343.)

When Jacob Feickert could no longer handle the mortgage on Lemp Mansion, William bought him out and moved his growing family and wife in. But not before he did some major renovating. His children now numbered 6 and they would require more servants to facilitate the needs of the family. For this reason, the attic was remodeled to include three large rooms, a bath and open area for the servants. Three cedar closets were installed to house the gowns, furs and seasonal clothing.

Servant's room in attic before remodeling. A closet is to the left, a door leading to the attic crawl space is to the right. Today this is the Louis Lemp Room. Photo courtesy of Lemp Mansion

If you look closely at the walls of the staircase leading from the 1st floor to the 2nd floor, you can see the old joist openings in the brick where there was once a floor. When William enlarged the house, he removed a floor to make a winding staircase that was easier to navigate than the old straight one with narrow, sharply angled rungs.

While interviewing Paul Pointer for this book, he told me that during the renovation work on the mansion they took down the old plaster and found the brick wall in the stairway area. "We decided to leave it as exposed brick," he said. "I liked the look of it."

Photos are looking down from the 2nd floor landing. You can
see the old floor joist indentations in the brick.
–Photo Rebecca F. Pittman

Three massive vaults were constructed at the rear of the
home, measuring 15' wide, 25' deep and 13' high. They were
fireproofed with glazed tiles and a concrete floor and ceiling.
These formidable rooms would house the Lemp's growing
collection of art and priceless keepsakes. When the home was
converted into brewery offices in 1911, the vaults housed the
records and revenue of the William J. Lemp Brewing Company.
During the boarding house years, from 1950 to the 1970s, the
vaults were kept locked, probably by Edwin. When the vaults
were opened years later in the 1970s, many of the mansion's
fixtures were still safely stored there. Original doors, chandeliers
and fittings sat untouched and unharmed. Today, the vaults are
used for three purposes: a Museum and Gift Shop on the first
floor, Offices on the 2nd floor, and restaurant food storage on
the basement level. The attic utilizes the roof of the vaults as a
wonderful balcony patio that looks out over the Mississippi
River, Saint Agatha Church, and ironically, the Anheuser-Busch
Brewery.

Julia's parents, Jacob and Elizabeth Feickert, also lived with the Lemp Family until their passing, in 1892. Today, their room is called the Charles Lemp Room. From that time until the home became brewery offices in 1911, it was considered an opulent residence, replete with every new convenience that heralded the Gilded Age of St. Louis. The street was known as Mansion Row. When the city's businesses began encroaching on the stately homes, the millionaires moved to the Central West End and created newer subdivisions of jaw dropping estates.

LEMP MANSION: ROOM BY ROOM

When you enter through the vestibule of Lemp Mansion, there is an immediate sense of time traveling back to the past. The integrity of the mansion is intact, thanks to the monumental efforts of the Pointer family to maintain the home's original motif. During the renovation of the home, after its period as a boarding house, the Pointers found original hardwoods, wall colors, murals and hinges buried beneath layers of paint. Through these discoveries, they were able to bring Lemp Mansion out of the shadows of the past, restore the original features, and breathe new life into her bones.

I visited Lemp Mansion for the second time in December of 2014, and thus many of the photos show the lovely holiday decorations of the home. Others are from my original visit in May of 2012. My partner Ron Bueker shot many of the images as well. You can visit the Facebook page, The History and Haunting of Lemp Mansion, to see many of these beautiful rooms in full color photos.

View from stairway landing to front door. The open door to
Billy's office is to the right of the photo. To the left (out of view) is
the door to the double parlor. Note the double radiators and front
doors, all original to the house. Christmas, 2014
Photo courtesy of Rebecca F. Pittman

Hallway from front door leading past the bar (through door on the left next to the couch) to the dining room at the back. A built-in display case of Lemp memorabilia, to the right, takes advantage of the open space that was once stairs to the basement, and later, an air-lift elevator. Photo courtesy of Rebecca F. Pittman

The twin doors leading into the front hallway from the outside are original to the house. Dick Pointer, son of Richard Pointer, who helped purchase the mansion and began the restoration process in 1975, told me the glass in the right panel of the front door is authentic. The pane on the other side was damaged and replaced. The crackle effect you see in the original was created by using a process that involved using glue made from horse hooves. The glass was coated with the mixture and then baked in an oven. As the glue baked it made a snapping sound, like walking on bubble wrap. The finished product was this beautifully intricate design you see in the door's glass today. Every pane was one-of-a-kind.

Front door of Lemp Mansion with crackle glass panes.
Photo courtesy of Rebecca F. Pittman

Lady's Parlor/Billy Lemp Brewery Office

When Lemp Mansion was first constructed in 1868, it followed the dictates of the Victorian era as far as lay-out and function. A small parlor was usually to the left of the main entrance where the lady of house would receive female guests and have intimate gatherings. These rooms were often feminine in design and color, with parlor chairs, couches, tiffany-style lamps and ornate bric-a-brac. The Lemp daughters would have received male suitors here, under the scrutiny of the elder Lemps. A small table was usually set just outside the door to this room, holding an elaborate silver tray to receive calling cards.

Lady's Parlor/Billy's Office. Photo Rebecca F. Pittman.

The dainty pale mint green striping of the wallpaper is complemented by soft pink lace draperies. Above the painting rail the frieze work is original and showcases medallions of brilliant blue with soft green fern work.

During the Gilded Age, nature was brought inside and highlighted in wallpaper, fabric and paintings. Small stuffed birds and animals were placed beneath glass domes and set atop marble tables.

Lady's Parlor/Billy's Office West wall.

A portrait of the Lavender Lady hangs between the two windows facing the street. Twin radiators sit beneath the windows. This is where Billy Lemp conducted his business affairs when the room was later used for brewery business.

Lavender Lady portrait by May Alsop hanging in the Lady's Parlor.
Photos by Rebecca F. Pittman

Close-up of the detailed marble fireplace in Lady's Parlor.

Today the Lady's Parlor/Billy's Office is used for dining at the Lemp Mansion Restaurant & Inn.

Double Parlor

Across the hallway from the Lady's Parlor, just right of the main staircase is the entrance to the double parlor. This room would have been used for formal gatherings and the important events of the family. Annie Lemp's wedding reception was held here, William Sr. and Billy's funerals, and those of Julia's parents, Jacob and Elizabeth Feickert. Typically, in the Gilded Age, if one did not have a formal ballroom, parlors served as the entertainment venue by removing the furniture or pushing it to one side to allow dancing.

The double parlor at Lemp Mansion is, in a way, the reason the home has been restored to its elegance today.

Richard Pointer, the patriarch of the Pointer family, was at one time working on a road crew near the DeMenil Mansion. His son, Richard L. Pointer, Jr. (Dick) had always wanted to turn an historic landmark into a restaurant. Richard Sr. was working one day at the end of DeMenil Place and happened to glance over at the old Lemp home. It was a flop house at the time and in run-down condition. From his vantage point at the end of the road he could see the place was actually much larger than it appeared from the front.

The side of Lemp Mansion on the north. The ad is painted on the exterior brick wall of the vault room. Photo byRon Bueker.

The house went fairly deep into the wooded property. He had heard rumors the place was haunted. It was considered by St. Louisans to be "the haunted house on DeMenil Street," but he shrugged it off.

According to Dick, who related this story to the author with a grin on his face, he and his father Richard went one day to the door of the mansion and were greeted by the person running it as a boarding house. Richard had already taken Dick aside and told him his part to play. He was to pretend to be mute, and to let his father do the talking. Richard would say he was looking for a room to rent for his son, Dick.

When they stepped inside the entry, Dick surreptitiously looked around as his father engaged the lady in conversation. The first thing he noticed was the fireplace he could see through the open parlor door.

The room was being used as a boarder's bedroom at the time. Dick was surprised to see the mantel was intact, although covered in paint. It looked like some form of carving was beneath the layers of latex. As a historian, he knew the first things to be stripped from a house were the mantels, as they were usually made of marble or expensive hardwoods. Yet here they sat.

When they left, he told his father that if those fireplaces were intact, the rest of the place may be in pretty good condition, although in need of extensive renovation. They turned to the rest of the Pointer family, nine children in all, who pitched in the needed amount to buy the place: $40,000, ironically the same amount the Landmarks Association paid to save the DeMenil Mansion from falling prey to Interstate 55's construction in 1960.

During the time the mansion was converted into offices for the brewery the parlors were used for the accountants, and as a waiting area. If you look inside the fireboxes of the two fireplaces in that room, you will see they were once small vaults. The hinges for the doors are still visible. This was probably for petty cash and important documents, deeds, etc.

When the brewery operations closed in 1922, after Billy's death, Charles renovated the home and returned it to its former glory. He moved back into it as his permanent residence in 1929. It was at this time, he may have removed the elevator, reinstating the grand staircase that accessed the basement and 2nd floors. If not, then it was taken out during the boarding house era in 1950, possibly due to its age or not complying with safety regulations of that time for a commercial establishment. Dick Pointer told me it was a staircase again when he and his father first peeked at the interior in 1975. As Charles Lemp was living on the first floor in his final days, I tend to believe the elevator was gone, or he would have remained upstairs in the bedroom area, using it to help with his arthritic condition.

During the boarding house period, a partition wall split the parlor into two rooms to act as bedrooms. You can see the slight indentation in the room's gold molding near the ceiling, about midpoint. When the Pointer's removed the wall during the renovation, a large portion of canvas covering the ceiling came down. Paul Pointer said it was very common in those days to paint on canvas and then adhere it to the ceiling or walls. The problem with this was, one side of the ceiling, nearest the street side, had the remains of a mural, the other side of the ceiling was painted green.

They removed the green paint and the rest of the mural began to appear. It showed striations from the canvas glue and was in bad shape.

Mural before refurbishment.

Ceiling mural after St. Louis artist Claude Breckwoldt restored it. (r)Detail of African mahogany fireplace column in parlor.

One of two fireplaces in the double parlor made of hand-carved African mahogany. The fire box was used as a small vault during the brewery era. Photo courtesy of Rebecca F. Pittman

The double parlor is most noted for its twin fireplaces carved from rare African mahogany. The detailing is intricate and showcases the Lemp's love for artistic creation, as well as travel. Charles was especially fond of Africa and made many trips to that continent.

William Morris, a designer who greatly influenced the Victorian period with his tapestries, wallpaper, fabrics, furniture, and stained glass, was perhaps best known for his wall coverings featuring finely crafted weavings of leaves, flowers and repeat patterns in pastel, as well as the popular bright reds, blues and greens of the era. The Pointer family have brought Morris' simple stripes and color themes alive to truly replicate the time when William and Julia lovingly decorated their new home.

Today the room is used for banquets, but just to make sure you don't forget where you are, a Falstaff charger smiles down at you from its place above a hand-carved art niche. The room is covered in soft green hues to complement the ceiling mural. The ball light fixtures and ceiling medallions are original to the home.

Ball light fixture in parlor with the beautiful mural behind it. Photo courtesy of Ron Bueker.

THE ATRIUM

The Gilded Age was also known as the Victorian Era. This was a time when nature was revered and the colors seen throughout the home mirrored the outdoors. Paints were ground from plants, bark, and berries and hence, the colors found in fabrics and wallcoverings were usually seen as ochres, russets, reds, greens, taupes, and browns. Boston ferns and large towering plants were found in almost every corner.

Lemp Mansion Atrium. –Photo courtesy of Louise Meyer.

The Lemps, with their love of the outdoors and animals, built a round atrium at the back of the house when they expanded the home in 1876. Its tile floors are still seen there today in their mini-mosaic motif. Here the Lemps filled the room with plants and cages of birds. The many windows let in an abundance of light. A bubbling fountain sat in the center of the room. Its copper tubing can be seen in the tile flooring.

Artist May Alsop, who painted the Lavender Lady portrait in the Lady's parlor, also painted the atrium during the renovation to bring back the feeling of a lush world of plants and birds.

Two folding doors with the horse glue cracked glass panes open into the parlor from the atrium. During the Lemp funerals plants were brought into that room from the atrium to add a sense of serenity and beauty.

Two other doors lead out into the hallway, and into the dining room, respectively. A final door leads outside to a metal spiral staircase that takes one down to the courtyard.

Metal spiral staircase to courtyard.
Photo courtesy of Rebecca F. Pittman

The property was purchased in 1975. Two years later the Pointers opened the basement as a restaurant. In 1980, they expanded to the newly renovated main floor, with offices and storage on the 2nd. In 1990, it became a full-service restaurant and Inn, complete with St. Louis' best acting troop, JEST Murder Mystery Co., putting on Mystery Dinner Theaters. You can see the sign at the front of the house pointing to the stairs that lead to the basement entrance for the theater productions.

The Bar/Library

The large double parlor was once home to the restaurant's bar. It was later moved across the hallway to the room sitting east of the Lady's Parlor/Billy's Office. It's most striking assets are the two stained glass windows depicting Billy and Lillian Lemp. The brilliant glass flanks the room's fireplace and warms the polished wood fixtures with its brilliant tones.

Sitting above the fireplace is a sportsman's trophy: a very large tarpon, mounted on a wood plaque. The lucky fisherman's name is engraved on the brass plate at the bottom. One would think the honor would fall to Billy, William Sr., Louis, Edwin or Charles. In fact, the name adorning this prize catch is Lillian Lemp.

Lemp Mansion bar. Photos courtesy of Lemp Mansion.

Lillian's tarpon.
Photo courtesy Ron Bueker

Stained glass windows of Lillian and Billy in the bar.

This room was originally the Lemp's library, and primarily William's domain. While bookcases housing the latest works of the 19th century, as well as classics and rare first editions would have lined its walls, there was probably a desk here as well where the patriarch of the house held sway. Libraries of that era sported high-backed "Dickens" chairs, usually upholstered in rich red or brown leather. An inkwell, blotter and paper would have adorned a polished wood desk. Before electricity, an oil lamp or two would sit near chairs for reading light. Soon, it was replaced by gasoliers, and finally, the lightbulb. It may have been in this room William met with the anxious Gustav Pabst as the young man tried to convince Mr. Lemp to allow him to have Hilda's hand in marriage.

The bar today is a warm welcome to the Lemp Mansion guests. Colorful bottles adorn myriad shelves, and a local ball game is usually tuned in on the television that sits in the east upper corner; the only contrivance that gives a nod to the 21st century in this pub-like atmosphere. You can order sandwiches, appetizers, and dinner, if you wish, from the cozy tables positioned against the south wall.

WILLIAM LEMP'S PRIVATE BATH

East of the bar is William Lemp, Sr.'s private bathroom. It is a luxurious retreat with tall diamond-paned windows, a fireplace and marble detailing. A giant Italian black-and-white marble free-standing tub and shower dominate the center of the room. William had the amazing fixture imported from an upscale Italian hotel and installed in his home during the remodeling. It was the only one of its kind in St. Louis.

Not to be outdone, a sink with glass legs stands near the north-west facing window. Next to it, sitting low to the floor is an original foot tub. The room's water closet is enclosed within a marble cubicle.

This was William's domain, a place to escape from the hectic demands of his life. His personal barber chair once sat beneath the north-east facing window. Here he would receive custom haircuts and shaves, the room becoming perfumed with the scents of pomades. This room was locked during the boarding house era and today serves as the Ladies Room for the Restaurant and Inn.

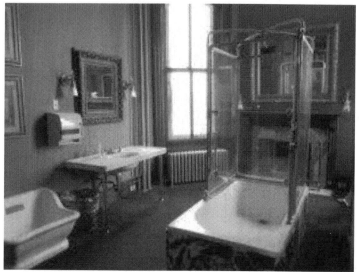

William Lemp, Sr.'s bathroom. Photo by Ron Bueker.

THE DINING ROOM

The dining room at Lemp Mansion is truly a work of art. The inlaid-parquet floors, floor-to-ceiling windows, hand-painted ceiling, and William-Morris style wallpaper make this room authentic to the Gilded Age motif.

The focal point of the room, however, is the magnificent fireplace with fired green glaze tiles. In exquisite detail, the features of a Bavarian hunter, country maiden, and hunting dogs come to life; images dear to the Lemp's heritage. Time spared this glistening craftsmanship, as it looks today as it must have over 100 years ago.

The chandelier in the room is the original and dates back to the mid-1800s.

Close-up of glazed tiles on dining room fireplace. Photos by Ron Bueker

Dining room fireplace with Bavarian hunting scene. Photo by Rebecca F. Pittman

The warm greens of the wallpaper and deep brown woods give this room a cozy feeling. You can almost hear the laughter and sounds of clinking glasses as William, Julia, Jacob and Elizabeth Feickert, and 8 children of various ages gathered here around an enormous dining table. Here the family caught up with each other's busy lives, shared gossip, and talked of the brewery business. Young gentlemen suitors would nervously join in the conversation, while children, and grandchildren in later years, would celebrate birthday parties.

A door east of the fireplace leads out to the hallway and back stairway to the basement kitchen. On the south side of the room a door opens to the lushly decorated atrium. Double doors mark the main entrance to this room from the 1st floor hallway.

During the brewery days, this room may have remained a place to dine. Records report, Billy used the "front of the house for offices, and the upper floors." Its purpose as a dining hall may have been maintained during the boarding house era as well.

Lemp Mansion dining room. Photo Ron Bueker.

Original Lemp Beer bottle hitching post from the front sidewalk.
It sits now outside the main Dining Room doors.

The servant's staircase leading to the 2nd floor. If you look closely you
will see the right side of the windows are cut off. This was due to moving the
wall to allow for the radiator installed in the bathroom next to it in 1884.

THE GIFT SHOP AND MUSEUM/VAULT

As you exit the dining room you will see the staircase leading
to the 2nd floor and basement levels. To the east of the staircase

is a second bathroom that today is used as the restaurant's Men's Room. Beyond that, is the first of three large vaults installed by William Lemp in 1876, when he remodeled the home.

Once used to house the family's priceless art collections and other valuables, the vault was constructed in fireproof glazed white tile. When the Lemp's traveled once a year to Europe, they locked away any of their valuable collections. Often gone for a month or more at a time, the vault offered the family peace of mind as they traveled.

During the brewery years, the vault was used for keeping the company's cash and important documents. Charles, no doubt, kept much of his extensive art acquisitions in the vaults, along with treasured family mementoes that were not on display.

When the house morphed again into a boarding house in 1950, these large rooms were bolted shut. Edwin Lemp held the keys, as he did the remains of his family's properties and "chattels."

Lemp Mansion gift shop in the first floor vault.

Green and white dish, circa 1870. Mr. and Mrs. William Lemp, Sr.
Handlan Family Silver spoons.—Ron Bueker photos

Butter dish of Julia Lemp.

Lavender hat belonging to Lillian Lemp.

Lavender Boot belonging to Lillian Lemp, the "Lavender Lady."
Some of these items are displayed in the main hall stairwell case.

Ceramic Box painted by Elsa Lemp at 16. It is purple, with red flower
blossoms on a white medallion.
Photos by Ron Bueker.

Jewelry box belonging to Annie Lemp, circa 1890.
Falstaff beer mugs, can and bottle.

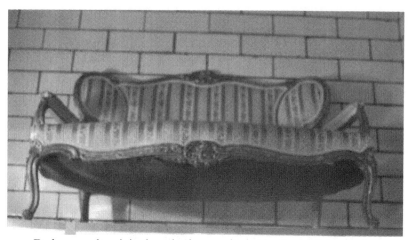

Parlor couch original to the house sits in the Lemp Mansion
Gift Shop and Museum. —Photo by Ron Bueker

Lillian Lemp table cloth, napkins, and large dinner plate. The square
Cherub dish belonged to Annie Lemp Konta.

Lillian Lemp cut glass dish, cake plate and tablecloth.
Portrait of Julia Lemp is in the background.

Falstaff collection in the Lemp Mansion.
Photos courtesy Ron Bueker.

Lemp Brewery memorabilia.

Typewriter from the Lemp Brewery, circa 1920.
Photo by Ron Bueker.

These are but a few of the treasures at the Lemp Mansion museum. They also offer merchandise for purchase such as t-shirts, mugs, custom Lemp board games, postcards, books and much more.

THE SECOND FLOOR

Main stairs to the 2nd Floor
Photo courtesy of Rebecca F. Pittman

The grand staircase led to two floors during the Lemp's lifetime at the house from 1868 to 1904, when it was removed to install an airlift elevator to help the aging, and ill, Julia Lemp navigate the giant house. At the time, before its destruction, it led to the basement level and the 2nd floor. When Charles Lemp remodeled the mansion, and moved back into the home in 1929, he removed the elevator and the stairs were reinstated.

At the top of the main staircase awaits the *Mona Lisa* of Lemp Mansion—a portrait of a smiling woman with a knowing look. She watches as you ascend the steps and her eyes follow you along the hallway to the various bedrooms. She is actually a portrait of Ellie Koehler Lemp, Billy's second wife, in later years. I nicknamed her "Moaning Mona" as there have been reports of low moaning sounds coming from the hallway at night. We will cover this in the next section of the book: The Haunting of Lemp Mansion.

Ellie Koehler Lemp, aka "Moaning Mona"
Photo by Rebecca F. Pittman

THE ATRIUM ROOM, 2ND FLOOR

At the top of the main staircase, to the left is the main door to the Charles Lemp Suite. To the right of "Moaning Mona" is a door leading to the room above the 1st floor atrium that Charles used as his private office when he occupied the bedroom next to it during his earlier days at Lemp Mansion. The etched glass in the upper half of the door allowed for privacy. The 2nd floor atrium addition was created by Billy Lemp when the house was converted into brewery offices in 1911. It may have been Henry Vahlkamp's office as we know his was on the 2nd floor, and with its abundance of windows and natural light, it would have been a premium place from which to conduct business as the brewery Vice-President. It has three doors accessing it: one from the hallway, another from the Charles Lemp Room, and a third from the William Lemp Suite, which is now sealed off. The atrium office door remains locked today and is used for storage.

Atrium Office door at the top of the main stairs, 2nd floor.

THE CHARLES LEMP SUITE

The Charles Lemp Suite is the most-aptly named of the rooms on the 2nd floor as it was truly his room during his lifetime. The other suites bear names of the people who featured heavily in the Lemp saga, but were not necessarily used by them.

Charles Lemp Suite with original sink, radiator & light fixtures.
Photos courtesy of Lemp Mansion

Charles Lemp Suite. Door to atrium office is at the left-hand corner.
Main door to hallway at top right. Photo by Ron Bueker

The Suite is a large room with three exterior doors: the main door off the 2nd floor hallway, one leading to a private bath across the hall, and the third to the atrium office. This is the only room with a private sink and mirror located within the suite, possibly due to Charles' fear of germs and his constant hand washing. He was known to take up to six showers a day. The windows look out over what would have been the two-story carriage house and the south courtyard. A south-facing window also looks out at the rooftop adjoining the atrium office, and is barred.

The room, painted in a warm magenta, features a King-size bed, antique armoire, couch, dinette table and chairs, and a piano that has been known to sound a few notes on its own.

Piano in Charles Lemp room. Photo Rebecca F. Pittman

When the Lemps and Julia's parents shared the home from 1878 to 1892, this was the Feickert's room. They gave the large master suite with the private bath to William and Julia, after they moved in with them for practical reasons. Julia would become pregnant twice more shortly after their arrival at 3322 and the proximity to the bathroom would be a nicety. During the brewery office days, this room was used for various business set-ups. In 1929, it became Charles Lemp's room, until his arthritis forced him downstairs.

THE WILLIAM LEMP SUITE

Down the hall from the Charles Lemp Suite, and to the left, is the William Lemp Suite. This is a double room separated by pocket doors. In the 1880s, it was used as the nursery and rooms for the Lemp boys and girls. As Annie was a good deal older than the others, it is possible she took over one room first, and was later joined by Hilda and Elsa. The five boys ran herd on the other room, with the pocket doors separating the two large areas. In the Victorian era, it was typical for boys and girls to share a room until they reached a certain age. Large nurseries that served as a play area and sleeping quarters was the norm, as depicted in *Mary Poppins* and *Peter Pan* novels, and movies representing that era.

This room was divided into offices when the brewery took it over in 1911. An extra window was added that is not seen in earlier photos of the house. It sits close to the newly added upper atrium room. It's possible this area was an office cubicle that wanted "a view." It is one of the few additions to the exterior of the house made after the Lemp family's timeline, other than the 2nd floor atrium office.

The mansion went from 22 rooms when the Feickerts owned it, to 33 rooms when William expanded it. It's possible he put in the pocket doors seen in the William Lemp Suite and Lavender Suite areas to separate the space into two rooms for his growing family on one side of the hallway, and as different apartments for himself and Julia on the other. The other additions were the attic rooms, atrium, three vaults and a wine cellar.

Small window looking out from the William Lemp Suite sits next to the 2nd floor atrium office. Photo by Rebecca F. Pittman

The William Lemp Suite is a beautiful room, boasting a King-size bed, antique armoire, chairs and amenities. You can see the recess where there was once a door leading out onto the atrium balcony before the brewery office was added, and then later into that same office.

William Lemp Suite. Sealed door is at upper left, new window at right. Photos courtesy of Lemp Mansion

Sitting room section of the William Lemp Suite.

The Suite offers two large areas, a bedroom and sitting room. The walls are done in hunter green with a gold-guilt trim at the painting rail level. The radiators are original to the house as are the light fixtures. Where the couch sits is a "bump-out" that was once the room's fireplace. It is walled over, as is the matching one in the bedroom side of this suite. The Charles Lemp Room and the Lavender Suite also have walled over fireplaces, although the sitting room of the Lavender Suite still boasts the original fireplace.

THE LAVENDER SUITE

Possibly the most-requested room at the mansion is the Lavender Suite, named for Lillian Handlan Lemp, the "Lavender Lady." While Lillian was a constant visitor to the house, and to this room during Julia Lemp's final days, it is doubtful she slept here. Her own mansion was cata-corner across the street.

Lavender suite. The sitting area is beyond the pocket doors.
Photo courtesy of Lemp Mansion.

This two-room suite boasts a bedroom, sitting area and massive master bathroom. The two living areas are done in soothing pale pink walls, with lavender-colored trim, and hand-painted roses in the same color encircling the frieze at the ceiling level. A King-size bed, burled wood armoire, and couch make up the bedroom side, while a dining table with chairs, original fireplace and side table invite the mansion's guests to stay a while.

The sitting room area of the Lavender Suite was William Lemp, Sr.'s bedroom. It was here he ended his life on February 13, 1904. His bouts with insomnia, stomach issues, and other illnesses necessitated a private room, and it was the norm of that era for the husband and wife to have separate quarters. From the west-facing window of the room he could see the tower of the Lemp Brewery across the street. It was a constant reminder of his stewardship.

The sitting room fireplace showcases a beautiful mantle surround with places for books and objects d' art. These were extremely popular in the Victorian period with their ginger breading and spindles. Both rooms are heated by the original radiator system. Velvet curtains complement these apartments in tones of lavender.

Lavender suite sitting room. Photo courtesy of Lemp Mansion

Fireplace surround in Lavender Suite sitting room. Photo Ron Bueker

Julia's room was on the other side of the pocket doors where the bedroom is today. During Julia's many pregnancies and at-home deliveries, this room also gave her a birthing area and temporary nursery while the baby was small. It also allowed her the closest access to the master bath. It was here she passed away from cancer, with her children gathered around her, in 1906.

The original chandeliers in these two rooms are beautiful examples of the Victorian era. They would have originally housed candles, then gasoliers fittings, and finally electrical bulbs. I had an unusual experience with the chandelier hanging above the master bed I will recite in the section on the hauntings of the house.

LAVENDER SUITE MASTER BATH

The master bathroom adjoining the Lavender Suite is amazing...and original to the house. The plumbing shows the ingenuity of that era. I was fascinated by the tub stoppers and how they worked.

The large marble shower in the Lavender Suite bathroom was the newest invention at the time William remodeled the mansion. It is the predecessor of today's multi-head shower. Invented in the late 1800s by J. L. Mott Iron Works, manufacturers and importers of "the latest and most approved plumbing appliances for all classes of buildings," the shower stall is described as "a patent combination unit with needle shower, descending douche, liver spray and bidet bath." The bather was showered by warm water from every angle. He or she was surrounded by pipes that moved the water to various outlets. None of the piping was concealed behind walls or in the floor. It was all exposed and formed a sort of cocoon, or shield around the user.

Lavender Suite marble shower with surrounding pipes and water jets . (R) Original design illustration.

Close-up of water pitcher in the Lavender Suite.

Lavender Suite bathroom with original tub, shower (l),
sink & fireplace.

The master suite bathroom has all the amenities. An antique
dressing table with mirror sits near the marble shower. Antique
perfume bottles, men's hair accessories, and more are
showcased in a wall recess with glass doors. The marble table
sitting in the center of the room offers current selections of
magazines. Diamond-paned windows look out over the
inspiring view of St. Agatha's spire which can be seen as one
walks into the room.

457

The fireplace has a surprise waiting for those who peer within. The original firebox houses a relief of Falstaff, the jolly mascot after whom Billy chose to name his famous beer. It has withstood the myriad fires that once warmed this room as Julia soaked in her marble tub or dressed for a ball.

Falstaff relief at the back of master bathroom fireplace.

GUEST BATH

At the back of the 2nd floor hallway is a lovely guest bath all with the original plumbing. The azure and cobalt blue fire-glazed tiles give the room an aquatic feel. An original claw-foot tub in dark blue boasts a beautiful white medallion of twin fish. Two windows flank the tub and look out over what was once the north grounds. Take a close look at the unique plumbing fixtures adorning the wall beneath the shower head. They still work and are a nod to the craftsmanship of the 19th century.

Guest bath with blue claw-foot tub.—Courtesy Elly'sDollhouse.com

Radiator in Guest Bath

Just outside the bathroom door, to the west, you will find the servant's staircase to the attic, or 3rd floor (4th if you are counting the basement).

At the back of the 2nd floor hallway, past the Charles Lemp Suite, is the 2nd Vault. It is now home to the mansion's offices. It is private and guests are asked to respect the operational hours of the staff.

THE ATTIC/3rd FLOOR

Access to the 3rd floor attic area is by the servant's staircase at the rear of the 2nd floor. It spirals up to the landing where the female staff during the Lemp's era would stay. In those days, there were three bedrooms, each with a fireplace, a common area for relaxing, a bathroom, access to a balcony with a view of the Mississippi, St. Agatha's church, and the burgeoning Anhueser-Busch brewery.

There were also three large, walk-in cedar closets to store the family's seasonal clothing, as well as expensive gowns, suits and furs. In the Gilded Age the females of the house always had a lady's maid. It was her duty to retrieve the desired dresses from the attic closet and lay them out for the day, or event. The wardrobes that acted as closets in each of the family's bedrooms could hold only a limited amount of clothing, especially the elaborate dresses of the day. They had drawers for underclothing, handkerchiefs, stockings and costume jewelry. Typically dressing gowns and nightshirts were kept here and possibly a day dress. All other clothing had to be fetched by the servant from the closets upstairs.

The furnishings in the servant's rooms were usually handed down by the family as new ones arrived. By the time a rug appeared in a maid's room, it had been through several decades of use: first, when it was new, in the parlor, then as it aged, moved up to a family member's room, and once thread-bare, to the attic. Children's brass railing beds usually ended up in the servant's quarters as they outgrew them or moved out to start lives of their own.

THE ELSA LEMP ROOM

At the top of the servant's stairs you will find the first of the three bedrooms on this floor. The Elsa Lemp Room is named for the youngest of the Lemp daughters, whose life was tragically ended on March 20, 1920, at her home at 13 Hortense Place. While all three rooms had fireplaces when the Lemp female staff stayed in these rooms, only the Elsa Lemp Room boasts one today.

The room has a private bathroom which was once a walk-in cedar closet. Its bump-out brick walls make it an unusual design with a Queen-size bed, dresser and cheval mirror. Its windows face the north with a stunning view of St. Agatha's church. Pale cream walls, warm brick and a floral rug give the room a welcoming feeling, even though it is purported to be the most-haunted room in the mansion.

Elsa Lemp Room at Lemp Mansion. Photo courtesy of Ron Bueker

The laundry room, service area, guest bath and balcony are outside the door to the Elsa Lemp Room. Actors for the JEST Mystery Dinner Theatre often change in the large Laundry Room and use the adjoining guest bath during performances.

THE LOUIS LEMP & FREDERICK LEMP ROOMS

The Louis Lemp and Frederick Lemp Rooms are joined by a pocket door which can be unlocked to offer a party of guests adjoining rooms. They are mirror images of each other with matching dormer windows, closets, Queen-size beds, armoires, dinettes and chairs, and cedar lined bathrooms with Jacuzzi tubs. These are the most recent rooms in the mansion to be remodeled and they have all the amenities.

The two rooms are named for Frederick, William's favorite son, who was to become heir to the brewery throne, and who died suddenly in 1901, and Louis Lemp, the famous horseman of the family.

Frederick Lemp Room on 3rd Floor. Photo Lemp Mansion

Frederick Lemp Room. Photos by Ron Bueker

Louis Lemp Room on 3rd Floor. Photo courtesy of Ron Bueker

Jacuzzi tub in both Louis and Frederick Lemp Rooms.
These were once the Lemp family's cedar clothes closets.

Cedar bathrooms on 3rd floor.

3rd Floor/Attic hallway leading from sitting area.
Photo by Ron Bueker

View of St. Agatha's church and Anhueser-Busch brewery
from rooftop balcony on attic floor.

Doors to the Louis and Frederick Lemp Suites
from the attic sitting area.—Ron Bueker

THE BASEMENT

The basement of Lemp Mansion was used for many things
in the Gilded Age of the Lemp's lifetime. Here we would find
the kitchen which contained several rooms: the kitchen proper
which revolved around the fireplace, a scullery for washing
dishes and storing them, a pantry for canned goods and
sundries, such as flour, sugar, etc., an ice box and a larder.
Game, such as fowl, deer, etc. would have been dressed in the
wood shed and brought into the house.

A servant's hall was usually offered on this level of the home.
The room near the stairs with the brick fireplace probably
served this function. Here there would be a large table for the
servant's meals, mending, reading, polishing shoes, and other
service details. The laundry, which would have been washed in
the scullery using a rotating tub, could have been placed before
the fireplace here to dry on racks during the winter months.

View from the top attic floor down to the basement level
through the servant's spiral staircase. Note the strange lights in the
center. They showed up as green on my camera.
Photo courtesy of Rebecca F. Pittman

The door leading from this room to the outdoor patio
beneath the atrium made it convenient for deliveries of food
and other household items. It also afforded easy access to
clothes drying on lines before the advent of dryers. The family
could come and go through this door when their shoes were too
muddy to come through the main entrance on the first floor. It
was also easy access from the stables and carriages.

The brick fireplace in this room is original and sports a hand
painted landscape. The polyurethane coating makes it look as if
the mural is beneath glasswork. Today this room is used for
extra dining accommodations.

Fireplace in Servant's Hall of Lemp Mansion with Landscape scene.
Photo courtesy of Ron Bueker.

Detail of fireplace mural scene done in vibrant blues
and forest greens against red brick. – Photo Ron Bueker

Servant's Hall now serving the Lemp Restaurant & Inn patrons.--
Photo courtesy Ron Bueker

Basement hallway with faux back-lit stained glass ceiling.
Photo courtesy of Rebecca F. Pittman

Outside the Servant's Hall runs a long hallway connecting
the east side of the building to the west where a private entrance

running beneath the front porch is used for dinner theater guests.

Lemp Mansion Dinner Theatre Entrance
Photo courtesy Lemp Mansion

The ceiling of this hallway has a beautiful back-lit faux stained glass mosaic of roses. To the north is the large kitchen, used today to service the mansion restaurant. Against the wall to the left was once the grand staircase, and later, the open air-lift elevator. You can still feel the cement pad beneath the carpeting where the elevator sat.

The original elevator doors belonging to this wonder of technology in the 19th century still stand in the basement hallway.

Original elevator doors in basement. Photo Rebecca F. Pittman

Just before one gets to the elevator doors, a door to the south opens into to the Lemp Mansion Rathskeller. It is here that the Lemp men enjoyed a game of billiards, a cigar, or a card game. It was the Gentleman's Parlor, with easy access to the wine cellar sitting just across the hall.

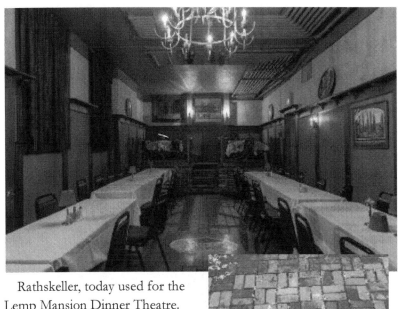

Rathskeller, today used for the Lemp Mansion Dinner Theatre. Falstaff chargers adorn the walls. Photo by Rebecca F. Pittman

The Rathskeller has many unique features, one of which is the floor. Paul Pointer related that when they first began renovations for the mansion, he was in the Charles Lemp Room and happened to look out the window to the courtyard below. Over the years, sod had been laid over the original bricks. It was fall and Paul noticed something from his vantage point on the second floor. The grass seemed to be dying in square patterns. Intrigued he went out to the area and scraped away some of the dying grass. Sure enough, there was the original brick from when the Lemp carriages rode across this courtyard.

Today that brick has been preserved and laid out as the Rathskeller flooring. In the middle of the floor in this room is a large hand-painted reproduction of the Lemp shield.

The stage was constructed by the Pointers to facilitate their Murder Mystery Dinner Theatres, as well as other events. Hanging above this area is an authentic mirror from the William J. Lemp Brewing Company.

The room has several windows, including two overlooking the patio beneath the atrium, giving this area a warm inviting feeling.

In the 19th century people were embracing color. The "painted ladies" of San Francisco are a good example. These homes exploded with bright blues, pinks, greens and yellows. The ginger breading was painted in bright contrasting shades. In the Lemp Mansion Rathskeller, you will see this blending of bright colors. The walls are a cornflower blue trimmed in purple. The courtyard brick, wrought iron railing of the stage area, and many Falstaff chargers, hung at the picture rail area, all combine to make this an authentic nod to that era.

Lemp shield on brick floor of Rathskeller.—Rebecca F. Pittman

Lemp Mansion Rathskeller's chargers

William Lemp's drinking horn and steins found in the house
after Charles' death. Christy Hawes Bond Collection

Wine cellar with white glazed brick in a barrel-vaulted ceiling.
Behind the twin doors are the mechanicals.—Photo Ron Bueker

After Charles Lemp's death, probate records noted the basement area as housing a Game Room filled with fishing tackle, tennis rackets, guns and other remnants belonging to a long-ago period of activity. They also found expensive china and crystal stored here, as well as linens and miscellaneous furniture.

Rumors that Charles Lemp shot his dog in the basement persist. Although there seems proof he did kill his pet before ending his own life, it was not determined where in the mansion that occurred.

A beautiful stained-glass window sitting atop the landing leading from the basement to the 2nd floor.—Photo Ron Bueker

Basement stairs leading up.
Photo by Ron Bueker

THE COURTYARD

Lemp Mansion's courtyard area is truly lovely. It can be accessed from the house through the basement door in the Servant's Hall, or down the winding metal staircase leading from the atrium.

Spiral staircase from atrium to courtyard.
Photo by Rebecca F. Pittman

Before Interstate 55 tore a swath through the back yard of Lemp Mansion, there stood three structures: a wood shed, a two-story carriage house, and the stables. A laundry house was mentioned as well. Today, the stables' structure remains and is now the Carriage Haus bar area serving the gazebo events. It also houses restrooms and offers air conditioning and heating for the outdoor entertainments and weddings.

View from the top of the spiral staircase:
Coach Haus and edge of Gazebo.

Lemp Mansion Gazebo. The atrium and basement patio are on the left. The Coach Haus can be seen through the open gazebo. Photo courtesy of Lemp Mansion.

The giant gazebo dominating the center of the courtyard is actually an architectural wonder. Paul Pointer related that architects from Washington University often came to sit and study it, make drawings, and marvel at its infrastructure. "It isn't that we invented the design," Paul said. "My Dad and Dick built it, and typical of both of them, the bigger the better. I guess it's the massive size and the way it's supported that holds architects' interests. We use it for weddings, summer events, and other outdoor functions."

The Pointers have carried on the long-standing tradition handed down by the Lemps, that of keeping the park-like atmosphere of the acreage intact. When Billy turned the residence into brewery offices, he made sure the trees and park setting surrounding the house remained unscathed. Today, it is still home to some of the landscape that was there from the beginning.

One of this author's favorite things at Lemp Mansion is the old willow tree that stands at the south side of the house. It has been there since the home was created. It appears in every photo of Lemp Mansion, from the newspaper pictures of William Lemp, Sr.'s funeral, to Billy's, to the boarding house years…it oversaw every major event that paraded through the home's timeline. It is called a Corkscrew willow, or "Dragon Claw." The tree's gnarled branches look as though as they have twisted along with the many mysteries surrounding this family.

Willow tree at Lemp Mansion stands before a wedding tent in the courtyard.—Photo courtesy of Lemp Mansion

(L) View through atrium patio to courtyard.

(Bottom) A fountain at Lemp Mansion. DeMenil Mansion is to the rear. Most of the trees are original to the property. Photos by Ron Bueker.

Chapter Twenty-Three

THE RESTORATION OF LEMP MANSION

It is hard to believe the transformation Lemp Mansion underwent from boarding house to the beautiful home we see today. Paul Pointer contributed the following "before" pictures. Those of us who have had the chance to enjoy this Restaurant and Inn, and those who have yet to discover it, owe them a debt of thanks.

Here are a few of the images as the Pointer family tackled what felt like an insurmountable task in 1975.

Charles Lemp Room

Lemp Mansion Rathskeller

Paul Pointer in basement with backlit rose ceiling overhead.

Coach Haus

Mathew Pointer in 1st floor hallway near the dining room.

Dining Room photos

Men's Room on 1st floor

Ceiling before restoration work

Paul Pointer during restoration of Lemp Mansion in 1975.

I asked the Pointers what their vision is for Lemp Mansion down the road. Here are their comments:

Paul: "We maintain the property and continually ask 'how can we do that with authenticity?' At this time, we are painting the exterior of the house, keeping it authentic to its original color. We follow the colors that were here. We redid the ceiling in the William Lemp Suite. When we took down a thick painted canvas there we found markings on the ceiling from an original mural. We will have it painted with stencils as they did in that era. If a customer base sees you hustling— they know you're here and you're going to be here. If we see a scratch, we fix it."

"When we started this project, we were too ignorant to know it was going to be this big an undertaking. My favorite sentence is 'With ignorance and persistence, success is insured.' Besides, the house saved us too."

Patty: "We get a lot of attention for the haunted reputation and that of the Lemp suicides. I would like people to remember this was a family who lived here, and had a huge impact on this city. They had some tragedy, but they also had nine children, many grandchildren and they loved this house. We feel a responsibility to care for it, and we hope the people who come here feel that love we have for our customers and the Lemp family heritage."

Matt Bell: "I'm reminded everyday this is a special place. I talk to people from all over the world. They tell me 'We have a list of places to see…the Arch, the St. Louis Zoo, the Cardinals, and Lemp Mansion.' You realize just how far a reach this place has. We put in a full 40-60-hour work week. And we love doing it.

"As for ghost stories, I would say the one reported most-often is that of people hearing a dark bark when there isn't one here. It's funny to have people ask you what they should expect to see or hear when they rent a room for the night. I really can't say. Ghosts don't usually perform on demand. I will say, there is a lot that tends to happen here."

Trip Advisor and other online review sites consistently tout the efforts of the Pointers for their excellent food and service. Each guest room has an added gift of a table strewn with snacks, wine, juices and complimentary tote bag, imprinted with the Lemp shield. This is hospitality at its finest.

Complimentary snacks and tote. Photo by Ron Bueker

An old photo of Lemp Mansion. The unusual horn hanging above the mantel belonged to William Lemp, Sr. It was a drinking mug. It's possible this was the Charles Lemp Room in the early years before the radiators were installed. The horn mug is featured on page 472.

Photo courtesy of Christy Hawes Bond, *Gateway Families*.

Chapter Twenty-Four

LEMP'S GRAND HALL

Lemp's Grand Hall, located at the corner of Cherokee and Lemp Avenues, is situated in one of the historic brewery buildings.

Lemp's Grand Hall Entrance. Photo courtesy of Lemp Mansion

Once the Wagon House and Stables for the mighty Lemp Brewery, the Pointers have turned this beautiful brick building into an event center, maintaining the integrity of the original maple flooring, caged elevator, and soaring buttress beamed ceilings.

Remnants of the wagon house and stables remain in the Hall's hidden secrets. The trap door, where hay was once dropped down to the horses, is still there on the top floor. Scribbled across a metal beam are some of the names of the men who worked there during the brewery days, faint, but still legible. William Lemp built these structures to last, and we can still see his eye for detail today.

Lemp's Grand Hall. The original brewery safe is at the right with the Lemp shield emblazoned upon it. Photos by Lemp Mansion

A wonderful feature of Lemp's Grand Hall is the rooftop patio. With the Lemp tower looming just to the south, the view of St. Louis from here is nostalgic. The patio is used for weddings, special events, parties and much more.

Lemp's Grand Hall rooftop. Lemp brewery is to the south. Photo by Lemp Mansion

Lemp's Grand Hall offers several venues for entertaining and wedding events. The Hall itself is a large, sweeping expanse with murals, a polished bar and even the original safe from the brewery days. A St. Louis favorite destination, it is regularly booked. Ample parking and an historic setting are just some of the amenities that keep the music and beverages pouring.

The Lemp's affinity for horses made this area of the brewery one of their favorite places to be. The wagons used for hauling the popular lager were kept here as well. It was a bustling center for the William J. Lemp Brewing Company. When Packard Trucks and railroad cars replaced the wagons, it was transformed to house the latest contrivances.

The Loft at Lemp's Grand Hall. The original steel beams are visible.

Lemp's Grand Hall with its maple floors, flying buttress beamed ceilings, fireplace and bar. Phot courtesy of Lemp Mansion.

The Pointer family brings the same integrity and love for the Lemp heritage to Lemp's Grand Hall as they have done to recreate Lemp Mansion's glory days. Only steps apart from each other, they give us a rare glimpse of the days of beer barons, and the introduction of a lager that put St. Louis on the forefront of national breweries. For weddings or special events, please contact Lemp Mansion at 314-664-8024.

From left to right top: Lemp's Grand Hall and Lemp Mansion. From left to right bottom: Lemp's Grand Hall and the Courtyard at Lemp Mansion. Photo courtesy of Lemp Mansion

Chapter Twenty-Five

LEMP MANSION TODAY

Today, the beautiful mansion at 3322 DeMenil Place, in St. Louis, Missouri is registered as a Historic National Landmark. It is also a famous Restaurant and Inn. Renowned for its excellent food, it is a popular destination for those wanting a chance to dine, and sleep, in the style and comfort of the Gilded Age era when a beer baron named William J. Lemp created a brewing empire.

Lemp Mansion events are always evolving. From wedding receptions to summer concerts, haunted tours to banquets, there is always something there to entertain and mystify. The restaurant's food reviews leave no doubt that the menu here is excellent. I can personally speak for the prime rib! Six beautifully decorated guest rooms in authentic period styling are available, each with complimentary snacks, television, and sumptuous beds.

"We care about our customers," Paul Pointer told me. "We listen, we change things, and we take it a day at a time...a season at a time." The Lemp Mansion Restaurant and Inn is also home to the popular comedy-mystery dinner theaters put on by St. Louis' own JEST Murder Mystery Company. They have been entertaining Lemp Mansion guests for 11 years.

www.jestmurdermystery.com

For information on Lemp Mansion events, room reservations or dining, please call 314-664-8024, or visit their web site at www.LempMansion.com. You can also follow them on Facebook and Twitter.

Another wonderful offering is the Ghost Tours hosted by St. Louis psychic and ghost hunter, Betsy Burnett-Belanger. For over an hour she leads you through the haunted halls of Lemp Mansion after dark, instructs on the use of dowsing rods to register energy, and relates the background of the amazing family who lives here. You can contact Betsy at 314-644-1814 to schedule a tour or lecture.

MEET THE PEOPLE BEHIND THE LEGACY

Here are the people who saved and renovated Lemp Mansion in 1975. From that time, they have poured their passion into creating a place that welcomes the public with the hospitality and opulence that was the Gilded Age.

Patty Pointer-Brinker and her son, Tom Pointer

Matt Bell

Mary Pointer-Wolff, Paul Pointer and Patty Pointer-Brinker

Paul and Carolyn Pointer in Lemp Mansion's parlor

Paul Pointer, Ernesto, Luis, Scott and George

Betsy Burnett-Belanger, Lemp Mansion Tour Guide
and owner of St. Louis Spirit Search

Images of Lemp Mansion

The juxtaposition of a Lemp beer bottle hitching post and modern parking meter (l) sums up Lemp Mansion: "Where the past meets the present."

Chapter Twenty-Six

THE LEMP BREWERY—YESTERDAY & TODAY

Today, the magnificent structure of the William J. Lemp Brewing Company still stands proudly at the corners of Cherokee and DeMenil Place. LEMP is still emblazoned upon the Malt House Tower, defying all to forget its impact on the beer brewing industry. Shashi Palamand, of Historic Lemp Brewery, L.L.C., has taken the helm and breathed new life into the Italianate architecture of the building. Over 100 tenants now run their creative businesses from within its walls.

"We call it 'creative industrial', or 'micro-manufacturing'," Shashi Palamand told me. "We specialize in businesses here that are more small-to-midsize, and somehow factor into the creative entrepreneurial arena. Some have international reach, but what we offer here through these businesses is a design aspect that overseas' manufacturers can't provide. We have artist studios that feature 3-D mural art, commercial artists, amusement park creations, and much more. We also have distribution centers and storage facilities. Microbreweries is something we would like to incorporate here…for obvious reasons."

When the Lemp Brewery shut its doors in 1919, and was later auctioned off, the International Shoe Company bought up most of the buildings. For 75 years, they operated the old brewery for the creation and distribution of shoes. When they began moving business overseas, they lost interest in maintaining the building and eventually sold it. Shashi Palamand took over Historic Lemp Brewery, L.L.C. in 2004, and has poured his passion into hearing the brewery walls ring once again with the sounds of creation.

"If International Shoe Company hadn't purchased the brewery," Mr. Palamand said, "it might not be here today. It was too big to house many operations, and I believe, despite its sturdy structure, it would have been torn down. It's over one million square feet and has 29 buildings. So far, 25 of the buildings have new roofs and we work daily on the remaining areas as we refurbish this amazing complex."

Model of Lemp Brewery in the brewery office.
Courtesy of Shashi Palamand. Photo by Ron Bueker

Adam Lemp's first beer kettle in 1868.

Aerial view of Lemp Brewery circa 1960s. Courtesy Shashi Palamand

The future looks bright for the Historic Lemp Brewery at 3500 Lemp Avenue, Saint Louis, Missouri, 63118. Mr. Palamand is excited about the endless possibilities for the remaining buildings' usage. From entertainment venues to commercial concerns, he loves brainstorming the creative revitalization of a complex that meant, and means, so much to St. Louis, and around the world.

Rebecca F. Pittman

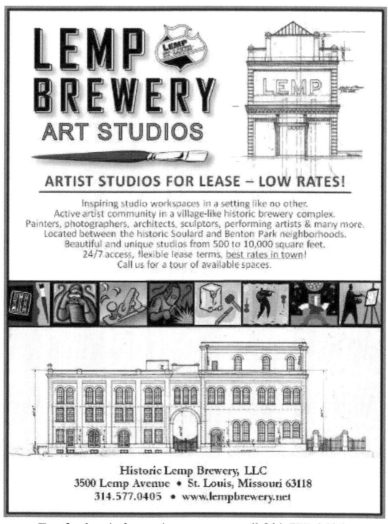

For further information, you can call **314-577-0405**.

The Haunting

THE HAUNTING OF LEMP MANSION

"Houses are memories of the people who dwelled there. Their brick and mortar absorb the emotions and events as surely as if they were recorded, to be played back when time's ticking clock dictates.

The floors recall the footsteps pressed upon them, releasing their soft paddings at night when the house is at ease. Windows, the eyes of the home, witness it all, and reflect the shadows of things that played across their glass. The velvet of draperies, the soft silk of a settee, or the down of a pillow retain the imprints left there, and once again feel the warmth of a bygone touch.

When it's still—when the doors are bolted and the lights dimmed, the vestiges of past souls reclaim their rooms, and breathe once more." Rebecca F. Pittman

The stories of Lemp Mansion's hauntings started long before the Pointer family took her under their wing. During the boarding house era, from 1950-1975, the house was considered to be haunted. Tenants staying in the rooms there reported knocking sounds, people walking along the darkened hallways, when no one was there, missing objects, and the lights having a life of their own. Though the rent was cheap, tenants packed up and left more often than is normal. The neighborhood surrounding the mansion was falling on hard times and the dilapidated feeling of the other homes, which were once mansions in the brewery's glory days, added to the dreary atmosphere.

"Mental Mary"

Margaret Mathers, an elderly woman from Illinois, wrote to me to say she had an uncle who lived at the mansion during its time as a boarding house. She said it was in the late 1950s. He used to tell her about the place, and how many of the people staying there would get "spooked" about the noises that seemed to happen frequently.

"His room was at the top of the stairs," she said, "and it looked out over the old courtyard." I told her that sounded like the room Charles Lemp lived in. She said her uncle told her that he would hear someone pacing around his room at night while he was trying to sleep. Each time he turned on the lamp beside his bed, the sound stopped. There was never anyone there. He also said his things would disappear, only to show up in strange places.

"One such occurrence involved his shaving razor," Margaret related. "It was silver and he had owned it a long time. He kept it on the sink in the room. When he went to shave one morning, it was gone. A search turned up nothing. Three days later, while sitting out back in the courtyard having a cigarette, he noticed light glinting off something over in the weeds by the old stable house. When he investigated, he was shocked to see it was his missing razor. Of course, my first question to him, Margaret said, was 'Wasn't it possible some other tenant stole it from his room?' He was emphatic that his doors were always locked. 'And besides,' he said, 'why steal it only to toss it into the weeds?'

"He remembered a strange woman who lived there at the time," Margaret continued. "The others nicknamed her "Mental Mary." She was always talking to herself and kept a list of everyone's movements. She had hundreds of cheap notebooks filled with entries such as 'Hank lost his shoelace last night in the basement,' or, 'Donna ate oatmeal again at 7:05/morning.' She had all these notes about someone named 'Ellie.' My Uncle said no one named Ellie lived there. But here were all these entries about Ellie's movements. 'Ellie keeps leaving the water running in the tub.' 'Ellie won't shut the curtains. 11:43/night.' One said, 'Ellie was looking for her sapphire hair comb again. It's behind the brick.' My uncle said he had nightmares about a woman floating along the hallway looking for a hair comb. He lived there about 8 months and moved out."

Stories sent to me at the Facebook page for this book were varied and interesting. Most were sent in private messages, some were openly posted. One story, that seemed to repeat often, was that of missing room keys. In some cases, people asked not to have their full names listed. To protect these guests' privacy, I am using their first name and last initial.

Missing Keys

Dawn H., Wisconsin. 2010.

"I was at Lemp Mansion with my friends. We got the William Lemp Suite. There is definitely a feeling of presence in that room. It feels 'heavy.' We were there one night but we mislaid the room key five times! Even when we put it all alone on a table, it would disappear, then show up in someone's purse or on a chair. We checked out early and left it on a table downstairs."

Michael Chambers, Utah. 2009.

"I got a call from my sister who was staying at Lemp Mansion in St. Louis, in 2009. She said she was staying in the 'purple room' and things kept happening to her. She said she would go into the bathroom and find towels lying on the floor when she had just seen them hung up. The bathroom was private to the room so no one else was using it. She said she would find the toilet paper roll undone with a strand of tissue stretched across the floor. The room key kept moving, she said. I think this is when I asked how much she'd had to drink, but seriously, she sounded scared. The key would change places and even end up sticking out of a different door in the room, one she wasn't even using."

Barb Orlier, Florida. 2012.

"My girlfriend gave me a trip to Lemp Mansion as a birthday present. I love haunted houses and this is one I've been talking to her about. I was so excited! We got the Lavender Suite which is so big! You get the whole wing to yourself. We were sitting at that dining table in the room, in front of the fireplace, snacking on all the stuff they lay out on the table, when we heard something go 'clink.' It came from the bathroom which is on the other side of the bedroom. It sounded like something landed on the tile floor. She got up and went to look and came back holding our room key.

'How'd this get in the bathroom?' she said. 'I have no idea. Where was it before?' 'It was over there on that table by the door. I put it there so I wouldn't forget where it was.' She stared at it a minute, shrugged, put it back on the table and we forgot about it. The next morning, we were getting ready to head down to check out and the key wasn't there. We found it on the dressing table in the bathroom. That is really spooky to me. We kept wondering if the key used to belong to the bathroom door and 'someone' wanted it left in there."

Many stories have been reported of people returning to their rooms to see their door standing open, even though they locked it and the staff has gone home for the night. Some have found their key hanging from the lock...on the other side of the door...when they are in their rooms. Obviously, the 'former caretakers' of Lemp Mansion have their own rules about who handles the opening and closing of doors.

Melissa Widman, a housekeeper at Lemp Mansion reported disappearing keys on numerous occasions.

"I was cleaning the Elsa Lemp Room on the 3rd floor, the attic area. I always lay my ring of keys on the table in the room when I walk in. After you clean these rooms as often as I do you have a routine. There are a lot of keys on the ring; they open every door at the mansion.

"I cleaned the Elsa Room and went to lock up. The keys weren't on the table. I looked all over that room. I looked in the trash, through my supplies, under the furniture...they were gone. I was getting really flustered, and a little nervous, because if I lose those keys, I'm screwed. They would have to replace every lock in the mansion since we wouldn't know who had them.

"By now I am going through every inch of that room. When I lifted a pillow on the bed, I heard them clink. They were tucked inside the pillow case! There is no way they would be tucked inside that pillow case."

It seems the Elsa Room isn't the only place on the attic floor that acts like a Black Hole for keys. Melissa related this story to me as well:

"About three years ago, I was working on a Sunday. I brought my daughter and niece with me. We were the only ones there, which is typical on a weekend during cleaning hours. We had finished the Elsa Room and headed for the Frederick and Louis Rooms at the back. There is a little table in the area between their two doors in the hallway there where I always place the keys after I unlock their doors.

"I unlocked the rooms, put the keys on the little table and started cleaning the rooms. When I was finished, I went to get the keys to lock up and they weren't there. I asked my daughter if she had  them, and she said 'No, you put them on the table.' We looked everywhere for them. We checked both rooms. The pocket door that separates the two rooms was open and I rushed back and forth between them looking for the keys.

"I left the Frederick Room and was looking through the Louis Room again when I heard a crinkling sound come from the Frederick. It sounded to me like a bag of chips crinkling. I went back in there to where I thought the sound had come from. I opened the TV cabinet and there were the keys, dangling there. My daughter bursts out 'Mom, you already looked in there!' We had searched that cabinet and everywhere else before. I think the crinkling sound was the keys "appearing" inside that cabinet.

"I used to be scared about working on the 3rd floor. There is just a different feeling up there. But now I realize it isn't a negative energy I feel, it's a positive one, although they like to mess with you. I love working here, and you get kind of used to the weird stuff."

I (the author) told Melissa during this conversation that I knew what she meant. There is a different feeling when you climb the steps to the attic and step onto that landing. I said 'there is a crowded feeling, like you just entered a room filled with people, only you can't see them." She agreed...it felt 'crowded,' not because of the walls or rooms or hallway, just a sense you are not alone.

SPOOKY GOINGS-ON IN THE ATTIC

Amber Hilt stayed at Lemp Mansion on October 20, 2014. Here is her story:

"I went on the ghost tour and stayed the night in the Frederick Room. I am an avid ghost hunter. We came from Kansas City to St. Louis for my birthday. Around 2 am I did an EVP recording with a camcorder, digital recorder, and I had an EMF reader. I picked up a girl saying ' lalala' and a dog making a soft 'urg' noise. I had brought dog toys and plush toys and was appealing to them. I love animals so I was really focused on connecting. I was also able to capture the EMF reader going off when I turned my back. I think they were playing with me. Also, I went down to the first floor by myself at 2:50 am with my camcorder and EMF reader. The other house guests were long asleep and the house was dark and quiet. I was on the main stair case in the midway landing and asked if anyone was there and my EMF meter went off. I was only downstairs for 6 minutes because my reader kept going off when I said things. I know they were there with me. As I went back up to my room, a shadow figure is leaning on the wall near the bathroom by the employee area. He goes ahead of me and on the camcorder, you here a groaning noise that was not on the spiral staircase when I descended. Very spooky! I was scared by myself but it was worth it! When I got back to my room, the bathroom light was on. I turned on the TV to go to bed and within 1 min, the batteries died. I had brought my own batteries so I switched them out, found something to watch, and went to sleep. The next morning I tried to debunk my EMF reader but instead of going off in the places it had, it went crazy in the garden room as I said goodbye!"

Rebecca F. Pittman (author). I met **Catherine, Cheryl, Donna and Susan** at Lemp Mansion in May, of 2012, during my first visit there. They were celebrating a birthday and were staying in the William Lemp, and the Charles Lemp Suites. I was in the Lavender Suite, along with my sister (who lives in St. Louis) and her son. I took the tour with a group of people earlier that evening, including Catherine, Cheryl, Donna and Susan. When the tour headed for the attic, I decided to return to my room, as I had stayed in the Frederick Lemp Room on that floor the evening before, and had seen the attic.

A little after 10:00 p.m., there was a knock on my door. The four ladies mentioned previously were standing there, very excited. They were holding out their camera and asked that I look into the viewing window. In the picture, you can see their legs, and in the foreground, is a shadow figure of someone with pants and what looks like a suit coat. The odd thing about the photo, is that they are all standing in the same vicinity, but while they are plainly seen, the person in the middle is shadowy and black.

The ladies told me that while they were up in the attic, a few minutes before on the tour, they saw a black shadow move around past their feet. They are wearing sandals and each claimed to have felt hot wet breath on their feet as the shadow moved past. It was low to the floor and they had the distinct impression of it being a dog. When one of them took the photo, they were showing me, there was a shadow man standing there.

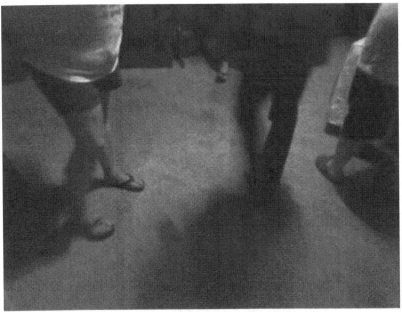

Photo taken in attic sitting area of the shadow man.
Photo courtesy of Cheryl Pearson

Reports of a man wearing a top hat and suit-length coat have been reported often from guests staying on the attic floor. His shadow has appeared against a wall in some photos, and clearly, as in this one. This floor housed the cedar closets containing the Lemp's evening attire. Perhaps it is William Lemp, all dressed up to go out.

Melissa Wideman is a housekeeper at Lemp Mansion. During my stay there in December 2014, I stopped to complement her on how nice she always kept the rooms. There was never a day she wasn't vacuuming after a guest left and making sure the rooms were in pristine condition.

While talking to her I asked if she had any experiences at Lemp she would share with me for the book. I've already related two of her reports. Without hesitation, she related the following story:

"I've been working here at Lemp Mansion since 2011. About two months after I started, I was working a Saturday alone here. I did have my 12-year-old daughter with me but the rest of the staff wasn't here. We had cleaned the William, Charles and Lavender Suites and locked their doors. We then went upstairs to the attic floor. I unlocked the Elsa Lemp Room and went in and set my cleaning supplies down in there. I decided to check the Frederick and Louis Rooms at the back of the hall on that floor to see how much needed to be done in there.

"My daughter and I went and checked out the two rooms. They were empty and no one was around. We went back to the Elsa Room to start cleaning. It had only been about 30 seconds since I was down at the other two rooms. All of a sudden, we turn and see this man walking toward us, coming from the direction of the Frederick and Louis Rooms. I had just come from there. There was no one there and no place to be hiding. He was wearing an old-style suit, like some of the kids go for today. He had on a hat and he had a beard. He walked right past us with no eye contact at all.

"He wasn't transparent or anything, he looked as real as anyone. My daughter saw him too and got really frightened. I was really scared too. I called Mary (one of the Pointer's) and asked 'Are you coming in?' She said 'No, why?' I told her I had just seen a man walking around on the 3rd floor when there was no one there a few seconds before. She asked if I had locked the outside doors after me, and I said 'Of course I did.' Since then, I've heard others say they've seen this same man with the old-fashioned hat and suit. When I later saw a picture of William Lemp, I thought he looked just like the man I saw."

One guest reported seeing a man's reflection in the glass as she stood looking out through the windows over the attic balcony atop the vaults. She saw his outline, a top hat and what looked like a fuzzy area around the chin, which she interpreted as a full beard. When she turned to look at him there was no one there.

While shadow people are more commonly reported than full body apparitions, they are still rare enough to make it a surreal experience.

The following story also relates an event with the shadow man, as well as an encounter with the Lavender Lady on the 2nd floor.

Stephanie Neal took this photo of what she said appeared to be the Lavender Lady's figure and hat. In another shot, the figure is headed down the stairs:

Lavender Lady's shadow on the 2nd floor. Camcorder still shot.

Here is Stephanie Neal's story:

"I recently stayed at the Lemp Mansion and have some really interesting photos. On the second floor, I believe I have an almost full body photo of Lillian Lemp. Her dress is the same as one I have found on the Internet as being her actual gown.

Another photo on the second floor looks like a sleeve of Lillian's gown in the long mirror in the hallway. The final picture is on the 3rd floor. I was using my night vision camcorder and my friend was using her flash camera. When her flash went off, I captured a man with a drape coat and top hat walk right in front of us." (Unfortunately, this photo was not clear enough for inclusion.)

I (the author) stayed two nights at Lemp Mansion on May 21, 2012, while researching this book. The Pointers have been very kind in allowing me access to their stories and the mansion rooms. I had heard a little about the house and the Lemp saga, but nothing prepares you for the atmosphere of the place. Even with 12' soaring ceilings, you have the feeling the house engulfs you as you come through the front door.

On my first night at Lemp Mansion, I was given the Frederick Lemp Room on the 3rd floor/attic level. I was later told I would have the house to myself. This happened to me while researching the Myrtles Plantation, and I had the entire Manor House to myself at the Stanley Hotel, while writing that book. It was becoming a habit.

The room was wonderful, and the Jacuzzi bath even better. I was tired after a plane flight from Colorado, so I went to bed around 10:00 p.m. I'll admit I listened to every groan of the house, and I watched the open bathroom door for signs of shadows. I finally fell asleep not long after.

Sometime, between midnight and 12:30 a.m., I awoke to something kicking my bed. At first, it didn't register what was happening, but as my body jerked sideways with every kick, I realized I wasn't dreaming. The room was dark, with only a ray of light coming from beneath the locked door leading out into the old attic crawl space where there are small windows letting in the moonlight. I froze, my heart pounding. As it continued, I realized my impression was that it was a child, as the kicks felt fumbling and low...like a petulant child kicking the wall after you tell them to stop. After several moments, it stopped. I laid there in the darkness trying to breathe.

After what seemed like an eternity, I mustered the courage to spring from the bed and run for the bathroom, where I quickly turned on the light. It shone out onto the bed. There was nothing there. I left the door partly open to leave a night light on, and crawled back beneath the covers, my eyes glued to the light coming through the open door.

I must have fallen asleep. Sometime later, I awoke to a pressure bearing down next to my feet. It was trapping my feet beneath the blanket. It was followed by something patting my lower legs with soft little fluttering movements. As my eyes flew open, I could see light coming in through the dormer window near me. It must be early morning, I thought. The room was still somewhat dark and I couldn't see the end of the bed. I reached carefully for my cell phone lying next to me. With every nerve fiber firing, I turned the phone's face toward my feet and clicked it on. The light lit up the room. That was the scariest moment for me…wondering what I would see when that light shot out.

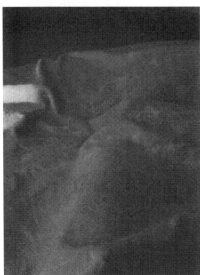

Photo of imprints in blanket in the Frederick Lemp Room.
Photo by Rebecca F. Pittman

There in the covers, like two small shoe prints, was an impression next to my feet. There is no way those could have been there the entire time. My getting in and out of bed, tossing and turning, etc. would not have allowed those two perfect impressions. Again, they seemed child-like in appearance. On the preceding page is the photo I took that early morning:

You can clearly see the two imprints at the bottom of the bed. My knee beneath the blankets is in the middle of the photo. I had shifted my feet to the right to take the picture.

BETSY BURNETT-BELANGER

My second day there, I interviewed Paul Pointer, and Betsy Burnett-Belanger, the resident tour guide and a remarkable woman with psychic ability.

Betsy owns the St. Louis Spirit Search, and is a paranormal investigator, lecturer and professed ghost hunter. She has been the tour guide at Lemp Mansion for over 17 years. She began there doing history tours, but later, as haunted reports kept flooding in from guests and the staff, she asked to include a ghost tour to the offering. She had experienced enough activity to warrant an authentic tour to the thousands of people who find their way to Lemp Mansion's doors each year.

She founded the St. Louis Spirit Search in 1993, but has been a ghost hunter since the 1980s. Betsy is sensitive to things going on around her that most of us don't experience. She, and Lemp Mansion, have been featured on such shows as TAPS, National Geographic, Ghost Hunters, Ghost Adventures and more. She mentioned the mansion's listing in CNN's "most-haunted places in the world," and said they listed it at #5. She gave it an 8.

During the interview, she mentioned someone named Zeke. I said I didn't know who that was. Speaking into my tape recorder, this is her story of yet another Lemp mystery:

"Zeke was a boy born late in life to William and Julia Lemp. Due to their age, he was born with some mental and physical challenges. His face had some deformities as well. The Lemp's kept him a secret, I believe in an effort to protect him from the mean taunts of others. He stayed in the attic in what is today the Louis Lemp Room. He liked it there and felt safe. He had the run of the house, but enjoyed this room and could look down from the dormer window at the people passing along the sidewalk below. Some people saw him and the nickname "Monkey Face Boy" began to circulate.

"At one time, the middle of the attic area was open for the staircase. In the Louis Lemp Room bathroom there is a little staircase that goes up to the roof. It is locked now behind the French doors. He liked to hide on those stairs as he felt safe there from people coming and going in the mansion.

"He died at 16, from a fall down the stairs. Charles Lemp was living alone with him at the time,, after Julia died and everyone moved out. I'm sure there were still some servants there. I've heard rumors that people think he was an illegitimate son of Billy Lemp's and was kept there. Why would Billy keep his son at the house when he had his own? All the newspapers jumped on Billy at the time and that's how the gossip started.

"The Booth Brothers had a TV documentary called "Children of the Grave." It was about ghost children. They came here and interviewed me. They set up fancy equipment and got Zeke to move things when they asked him to, captured his voice on EVP's, and I've seen a few photos of him."

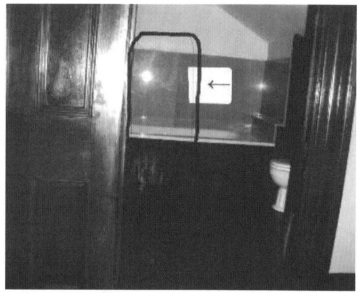

In the above photo, next to the bright light, you can see the profile silhouette of a small boy. He is facing right. This was taken in the Louis Lemp bathroom where Zeke was known to play when it was a closet off the servant's room. Photo Betsy Burnett-Belanger

It was at this time, I told Betsy about my stay the night before in the Frederick Room and the sensation of someone kicking my bed, sitting on my feet and patting my legs. I told her my impression was that it was a child. She said that while Zeke preferred the Louis Lemp Room she wasn't' surprised that he gravitated to a woman he felt was sympathetic.

I ran the dates against a census and found Charles did indeed live in the mansion after Julia's death from 1906-1910. If Zeke died at 16 from a fall, it means he was born in 1894, when Julia was 53 and William, 58. Their advanced years for conceiving very possibly resulted in a child being born with challenges, as we still witness today. After the boy's death, Charles moved out, and Billy turned the home into brewery offices.

I do know that a plethora of recordings have been captured in the attic area of a child's voice. Toys move, sounds of small feet running in the hall are reported. And after my own experience that night in the Frederick Lemp Room, I'm open.

As the interview continued, I found Betsy has an affinity for Billy. As she and I sat talking in the double parlors, the large ball light above us kept flickering whenever we mentioned Billy's name. I tape recorded the session and you can hear me pause and say, "That's not just me imagining that, right?" Betsy smiled and said it happens all the time there when Billy's name is mentioned, even though he died across the hall from where we are talking.

Later that evening, I attended Betsy's tour, and as I mentioned previously, I ended mine when we got to the Lavender Suite where I was staying and allowed the others to head up to the attic. My sister and nephew were waiting for me in the bedroom, watching a Cardinal's game. She was propped up on the bed and he was lying on the couch next to it.

I plopped on the bed and began telling them about the tour when all of a sudden, the chandelier above us began going crazy. It was flickering so fast it looked like a short circuit. We watched it for a minute, until I finally realized I should be filming it, so I grabbed my IPhone and turned it to video record. The light, which is the original fixture for this room, continued to flash erratically. I looked up at it and said, "If that is someone doing that, make it stop." It flashed once more and stopped. You can hear my sister on the tape gasping. I then said, "If you are someone who died in this house, please make it blink once." A few seconds passed and it blinked once. Now my sister is beating on me and telling me to "stop talking to it!" I asked if it was happy we were there and it stopped responding. The light remained still.

In an effort to debunk it, I got up and went to the dimmer switch on the wall and played around with the light, trying to mimic the erratic flickering, or see if it would start up again. It did nothing. I asked the ladies, after they showed me their picture of the attic ghost, if anyone on the tour had been turning lights on and off, as the floor was right over the light fixture, but they said the lights were already on and no one messed with them.

Lavender Suite light. –photo by Rebecca F. Pittman

CHARLES LEMP'S DOG

I received many stories about guest's hearing dogs bark, whimper, snort or snarl. I was impressed with the abundance of reports that came from all over the mansion. The Lemp's undoubtedly had several dogs over their lifetime in the house; they loved animals and it showed in their creation of the atrium, their obsession with horses, and later, Edwin's involvement with the St. Louis Zoo and his *Cragwold* farm.

People have sent me EVP's where you can distinctly hear a dog whimpering in the attic. Others, where a muffled barking is heard. As for me, I can with all honesty say, that what happened to me on the morning of May 22, 2012, will rank in my top chilling moments.

My sister and nephew spent the night with me the night we witnessed the strange activity with the lights. It was the same night the ladies captured the shadow figure on film during their trip to the attic. I was due to catch a flight early the next morning to Louisiana to wrap up the research for the Myrtles Plantation book. If you are like me, you don't sleep well when you have an early flight. You are always worried the alarm won't go off. So, I woke up at 5 in the morning, an hour before I needed to, and found myself running over all the details of the trip to Baton Rouge, as I lay there: What time to pick up the rental car, which flight, did I have all my notes, batteries, tape recorders, etc.?

It was 5:05 a.m. (I had just looked at the clock again), when I heard two loud gun shots followed by one sharp 'bark' just outside the door from the sitting room of the Lavender Suite, leading out to the hallway. I remember my eyes flew to that door when I heard it. It sounded like a gun had gone off in the hallway. I jerked my head toward my sister who was lying beside me and found her sound asleep. But just at that moment, my nephew raised up on his elbow from his place on the couch. He was 21-years-old at the time. I looked at him and said, "Did you hear those gun shots?" He said, "No, but I heard a big dog." I was elated! "You did? You heard a dog?" "Yeah, a big one." I wondered if the shots woke him in time to hear the dog.

Finally, I had someone to verify my story. I still felt as if someone had poured ice water through my veins as I listened for further sounds. Finally, I got up and walked to that door. I opened it and peeked out into the hallway. Nothing was there.

Later, as I carried my bags out into the hallway around 6:30 that morning, the ladies across the hall in the William Lemp Suite opened their door. I asked if they heard gun shots. They looked surprised and said '"No." I was shocked they had slept through something that loud. It wasn't muffled. It was as if someone had shot a gun just outside the door.

It wasn't until I began the heavier research for this book, that I began to understand what those two shots and a dog barking meant. It bothered me for a long time. Had I heard William Lemp, Sr.'s shooting? But then, why two shots, and what did the dog have to do with it? Was it an echo of Billy's suicide, one floor beneath the Lavender Suite sitting room? There were rumors he shot himself twice. Again, why the dog? When I received the coroner's report on William Lemp, Sr., I found he had actually fired three shots. That didn't fit. Charles Lemp's report listed only one shot, just the one spent cartridge. I was going nuts trying to figure this out. I had heard rumors Charles had shot his dog and then himself, but I couldn't find proof of it.

That is until my interview with Paul Pointer, when he told me Charles's servants, the Bitner's, told him themselves years later, that Charles left two notes. The one he left for their eyes only confessed to shooting the dog. There were my two shots and a dog barking. I'm not sure why I heard them outside the sitting room door in the Lavender Suite. Perhaps he shot the dog there. Maybe it saw the gun and was making a run for it. And why shortly after 5 a.m.? I learned Charles routinely woke guests staying at the mansion at 5 a.m. I don't know. I do know I will never forget being privileged to actually hear a residual haunting from another era.

CHILDREN IN THE ATTIC

My story of sensing a child in the attic rooms is not the only one. Many guests have heard children laughing in the hallways of the 3rd floor, singing and calling out "Come play with me." Others have said they've heard "Help Me!"

While I don't disallow that a boy named Zeke once roamed those hallways, I found it interesting that most of the reports from there were those of hearing a little girl, not a little boy.

Mary Neske sent me her YouTube tape of her time at Lemp

Mansion. It was very impressive. She and her friends had taken the Charles Lemp Room on the 2nd floor, and the Elsa Lemp Room on the 3rd. The Elsa Lemp Room is purportedly the most-haunted room at the mansion. Most of these hauntings revolve around a child. Guests in that room hear a little voice laughing or singing. Toys that have been brought in to tempt him, or her, are found missing or moved.

In Mary's tape, she films herself asking if anyone is there out in the hallway by the Elsa Lemp Room. When the recording is played back, you can distinctly hear a little girl's voice. Her group brought along a large rubber ball and left it in the Elsa Lemp Room while they toured the rest of the mansion, including the basement. Hours later, when they came back to the second floor and rounded the corner to the back door of the Charles Lemp Room, they stopped in their tracks. There in the darkened hallway sat the ball. It had traveled out of Elsa's room in the attic where they left it, rolled to the servant's stairs, traveled down the winding steps, turned right and ended up just outside Charles's door. If you would like to see the tape, you can go to YouTube and type in neskeparanormal.

MISSING PIECES

It seems Lemp Mansion has an affinity for shiny objects. People staying in the William Lemp Suite report missing coins on a frequent basis. Those who have dropped coins have found them mysteriously disappear as they go to retrieve them. Shiny combs, hair accessories, a silver knife…all end up in the ether world. Some reappear, but a good many do not.

Wanda P. Kansas. 2013.

"I was staying in the William Lemp Suite, during the fall. I wanted to experience the haunted house as it neared Halloween. My friends and I had a Ouija Board and we set it in the center of the bed one night. We turned off most of the lights and sat there with our hands on the planchette. Kacey, my friend, wouldn't stop giggling and we were getting mad at her. Finally, we started asking questions, like, "Did you die in here?" "Do you miss Alswel, Billy?" Stuff like that.

Someone knocked on the door and Kacey started freaking. It was after midnight and she thought we were going to get in trouble for being loud or having  a Ouija board in the room. We all got up and went to the door. I said, "Who is it?" No one answered. I asked again, but got no answer. Kacey is tugging at me not to open the door, but I did, and peeked out into the empty hallway.

We hurried and shut it, and made sure it was locked. Kacey started crying and saying we shouldn't be messing with the Ouija board and to put it away. As we turned toward the bed, we all stopped. The planchette was gone. We searched under the bed, the blankets, everywhere. It was gone. We never did find it. I was miffed because it was a really nice one with silver edges."

HAMMERS AND HAUNTINGS

During the restoration of Lemp Mansion, several workmen had difficulties completing their duties. Tools would go missing, equipment would stop working, and things would happen that caused more than one man to walk off the job.

While painting the elaborate ceiling in the double parlors, Claude Breckwoldt became more and more nervous about being there. Up on the scaffolding, lying on his back, he kept getting the impression that someone was standing below, watching him…and that someone was not happy he was there. He said it was hard to describe but he felt that his work on the mural was not appreciated, that he was not supposed to be messing with the ceiling at all. He finally stopped at one point and had to leave the building.

Paul said, in later years, he took an elderly man, familiar with the mansion, on a tour to learn more about the property. When they reached the twin parlor, the man looked up at the ceiling mural in surprise. He said, "It was my understanding that Papa Lemp got into an argument with the German artist who was working on the fresco, covered it with canvas and said it would never be finished." The negative energy Mr. Breckwoldt was feeling as he worked on the mural may have been coming from William J. Lemp, Sr.

Paul Pointer related a story about a large oak buffet that was original to the house that sat in the atrium. It was used to store silverware and things needed for service of the dining areas. One drawer in particular had trouble staying shut.

"At least three times a day one of us would say, 'Shut the silverware drawer,'" Paul told me, laughing. "You would walk by and it would be hanging open again, so we would shut it. One day, I noticed it was open, and called to Chris, "Shut the silverware drawer." I heard the usual sound of the silver clinking as the drawer was closed. I turned, expecting to see Chris shutting the drawer. Instead, I watched as the door sucked itself shut. I experimented with stacking silverware in it in different ways to see if it would cause it to close by itself, but nothing worked."

Patty Pointer-Brinker, Paul's sister and co-owner of the Restaurant and Inn, has had her own dealings with playful spirits. Her faulty item in the mansion is not a drawer, but a candle.

At one time, the bar, which is now in the old library, was in the double parlor. Patty was behind the bar when she happened to look across the hall into the Lady's Parlor where Billy died. The candle sitting atop the marble mantel suddenly lit by itself. She stared at it in disbelief. I asked her if it had been recently lit and blown out and maybe the wick rekindled. She said no one had lit it in sometime. After that, she said she had a hard time opening or closing the mansion by herself."

Patty's love for the mansion is tempered with respect for the unexplainable things that happen there.

"You always feel someone is watching," she said. "It's hard to put into words. It's a feeling. You turn and look, and no one is there."

Paul echoed her sentiments. "There isn't a day that goes by that you don't feel something here. It's more than atmosphere. You do feel like you're being watched over."

Matt Bell, Paul's nephew, says it is a prevalent feeling. He has been part of the team here since he can remember. "What I find funny," he said, "is that people ask me if they can expect something spooky to happen to them during the night when they rent a room here. It's like they think the ghosts are on demand." I laughed and said, "Yep, it's 6:00! Time for the ghosts to come out." While we both laughed, it is a prevalent thought for guests at haunted venues. They expect that every night will be Halloween. Paranormal just doesn't work on a time clock.

When Dick Pointer was first working on the renovations for the house, he would sleep downstairs to keep an eye on things.

"You have to remember this area was a little seedy then," he said. "We had a lot of tools in the house we were using, and I didn't' want anyone breaking in to steal them. So, I stayed here with my big red Doberman Pincher, Shep. I had him on a rope so he wouldn't run off. That dog would not go up the stairs here. He has no problem with stairs anywhere else, but here, he would shy back from them, and even if I pulled on the rope, he would not go up the stairs. One day, he just off and ran off. I never did find him. Rewind a decade and what do you find? Charles Lemp with a 'big red Doberman Pincher.'"

THE HALLWAYS AND STAIRCASE

Most venues known for their paranormal activity have "hot spots" of activity. Lemp Mansion's hallways and stairs are some of those places. With all the traffic using these areas over the years, it is not a surprise to find echoes of the people who passed this way.

Here are a few of the stories reported to me:

Catharine C. St. Louis, Mo.

"I was there again last year with a different set of friends who wanted to go after my stories. I did have one personal experience on my second visit. Everyone in the group was ahead of me as we left the William Lemp Suite. I was walking past the staircase when I heard a voice right next to me in a normal tone say "Hey!" There was no one near me. One friend saw me look around, look down the staircase to the lobby and she asked about it. When I told her, we both laughed, and I said it must be the house recognizing me and welcoming me back."

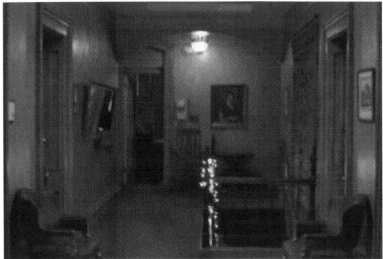

Lemp Mansion 2nd floor hallway at night.—Photo Ron Bueker

Ouran P., Pakistan. 2012.

"I have always wanted to stay in a haunted house. I was in St. Louis on business and my friends were renting a room at Lemp Mansion. They invited me over for lunch and I was excited to see this historic place. The lunch was really good, the people very friendly, and I thought the house was in great condition for being over 100 years old.

"After lunch, my friends showed me their room. They were staying two nights in the Lavender Suite. I could not believe how big these rooms are...even the bathroom. While we were walking along the hallway leading to their room, I felt someone walking behind me. It felt like they were in a hurry so I moved to one side and said, "Excuse me." When no one passed me, I looked behind me and the hallway was empty. I felt the hair stand up on my arms. My friend, who was unlocking the Lavender room door said "For what?" I was still shaken and said, "What?" He said, "What are you excusing yourself for?" I just shook my head and said nothing. I kept looking back at the hallway and stairs. I know someone was right on my heels. They had no time to go anywhere else."

Mason R., Rhode Island. 2009.

"Had lunch at Lemp in the atrium. I left to use the guy's room, which is at the end of the hall by the vault. Just before I got to the bathroom door, I feel this sense of someone coming toward me. I turned to look down the hall toward the bar and I see a shadow moving along the wall like it's coming my way. Only, no one was attached to the shadow! It disappeared when it got to the stairs going up to the next floor. I ran into the bathroom, locked the door and took a minute to get my nerve back. The shadow looked like a guy with a jacket...like a suit. I felt too stupid to tell my friends."

Drew H. Missouri. 2010.

"My girlfriend and I were at the DeMenil mansion and decided to stop in at the Lemp house. The people there were really nice and said we could look around on the first floor. My girlfriend decided to use the Lady's room as we passed by, so I waited in the hallway for her, just looking around at the old sink there and stuff. She poked her head out and said "You gotta see this tub!" I peeked in and when I did, something pushed me in my right shoulder. I jumped back, thinking maybe the staff didn't like me looking in the girl's bathroom, but there was nobody there. No one anywhere. Not in the hall, nothing. We left pretty quickly and she told me later that I was still white in the face and shaking."

These are two photos I took of the main staircase in 2012. They were taken back-to-back. I used my phone, so there was no camera strap. I barely moved and the lighting was the same. I can't explain the second photo. Rebecca F. Pittman

BASEMENT BILLIARDS

The basement at Lemp Mansion is used for special events such as their Mystery Dinner Theatres and other occasions. There is a sign posted on the stairs accessing this area that reads Employees Only. The people who have been in the Lemp Mansion basement, however, report hearing the sound of clinking billiard balls. I ran across this phenomenon when writing about the Stanley Hotel. F.O. Stanley's favorite room was the Billiard Room at the hotel and his ghost has been seen, and heard, still playing pool, even though he's been dead 75 years. It seems areas for which people had a special fondness carry echoes of their time there. We do know the Rathskeller was the Lemp's Gentlemen's Parlor and Game Room when they lived at the mansion. Guests today say they have heard men's laughter, the sound of billiard balls smacking into each other, and the smell of cigar smoke.

One woman, who did not want her name included, said she was attending a theater performance and was annoyed by the smell of cigar smoke coming from the table across from her. But when she looked their way, no one was smoking. It is a non-smoking facility.

Damion S. St. Louis. 2009.

"I was spending the night at Lemp Mansion, in 2013. I wanted to explore it during the night so I walked around with an EMF reader and a flashlight. The basement is really weird at night. It's super quiet and the lights feel strange. I was waving the EMF around and finally got to the old elevator doors. Just as I was touching the metal bars I heard the sounds of a pool game coming out of the room next to me. Thinking there was a pool table in there and maybe some of the staff was in there playing a game, I stuck my head in. The EMF reader went crazy. It was the only time it acted like that. But as soon I stepped around the corner into the room with the stage, the sounds stopped and so did the reader. I gotta tell ya…that is chilling stuff. There is NO pool table there. I asked one of the staff the next day if anyone said anything about a pool game going on in the basement and they said they hadn't. I would be curious to hear if others have heard that."

Mitchell W., Kentucky. "This isn't a story from firsthand experience. A friend of mine was at Lemp Mansion and he and his fiancée were looking around one night after everyone was asleep. He said when they got to the basement he heard the sound of an elevator lowering. Not thinking much of it, he looked around for the elevator but all he found was the old doors where there used to be one. He was told later there hadn't been an elevator there for over 60 years."

Donna Filberg., St. Louis, Mo. "I was on the tour at Lemp Mansion and while we were on the 2nd floor I kept hearing moaning coming from the far end of the hallway by the window that looks out over the front yard. No one else heard it. When I took the tour a year later, I heard it again on the 2nd floor, coming from the same place. I asked a couple of other people on the tour if they heard it and they said "no." Since then, I have spoken to others who have taken the tour or spent the night and they report the sounds of someone moaning coming from the hallway; sometimes near the painting by of the woman at the top of the stairs, and others hear it down at the other end of the hall."

LIBERACE IS IN THE HOUSE

While stories regarding pianos playing with unseen fingers are not new, the number of stories told about the music coming from this old instrument are quite prevalent. It seems no matter where the piano is housed in the mansion, people hear a plaintive note or two sounding from it, when no one is around.

Melissa Wideman, Lemp Mansion staff: "I have been cleaning at the mansion and heard music coming from the piano in the Charles Lemp Room. I thought it was Patty's daughter who sometimes went in there to watch TV. But whenever I checked to see, the room was empty and the music halted as soon as I opened the door. This has happened more than once."

HAUNTED CAVES & THE BREWERY

The Mansion is not the only place privy to supernatural occurrences. People who have been privileged to see the caves, before they were sealed over, have heard footsteps where no one was walking, seen flickering lights, and heard the voices of men talking.

The brewery has similar reports of phantom footsteps, the elevator moving on its own, and sounds from a long-ago era where workmen tended to the daily duties of the brewing business.

When Haunted House attractions used the old brewery during Halloween season, customers walking through the cave found more than the proffered props and costumed employees. They saw shadow figures, and heard people walking next to them when they were alone.

Reports of laughter coming up the staircase to the theater area of the caves have been rumored for many years. People have said they heard music, shouting and females laughing. When the entrance to the cave was sealed, the reports stopped. There were no parties in the cave during the days people heard residual hauntings from the past.

Stories continue to pour in from guests who find their way into the historic hallways of Lemp Mansion. The owners of the home don't go out of their way to promote the paranormal side of the mansion. They focus on their guest's comfort, serving great food, and providing quality entertainments. As Paul Pointer said about the house's haunted history, "There's no putting that Genie back in the bottle." With **CNN** calling it "one of the most-haunted places in the world," I would have to agree.

**A house is never silent in darkness to those who listen intently;
there is a whispering in distant chambers, an unearthly hand presses the snib of the window, the latch rises. Ghosts were created when the first man woke in the night.**

-- James Matthew Barrie, "The Little Minister"

An 1875 illustration of Lemp Mansion. You can see the two-story carriage house and stables in the back. Note there is no atrium at that time as William, Sr. had it built in 1876, when he took over the mansion. You can see a stone staircase leading from the courtyard to the second floor where the atrium is today. This was also before the 3 giant vaults were added to the back of the house. The park-like atmosphere is still there today.

Appendix I:

Lemp Mansion Floor Plans

1st Floor

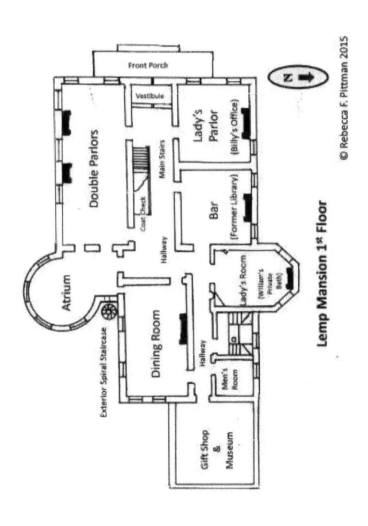

2nd Floor

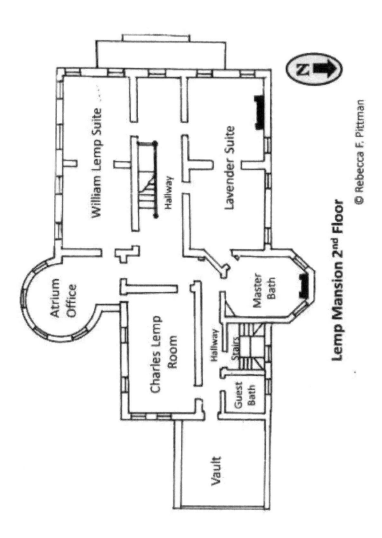

3rd Floor

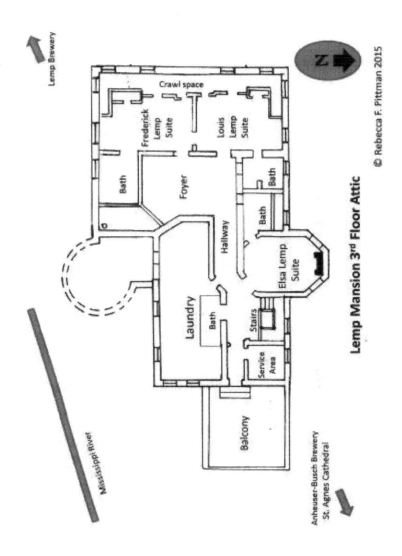

Basement

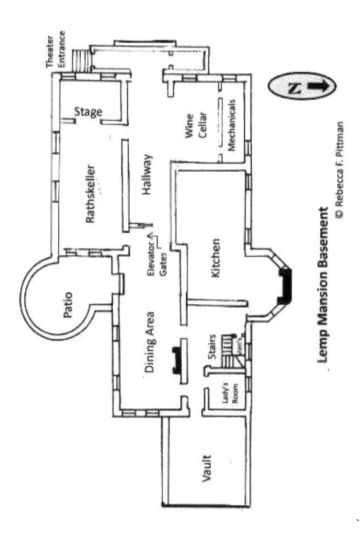

Appendix II:

Cave map:

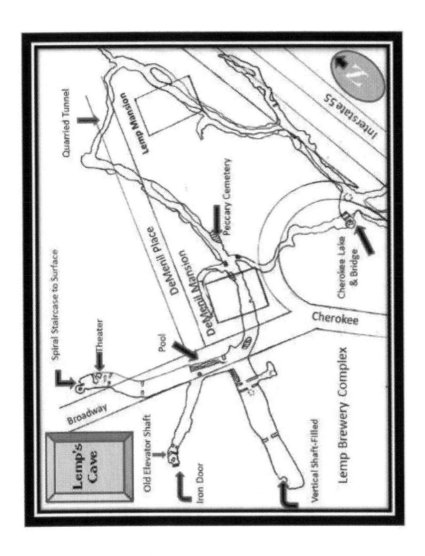

Appendix III:

Lemp Family Timeline:

Johann Adam Lemp. B: 1798 D: Aug. 23, 1862
Louise Bauer Lemp. B: 1808 D: March 14, 1893
William J. Lemp, Sr. B: Feb. 21, 1836 D: Feb. 13, 1904
Julia F. Lemp. B: July 26, 1841 D: April 16, 1906
Lemp Baby Boy. B: July 4, 1862 D: July 4, 1862
Anna Laura Lemp: B: May 27, 1865 D: Aug. 19, 1939
  Married Heinrich Julius Meyer Apr. 28, 1886
    Son: Geoffrey B: Nov. 13, 1887 D: 1942
  Married Alexander Konta 1895
William J. Lemp, Jr. B: Aug. 13, 1867 D: Dec. 29, 1922
  Married Lillie May "Lillian" Handlan Oct. 24, 1899
    Son: William J. Lemp III Sept. 24, 1900
    Married Agnes P. 1928
  Married Ellie Koehler Limberg May 18, 1915
Louis Lemp: B: Jan. 11, 1870 D: Oct. 17, 1931
  Married Agnes Walsh 1899
    Daughter Louise: June 12, 1909
Charles Adam Lemp: B: Dec. 30, 1871 D: May 10, 1949
Frederick William Lemp: Nov. 20, 1873 D: Dec. 12, 1901
  Married Irene Verdin 1899
    Daughter: Marion Aug. 29, 1900
Hilda Thusnelda Lemp: B: Nov. 20, 1875 D: July 8, 1951
  Married Gustav Pabst Sept 14, 1897
    Sons: Gustav 1899, William 1902 & Edwin 1908
Edwin Alvin Lemp: B: Aug. 28, 1880 D: Nov. 30, 1970
Elsa Justine Lemp: B: Feb. 8, 1883 D: Mar. 20, 1920
  Married Thomas Wright April 12, 1910
    Daughter: Patricia Lemp Wright B: Aug. 8, 1914
Jacob Feickert B: 1815 D: Jan. 5, 1892
Elizabeth Hoster Feickert: B: 1818 D: Jan. 21, 1892
Selected Bibliography

Books:

The Falstaff Story, Alvin Griesedieck. 1951
Gateway Families, Christy Hawes Bond, Marion Bond. 1994
St. Louis, Then and Now, Elizabeth McNulty. 2000
Saint Louis in the Gilded Age, Katherine T. Corbett and
  Howard S. Miller. 1993
Brewed in America: A History of Beer and Ale in the
United States, Stanley Wade Baron. 1962
Falstaff's Complete Beer Book. Frederick Alexander
Birmingham, 1970.

Websites:

BeerHistory.com. Great history of beer and the Lemp legacy.
MuseeGaleria.com. Parisian fashions from the Gilded Age.
EonImages.com. Nostalgic illustrations from the past.
PabstMansion.com. Learn about the Pabst history and
mansion.
Glamourdaze.com. Amazing website on women's fashions
through the ages.
Trickykegstands.com. Information and photos of Lemp
Cave.
LempMansion.com. Information on reservations & events.
Jestmurdermystery.com. Information on scheduling a murder
mystery entertainment.
CR3AT.com. Wonderful furnishings representing different
eras.

Recommended Reading:

Lemp: The Haunted History. Stephen Walker, 1989
Gateway Families. Christy Hawes Bond, Marion Bond, 1994

St. Louis Then and Now. Elizabeth McNulty, 2000.
Saint Louis in the Gilded Age. Katharine T. Corbett &
Howard S. Miller

Newspapers:

St. Louis Post-Dispatch
St. Louis Globe-Democrat
St. Louis Star
St. Louis Republic
Ogden Bee
New York World
Rock Island Argus (Illinois)
Salt Lake Herald
New York Daily Tribune
The Chanute Times (Kansas)
Honolulu Star-Bulletin
The Evening World
Ogden Standard Examiner

OTHER SOURCES:

Louis Lemp—Brewery Notebook. Missouri Historical
Library
Sprague Scrapbook. Missouri Historical Library
St. Louis Directories. Missouri Historical Library
Ancestry.com
Missouri Death Records
Missouri Birth Records
Missouri Marriage Records
Lemp Family Passports & Census Reports
St. Louis Medical Examiner's Coroner's Inquest Reports
Teresa Huelsing with Keller Williams Realty, St. Louis

About the Author

Rebecca F. Pittman had an unusual childhood: she was raised in a modeling agency and was on a fashion runway by the time she was 5, teaching modeling at 16, and designing events at 21. She credits her mother for her love of the entrepreneurial spirit that finds her making her careers in several arenas, including helping women.

As a muralist, she's painted artwork across the country for 39 years. This resulted in her first book, *How to Start a Faux Painting or Mural Business*. From there she wrote about the things that fascinated her: the creative arts, quantum physics, relationships, and the paranormal.

Her first work of fiction, *T.J. Finnel and the Well of Ghosts* was released in July of 2014. Geared to the Juvenile Fiction market, she's been delighted to find as many adults sending her requests for the sequel as the younger generation. It is book one of a five-book anthology and was courted by 4 major publishing companies.

The History and Haunting of the Stanley Hotel, The History and Haunting of the Myrtles Plantation, and The History and Haunting of Lemp Mansion are labors of love for Ms. Pittman. She adores researching the history of historic places, spending hours in Historic Societies, newspaper archives, and even dealing with coroners and police officers to get the facts she wants. *The History and Haunting of Lizzie Borden* has a November, 2016, release date. Books on the Crescent Hotel and Salem will follow in 2017.

Rebecca makes her home in the foothills of Colorado with her husband Ron, where she indulges her love of golf, boating, travel, and the delight of being a mother to four tall sons, 3 stepsons and a step-daughter, their spouses, and 11 grandchildren...so far.

Sign up for Rebecca's free monthly newsletter, *Ghost Writings*, at her website www.rebeccafpittmanbooks.com. It' brimming with reports of the paranormal, contests, and reader's accounts of their own ghostly encounters. It's always free and always spooky.

Rebecca F. Pittman brings you--
T.J. Finnel and the Well of Ghosts
Now on sale.

Something is climbing from the ancient well in Harmon's Wood. As moonlight falls upon the sleeping inhabitants of the old Finnel house at the forest's edge, the creature from the well scours the trees for its bottle of Lunar Potion. The Crone, an evil witch who governs the Spectre Lands, is also looking for the potion; along with her missing red crystal eye, an ancient map, and the Dark Orb.

T.J. Finnel, an 11-year-old boy, unwittingly has possession of the missing items, and his young life is about to be changed forever. Join T.J., Twicket (a talking troll head walking cane), and Mandolin Brandy as they take on the dark forces of another dimension where evil constellations come to life. And to do that, they must enter the Well of Ghosts.

Other books by Rebecca F. Pittman

Paranormal History:
The History and Haunting of the Stanley Hotel
(1st Edition, 23 House Publishing, 2011;
2nd Edition, Wonderland Productions)
The History and Haunting of the Myrtles Plantation
(1st Edition, 23 House Publishing, 2012;
2nd Edition, Wonderland Productions)
The History and Haunting of Lemp Mansion
(Wonderland Productions, 2015)

Creative Arts:
How to Start a Faux Painting or Mural Business 1st Edition, 2003.
2nd Edition, 2010. (Allworth Press, New York.)
Scrapbooking for Profit 1st Edition, 2005.
2nd Edition, 2014. (Allworth Press, New York)

Dating & Marriage Guide:
Troubleshooting Men: What in the WORLD do they want?
(Wonderland Productions, 2014)

Fiction:
T.J. Finnel and the Well of Ghosts
(Wonderland Productions, 2014)

Coming Soon:
The History and Haunting of Lizzie Borden (Nov. 2016)
The History and Haunting of the Crescent Hotel (Spring 2017)
The History and Haunting of Salem (Fall 2017)
Don't Look Now! (Paranormal Mystery) (2018)

90296365R00306

Made in the USA
San Bernardino, CA
17 October 2018